POWER VERSUS FORCE:

AN ANATOMY OF CONSCIOUSNESS

Also by
Dr. David R. Hawkins:

Orthomolecular Psychiatry
(with Linus Pauling)

Qualitative and Quantitative Calibration
of the Levels of Human Consciousness

POWER VERSUS FORCE:

AN ANATOMY OF CONSCIOUSNESS

The Hidden Determinants of Human Behavior

by
David R. Hawkins, M.D., Ph.D.

VERITAS

Published by Veritas Publishing
151 Keller Lane
Sedona, Arizona, 86336

Illustration, p.32, reprinted by permission of the William Morris Agency, Inc.
on behalf of the Author. Copyright © 1987 by James Gleick.

Cover and book design, editing and type
by **Bard Press**

LCCN: 94-90492
ISBN: 0-9643261-1-6

Manufactured in the United States of America
by Bertelsmann Industry Services

5ᵗʰ **Printing, April 2001**

The skillful are not obvious
They appear to be simple-minded
Those who know this know the patterns of the Absolute
To know the patterns is the Subtle Power
The Subtle Power moves all things and has no name

Contents

Foreword

IMAGINE—WHAT IF you had access to a simple yes-or-no answer to any question you wished to ask? A demonstrably true answer. *Any* question.

Think about it.

There's the obvious: "Jane is seeing another guy." (Y/N?) "Johnny is telling the truth about school." (Y/N?) But it's only a short step to: "This is a safe investment." (Y/N?) or "This career is worthy of my pursuit." (Y/N?)

What if *everyone* had such access?

Staggering implications suggest themselves immediately. Think again.

What would happen to our ponderous and all-too-often flawed judicial system if there were a clear, confirmable answer to the proposition, "John Doe is guilty as charged." (Y/N?)

What would happen to politics as we know it if all of us could ask the question, "Candidate X honestly intends to fulfill this campaign promise." (Y/N?) —and all of us got the same answer?

And what would happen to advertising, period?

You get the idea. But the idea gets bigger, fast. What happens to nationalism ("Nation X *is* in fact dedicated to the overthrow of Democracy.")? To government ("This bill *does* in fact protect the rights of citizens.")?

What happens to "The check is in the mail"?

If, as has been said, man learned to lie an hour after he learned to talk, then a phenomenon such as we are discussing would be the genesis of the most fundamental change in human knowledge since the beginning of society; the transformations it would wreak—in fields from communications to ethics, in our most basic concepts, in every detail of daily existence—would be so profound that it is difficult even to conceive what life would be like in a subsequent new era of truth. The world as we know it would be irrevocably changed, to its very roots.

kinesiology: —n. The study of muscles and their movements, esp. as applied to physical conditioning. [Gk. kinesis, movement (kinein, to move) + -logy.][1]

The study of kinesiology first received scientific attention in the second half of this century through the work of Dr. George Goodheart, who pioneered the specialty he called applied kinesiology after finding that benign physical stimuli—for instance, beneficial nutritional supplements—would increase the strength of certain indicator muscles, whereas inimical stimuli would cause those muscles to suddenly weaken. The implication was that at a level far below conceptual consciousness the body "knew," and through muscle testing was able to signal, what was good and bad for it. The classic example, cited later in this work, is a universally observed weakening of indicator muscles in the presence of a chemical sweetener; the same muscles strengthen in the presence of a healthful natural supplement.

In the late seventies Dr. John Diamond refined this specialty into a new discipline he called Behavioral Kinesiology. Dr. Diamond's startling discovery was that indicator muscles would strengthen or weaken in the presence of positive or negative *emotional and intellectual stimuli*, as well as physical stimuli.[2] A smile will make you test strong. The statement, "I hate you," will make you test weak.

Before we go any farther, let us explain in detail exactly how one "tests," especially as the reader will certainly wish to try this himself. Here is Dr. Diamond's outline, from his 1979 book, *Your Body Doesn't Lie*,[3] of the procedure adapted by him from the classic description in H.O. Kendall's *Muscles: Testing and Function* (Baltimore: Williams & Wilkins, 2nd ed., 1971).

> It takes two people to perform a kinesiological test. Choose a friend or a family member for testing. We'll call him or her your subject.
>
> 1. Have the subject stand erect, right arm relaxed at his side, left arm held out parallel to the floor, elbow straight. (You may use the other arm if you wish.)
>
> 2. Face your subject and place your left hand on his right shoulder to steady him. Then place your right hand on the subject's extended left arm just above the wrist.
>
> 3. Tell the subject you are going to try to push his arm down as he resists with all his strength.
>
> 4. Now push down on his arm fairly quickly, firmly and evenly. The idea is to push just hard enough to test the spring and bounce in the arm, not so hard that the muscle becomes fatigued. It is not a question of who is stronger, but of whether the muscle can "lock" the shoulder joint against the push.

Assuming there is no physical problem with the muscle and the subject is in a normal, relaxed state of mind, receiving no extraneous stimuli (for this reason it is important that the tester not smile or otherwise interact with the subject), the muscle will "test strong"—the arm will remain locked. If the test is repeated in the presence of a negative stimulus (for instance, artificial sweetener), "although you are pushing down no harder than before, the muscle will not be able to resist the pressure and the subject's arm will fall to his side."[4]

A striking aspect of Diamond's research was the uniformity of response among his subjects. Diamond's results were predictable, repeatable, universal. This was so even where no rational link existed between stimulus and response. For totally undetermined reasons certain abstract symbols caused all subjects to test weak; others, the opposite. Some results were perplexing: certain pictures, with no overtly positive or negative content would cause all subjects to test weak, while other "neutral" pictures caused all subjects to test strong. And some results were food for considerable surmise: whereas virtually all classical music and most pop music (including "classic" rock-and-roll) caused a universally strong response, the "hard" or "metal" rock that first gained popularity in the late seventies produced a universally weak response.

There was one other phenomenon which Diamond noted in passing, though devoting no deeper analysis to its extraordinary implications. Subjects listening to tapes of known deceits—Lyndon Johnson perpetrating the Tonkin Gulf hoax, Edward Kennedy stonewalling the Chappaquiddick incident—universally tested weak. While listening to recordings of demonstrably true statements, they universally tested strong.[5] This was the starting point of the work of the author of this volume, the well-known psychiatrist and physician, David R. Hawkins. In 1975 Dr. Hawkins began research on the kinesiological response to truth and falsehood.

It had been established that test subjects did not need any conscious acquaintance with the substance (or issue) being tested. In double-blind studies—and in mass demonstrations involving entire lecture audiences—subjects universally tested weak in response to unmarked envelopes containing artificial sweetener, and strong to identical placebo envelopes. The same naïve response appeared in testing intellectual values.

What seems to be at work is a form of communal consciousness, *spiritus mundi*, or as Hawkins calls it, following Jung, a "database of consciousness." The phenomenon seen so commonly in other social animals—whereby a fish swimming at one edge of a school will turn instantaneously when its fellows a quarter mile away flee a predator—pertains in some subconscious way to our species, also. There are simply too many documented instances of individuals having intimate acquaintance with information experienced firsthand by remote strangers for us to deny that there are forms of shared knowledge other than those achieved by rational consciousness. Or perhaps, more simply, the same spark of inner subrational wisdom that can discriminate healthy from unhealthy can discriminate true from false.

One highly suggestive element of this phenomenon is the binary nature of the response. Hawkins found that questions must be phrased so that the answer is very clearly yes or no, like a nerve synapse that is on or off, like the most basic cellular forms of "knowledge," like so much of what our cutting-edge physicists tell us is the essential nature of universal energy. Is the human brain, at some primal level, a wondrous computer linked with a universal energy field, that knows far more than it knows it knows?

Be that as it may. As Dr. Hawkins' research continued, his most fertile discovery was a means of calibrating a scale of relative truth by which intellectual positions, statements or ideologies could be rated on a range of one to one thousand. One can ask, "This item (book, philosophy, teacher) calibrates at 200 (Y/N?); at 250 (Y/N?)," and so on, until the point of common weak response determines the calibration. The enormous implication of these calibrations was that for the first time in human history ideological validity could be appraised as an innate quality in *any* subject.

Through 20 years of similar calibrations, Hawkins was able to analyze the full spectrum of the levels of human consciousness, developing a fascinating map of the geography of man's experience. This "anatomy of consciousness" produces a profile of the entire human condition, allowing a comprehensive analysis of the emotional and spiritual development of individuals, societies, and the race in general. So profound and far-reaching a view provides not only a new understanding of man's journey in the universe, but also a guide to all of us as to where we and our neighbors are on the ladder of spiritual enlightenment and on our own personal journeys to become who we could be.

In this volume Dr. Hawkins brings these fruits of decades of research and insight into the penetrating illumination of revolutionary discoveries in advanced particle physics and nonlinear dynamics. For the first time in our Western intellectual record, he shows, the cold light of science is confirming what mystics and saints have always said about the self, God, and the very nature of reality. This vision of being, essence, and divinity presents a picture of man's relation to the universe that is unique in its capacity to satisfy both soul and reason. There is a rich intellectual and spiritual harvest here, much that you can take, and much more that you can give yourself.

Turn the page. The future starts now.

E. Whalen, Editor
Bard Press
Arizona, 1995

Preface

T O EXPLAIN THAT WHICH IS SIMPLE can be difficult indeed. Much of this book is devoted to the process of making the simple obvious. If we can understand even one simple thing in depth, we will have greatly expanded our capacity for comprehending the nature of the universe and life itself.

Kinesiology is now a well-established science, based on testing of an all-or-none muscle response to stimuli. A positive stimulus provokes a strong muscle response; a negative stimulus results in a demonstrable weakening of the test muscle. Clinical kinesiological muscle testing as a diagnostic technique has found widespread verification over the last twenty-five years. Goodheart's original research on the subject was given wider application by Dr. John Diamond, whose books brought the subject to the public. Diamond determined that this positive or negative response occurs with stimuli both physical and mental.

The research reflected in this volume has taken Dr.

Diamond's technique several steps further through the discovery that this kinesiologic response reflects a capacity of the human organism to differentiate not only positive from negative stimuli, but also anabolic (life-enhancing) from catabolic (life-consuming) and, most dramatically, true from false.

The test itself is simple, rapid, and relatively foolproof. A positive muscle reaction occurs in response to a statement which is objectively true; a negative response occurs if the test subject is presented with a false statement. This phenomenon occurs independently of the test subject's own opinion or knowledge of the topic, and the response has proven cross-culturally valid in any population and consistent through time. The test results thus fulfill the scientific requirement of replication and, therefore, reliable verification by any investigator. This technique provides, for the first time in human history, an objective basis for distinguishing truth from falsehood which is totally verifiable across time with randomly selected, naïve test subjects.

Moreover, we found that this testable phenomenon can be used to calibrate human levels of consciousness so that an arbitrary logarithmic scale of whole numbers emerges, stratifying the relative power of levels of consciousness in all areas of human experience. Exhaustive investigation has resulted in a calibrated scale of consciousness in which the log of whole numbers from 1 to 1,000 calibrates the degree of power of all possible levels of human awareness.

The millions of calibrations which confirmed this discovery further disclosed a stratification of levels of power in human affairs, revealing a remarkable distinction between power and force and their respective qualities. This in turn led to a comprehensive reinterpretation of human behavior in order to identify the invisible energy fields that control it. The calibrated scale was found to coincide with sublevels of the hierarchy of the *perennial philosophy*; correlations with emotional and intellectual phenomena in sociology, clinical psychology, and traditional spirituality immediately suggested themselves.

The calibrated scale has been examined here in light of current discoveries in advanced theoretical physics and the nonlinear dynamics of *chaos theory*. Calibrated levels, we suggest, represent powerful attractor Fields within the domain of consciousness itself, that dominate human existence and therefore define content, meaning, and value, and serve as organizing energies for widespread patterns of human behavior.

This stratification of attractor Fields according to corresponding levels of consciousness provides a new paradigm for recontextualizing the human experience throughout all time. Practically, by accessing data to which there has been heretofore no avenue of approach, our method promises both great value in researching history and enormous possible benefit for man's future. In attempting to emphasize the value of this technique as a research tool, examples have been given of its potential uses in a wide range of human activities: speculatively, in art, history, commerce, politics, medicine, sociology and the natural sciences; pragmatically, in marketing, advertising, research and development; and empirically, in psychological, philosophic and religious inquiry. Specific applications have been suggested in such diverse Fields as criminology, intelligence, addictionology, and self-improvement.

But further uses and extrapolations of the research method detailed herein have been barely hinted at. Although the results described here are the product of twenty years of investigation and millions of calibrations on thousands of subjects by teams of investigators, this book represents only a beginning exploration of the method's potential to enhance our knowledge in all the arts and sciences. Perhaps most important is its promise as an aid in spiritual growth and maturation to the most advanced levels of consciousness, even enlightenment itself.

By use of the kinesiological testing procedure described herein, unlimited information about any subject, past or present, is universally available. But the realization that everything is knowable about anything or anyone, anywhere, at any point in time, creates at first a paradigm shock. This reaction arises, generally, from realization of the nonlocality, impersonality and universality of consciousness itself; and, specifically, from the realization of the observability of one's own thoughts and motivations, their transparency across time. That one's every thought and action leave an indelible trace forever in the universe can be an unsettling thought.

As in the case of the discovery of radio waves or x-rays, a sudden expansion of our awareness of the workings of the universe not only allows but demands a recontextualization of our world-view. Implications of new knowledge require a reworking of old ideas to form a larger context. Though it may occasion some intellectual stress, such scientific recontextualization of human behavior can expose the basic structures that underlie personal and social problems, thereby revealing their solutions.

Because this subject matter is, in fact, extraordinarily simple, it is difficult to present in a world enamored of complexity. Despite our mistrust of simplification, we may see two general classes of people in the world: believers and non-believers. To the non-believers everything is false until proven true; to the believers everything said in good faith is probably true unless it is proven false. The pessimistic position of cynical skepticism stems from fear. The more optimistic manner of accepting information arises from self-confidence. Either style works and each has its pros and cons. I have been faced, therefore, with the problem of presenting my data in a manner that will satisfy both approaches.

This book is, therefore, oxymoronic in style, written to facilitate both so-called "left-" and "right-brain" comprehension. In actuality we know things by a holistic pattern-recognition. The easiest way to grasp a whole new concept is by familiarity. This kind of understanding is encouraged by a style of writing characterized by "closure." Instead of using only sparse adjectives or examples to express thoughts, they are instead run out and completed by use of repetition. The concept is then "done," and the mind is left at ease. Such an approach is also desirable because the mind that reads Chapter 3 will not be the same as the mind that read Chapter 1.

For that matter, the idea of having to start from Chapter 1 and read progressively to the end is merely a fixed left-brain concept. This is the pedestrian path of Newtonian physics, based on a limited and limiting view of the world in which all events supposedly happen in an A→B→C sequence. This form of myopia arises from an outdated paradigm of reality. Our wider and far more comprehensive view draws not only upon the essence of the most advanced physics, mathematics and nonlinear theory, but, as well, upon intuitions that can be experientially validated by anyone.

In general, the challenge in presenting this material lies in the paradox of comprehending nonlinear concepts in a linear, sentence-by-sentence structure. The fields of science from which the data emerged are of themselves complex and difficult enough: advanced theoretical physics and the mathematics thereof, nonlinear dynamics, chaos theory and its mathematics, advanced behavioral kinesiology, neurobiology, turbulence theory, as well as the philosophical considerations of epistemology and ontology. Beyond this, it was necessary to address the nature of human consciousness itself, an uncharted area at the perimeter of which the sciences have all drawn back. To conclusively comprehend such subjects from a purely intellectual viewpoint would be a staggering enterprise requiring a lifetime of study. Instead of essaying so formidable a task, I have tried to extract the essence of each subject and work only with these essences.

Even a rudimentary attempt to explain the workings of the testing technique fundamental to this book, which seems initially to transcend known laws of the universe, inevitably leads us into the intellectual territories of advanced theoretical physics, nonlinear dynamics and chaos theory. I have therefore attempted, as much as possible, to present these subjects in nontechnical terms. There is no need to worry that some erudite intellectual capacity is required to digest this material. It is not; we will circle around the same concepts over and over until they are obvious. Each time we return to comment on an example, greater comprehension will occur. This kind of learning is like surveying new terrain in an airplane: on the first pass it all looks unfamiliar; the second time around we spot some points of reference; the third time it starts to make sense, and we finally gain familiarity through simple exposure. The inborn pattern-recognition mechanism of the mind takes care of the rest.

To quell my own fear that perhaps, despite my best efforts, the reader might not get the essential message of the study, I will spell it out in advance: the individual human mind is like a computer terminal connected to a giant database. The database is human consciousness itself, of which our own consciousness is merely an individual expression, but with its roots in the common consciousness of all mankind. This database is the realm of genius; because to be human is to participate in the database, everyone by virtue of his birth has access to genius. The unlimited information contained in the database has now been shown to be readily available to anyone in a few seconds, at any time and in any place. This is indeed an astonishing discovery, bearing the power to change lives, both individually and collectively, to a degree never yet anticipated.

The database transcends time and space and all limitations of individual consciousness. This distinguishes it as a unique tool for future research and opens as yet undreamed-of areas for possible investigation. It holds forth the prospect of the establishment of an objective basis for human values, behaviors and belief systems. The information obtained by this method reveals a new context for understanding human behavior and a new paradigm for validating objective truth. Because the technique itself can be used by anyone, anywhere, at any time, it has the capacity to initiate a new era of human experience based on observable and verifiable truth.

We have at our fingertips a means of accurately distinguishing truth from falsehood, workable from unworkable, benevolent from malign. We can illuminate the hidden forces, hitherto overlooked, that determine human behavior. We have at our disposal a means of finding answers to previously unresolved personal and social problems. Falsehood need no longer hold sway over our lives.

Though the subject matter has proved easy to teach in lecture or videotape (see Appendix C) my problem has been to work it into readable form. The proofs can be complex. The demonstrations, however, are ultra-simple. Children get it right away and follow with delight. There's nothing here that is surprising to them. They have always known they were connected to the database; we adults have merely forgotten it. The inherent genius of the child is close to the surface, which is why it was children who saw that the emperor was not wearing new clothes. Genius is like that.

I will have been successful if by the end of the book you exclaim, "I always knew that." What is contained herein is only a reflection of that which you already know, but don't know that you know. All I have hoped to do here is connect the dots to let the hidden picture emerge.

This book makes a huge promise, perhaps the biggest promise that has ever been made to you. It can provide you the means by which you may detect if you are being misled. (You need never read a book or buy into any major teaching again without testing it first—it's too dangerous and too costly.) The level of truth of this work itself has been calibrated at 750 (see Appendix A) which is unusually high for this time in this culture. I pray this is already a partial fulfillment of the promise.

My hope as author has been that this work might undo the very sources of pain, suffering and failure, and assist the evolution of human consciousness in each of us to rise to the level of joy that should be the essence of man's experience.

The work comprehended by this book began in January, 1965 and was finally finished in June, 1994. Much of the material was originally developed in the course of work on a doctoral dissertation. The findings reported in the study were independently derived by the use of the research tool elucidated herein, the kinesiological response. The work evolved spontaneously, without reference to outside sources of information; correlation with the work of others was incorporated at a later date to provide an intellectual frame of reference. Much of the work in this study has now been corroborated by worldwide research presented in independent studies at the first major conference on consciousness, "Toward a Scientific Basis for Consciousness," held at the University of Arizona Health Sciences Center, Tucson, Arizona, in April of 1994.[1]

Our research teams used the testing method the book describes to calibrate the levels of truth of every chapter, paragraph and sentence. (For instance, testing revealed an error in a list of celebrities who had destroyed themselves as a consequence of fame. When we checked each word, the name "John Lennon" was found to be in error: in fact, he was shot by an assassin. When his name was deleted, the level of truth of the sentence, and therefore the paragraph and the page, rose to match the rest of the chapter.)

Preliminary versions of the book were circulated among selected readers, from rank-and-file health care workers to heads of state such as Mikhail Gorbachev; some comments appear on the back cover. Each person's response to the presentation of the subject has been unique. (One interesting fact observed was that the scores of tested individuals increased after encountering the material; it appears that mere exposure to the data "raised" the subjects' level of consciousness.) Because the implications and practical applications of the work are so varied, and any aspect of the material can be expanded and focused to suit the interests of a given audience, portions of it have lent themselves clinically to presentations for various special-interest groups.

A segment of the material was presented by the author in the keynote speech at the First International Conference on Consciousness and Addictions in San Mateo, California, in 1986[2] and a summation was published in the Proceedings of that conference by the Brookridge Institute (*Beyond Addictions, Beyond Boundaries*, edited by Shirley Burton and Leo Kiley, 1986).[3] An expanded version was given in a four-hour videotaped lecture on Consciousness and Addictions at the Second National Conference on Consciousness and Addictions in San Francisco in 1987.[4]

Other parts of the material have appeared in a series of nationally published videotapes: *Handling Major Crises; Cardiovascular and Heart Problems; Depression; Alcoholism; Spiritual First Aid; The Aging Process; Pain and Suffering; Weight; Worry,*

Fear and Anxiety; Health; Illness; Special Relationships; and *Sexuality.* (Coleman Publishers, Amityville, New York, 1984-1986).[5]

Some of this material was presented during three-hour weekly lectures given at an alcohol and drug rehabilitation center over a five-year period (Sedona Villa of Camelback Hospital, 1984-1988).[6]

This is the first time the anatomy of consciousness itself has been delineated in pure form in its entirety, without attenuation to the interests of a specific audience.

David R. Hawkins, M.D., Ph. D.
The Institute for Advanced Theoretical Research
Sedona, Arizona, 1995

Introduction

ALL HUMAN ENDEAVOR has the common goal of understanding or influencing human experience. To this end, man has developed numerous descriptive and analytical disciplines: Morality, Philosophy, Psychology, and so on. Staggering amounts of time and money are invested in data collection and analysis in attempts to predict human trends. Implicit in this frenetic search is the expectation of finding some ultimate "Answer." The "Answer," we seem perennially to believe, will, once found, allow us to solve the problems of the economy, or crime, national health, or politics. But so far, we have solved none.

It isn't that we lack data; we are virtually drowning in data. The obstacle is that we do not have the proper tools to interpret the significance of our data. We have not yet asked the right questions because we have not had an adequate gauge of our questions' relevance or accuracy.

Man's dilemma, now and always, has been that he misidentifies his own intellectual artifacts as reality.[1] But these artificial suppositions are merely the products of an arbitrary point of perception. The inadequacy of the answers we receive is a direct consequence of the limitations implicit in the viewpoints of the questioner. Slight errors in the formation of questions result in gross errors in the answers that follow.

Understanding does not proceed simply from examining data; it comes from examining data in a particular context. Data is useless until we know what it *means*. To understand its meaning we need not only to ask the right questions; we also need the appropriate instruments with which to measure the data in a meaningful process of sorting and description.

Most of human behavior has remained indecipherable despite all attempts to understand it in depth. The systems we have created to achieve understanding may seem extensive and impressive, but each in turn has led us down a blind alley because of limitations inherent in its initial design. As we explore the nature of man's problems, it becomes clear that there has never been a reliable experimental yardstick with which to measure and interpret man's motivations and experiences over the course of his history.

Philosophy in all its branches attempts to comprehend human experience by creating abstractions and hypothecating their concordance with some ultimate reality. Political systems are all based on suppositions about relative human values lacking any demonstrable factual basis. All systems of morality resolve into arbitrary attempts to reduce the enormous complexities of human behavior to simplistic categories of right and wrong. Psychoanalysis, in exposing the unconscious mind, has compounded this muddle, giving rise to a bewildering array of treatments and psychologies derived from various viewpoints. This ongoing babble of man's attempt to understand himself finally produces a semantic morass in which, in the end, anything one might say is probably true to some degree. Because of uncertainty about the exact nature of causality, even when measurable results are obtained they are subject to being ascribed to factitious causes.

The fatal faults of all thought systems have been, primarily: (1) failure to differentiate between subjective and objective; (2) disregard of the limitation of context inherent in basic design and terminology; (3) ignorance of the nature of consciousness itself; and (4) misunderstanding of the nature of causality. The consequences of these shortcomings will become obvious as we explore the major areas of human experience from a new perspective with new tools.

Society constantly expends its efforts to correct effects instead of causes, which is one reason why the evolution of human consciousness proceeds so slowly. Mankind is barely on the first rung of the ladder; we haven't yet solved even such primitive problems as world hunger. The accomplishments of mankind thus far, in fact, are most impressive for having been achieved, almost blindly, through trial and error. While this random search for solutions has resulted in a maze of baffling complexity, true answers always have the hallmark of simplicity. The basic law of the universe is economy. The universe does not waste a single quark; all serves a purpose and fits into a balance—there are no extraneous events.

Man is stuck with his lack of knowledge about himself until he can learn to look beyond apparent causes. From the human record we may note that answers never arise from identifying "causes" in the world. Instead, it is necessary to identify the conditions that underlie ostensible causes; and these conditions exist only within man's consciousness itself. No definitive answer to any problem can be found by isolating sequences of events and projecting upon them a mental notion of "causality." There are no causes within the observable world. As we shall demonstrate, the observable world is a world of effects.

What is the human prognosis? Is society by virtue of its own chaotic subsystems a runaway juggernaut, inherently doomed? This prospect underlies a general social apprehension about the future. International polls indicate a high level of unhappiness everywhere on the globe, even in the most advanced countries.[2] While the majority resign themselves to a pessimistic view and pray for a better life "hereafter," the few visionaries who foresee a utopian future are unable to describe the means necessary to bring it about. Society needs *visionaries of means, not dreamers of ends.* Once we have the means, the ends will reveal themselves.

The difficulty in finding effective means reduces itself, on examination, to our inability to discriminate the essential from the nonessential. Thus far there has been no system affording a method by which to distinguish powerful and effective solutions from weak, ineffective ones. Our means of evaluation themselves have been inherently incapable of performing realistic appraisal.

Societal choices, more often than not, are the result of expediency, statistical fallacy, sentiment, political or media pressure, or personal prejudice and vested interest. Crucial decisions affecting the lives of everyone on the planet are made under conditions that virtually guarantee failure. Because societies lack the necessary reality base for formulation of effective problem resolutions, they fall back, over and over, on a resort to force (in its various expressions such as law, taxation, war, rules and regulations) which is extremely costly, instead of employing power, which is very economical.

Man's two basic types of operational faculties, reason and feeling, are both inherently unreliable, as his history of precarious individual and collective survival attests. Although we ascribe our actions to reason, in fact, man operates primarily out of pattern recognition; the logical arrangement of data serves mainly to enhance a pattern-recognition system which then becomes "truth."[3] But nothing is ever "true" except under certain circumstances and then only from a particular viewpoint, characteristically unstated.

As a result, thoughtful man deduces that all his problems arise from the difficulty of "knowing." Ultimately, the mind arrives at epistemology, that branch of philosophy which examines the question of how and to what degree man really knows anything. Such philosophical disquisitions may seem either erudite or irrelevant, but the questions they pose are at the very core of human experience. No matter where we start in an examination of human knowledge, we always end up looking at the phenomena of *awareness* and the nature of human consciousness. And we eventually come to the same realization: any further advance in man's condition requires a verifiable basis for knowing, upon which we may place our trust.

The main obstacle to man's development, then, is his lack of knowledge about the nature of consciousness itself. If we look within ourselves at the instant-by-instant processes of our minds, we will soon notice that the mind acts much more rapidly than it would acknowledge. It becomes apparent that the notion that our actions are based on thoughtful decisions is a grand illusion. The decision-making process is a function of consciousness itself; with enormous rapidity, the mind makes choices based on millions of pieces of data and their correlations and projections, far beyond conscious comprehension. This is a global function dominated by the energy patterns which the new science of nonlinear dynamics terms *attractors*.[4]

Consciousness automatically chooses what it deems best from instant to instant because that is, ultimately, the only function of which it is capable. The relative weight and merit given to certain data are determined by a predominant attractor pattern operating in the individual or in a collective group of minds. These patterns can be identified, described and calibrated; out of that information arises a totally new understanding of human behavior, history and the destiny of mankind.

The present volume, result of twenty years of intensive research involving millions of calibrations, can make such understanding available to anyone. That this revelation proceeds from a fortuitous connection between the physiology of consciousness, the function of the human nervous system and the physics of the universe is not surprising when we remind ourselves that we are, after all, part of a universe in which everything is connected to everything; all its secrets are thus, theoretically, at least, available to us if we know where and how to look.

Can man lift himself by his bootstraps? Why not? All he has to do is increase his buoyancy and he will effortlessly rise to a higher state. Force cannot accomplish that feat; power not only can, but constantly does.

Man thinks he lives by virtue of the forces he can control, but in fact he is governed by power from unrevealed sources, power over which he has no control. Because power is effortless it goes unseen and unsuspected. Force is experienced through the senses; power can be recognized only through inner awareness. Man is immobilized in his present condition by his alignment with enormously powerful attractor energy patterns which he himself unconsciously sets in motion. Moment by moment he is suspended at this state of evolution, restrained by the energies of force, impelled by the energies of power.

The individual is like a cork in the sea of consciousness—he doesn't know where he is, where he came from, or where he's going, and he doesn't know why. Man wanders about in his endless conundrums, asking the same questions century after century, and so he will continue, failing a quantum leap in consciousness. One mark of such a sudden expansion of context and understanding is an inner experience of relief, joy and awe. All who have had such an experience feel afterwards that the universe has granted them a precious gift. Facts are accumulated by effort, but truth reveals itself effortlessly.[5] Hopefully, through this book the reader can comprehend and then prepare the conditions for such a personal revelation; to do so is the ultimate adventure.

PART ONE: TOOLS

I
Critical Advances in Knowledge

THE EVOLUTION OF THIS WORK, which began in 1965, was fostered by developments in numerous scientific fields, of which three were of special importance. Clinical research on the physiology of the nervous system and the holistic functioning of the human organism resulted in the development in the 1970s of the new science of *kinesiology*.[1] Meanwhile, in the technological arena, computers were being designed that were capable of millions of calculations in milliseconds, making possible the new tools of artificial intelligence.[2] This abrupt access to formerly inconceivable masses of data begot a revolutionary perspective on natural phenomena, *chaos theory*. Simultaneously, in the theoretical sciences, quantum mechanics led to advanced theoretical physics; through associated mathematics, there emerged a whole new study of *nonlinear dynamics*, one of the most far-reaching developments of modern science, the long-term impact of which has yet to be realized.[3]

Kinesiology for the first time exposed the intimate connection between mind and body, revealing that the mind "thinks" with the body itself. Thence, it provided an avenue for the exploration of the ways consciousness reveals itself in the subtle mechanisms behind the disease process.[4]

Advanced computers permitting the depiction through graphics of vast amounts of data disclosed unsuspected systems within what had been ignored by Newtonian physics as indecipherable or meaningless data (chaos).[5] Theoreticians in diverse fields were suddenly able to intimate coherent ways of understanding data that had been considered incoherent, or *nonlinear*—diffuse or chaotic, and therefore inaccessible through conventional probabilistic logical theory and mathematics.

Analysis of this "incoherent" data identified hidden energy patterns, or *attractors* (which had been postulated by the advanced mathematics of nonlinear equations) behind apparently random natural phenomena.[6] Computer graphics clearly demonstrated the designs of these attractor fields. The implicit potential for analyzing supposedly unpredictable systems in such disparate areas as fluid mechanics, human biology and stellar astronomy appeared to be limitless. (Though as yet, except for the appearance in the marketplace of some intriguing new computer graphics patterns generated by "fractal" geometry, the public has remained generally unaware of this new field of nonlinear dynamics.)

During the era preceding these revelations, linear science had grown progressively divorced from concern with the basis of life itself—all life processes are, in fact, nonlinear. This isolation was also characteristic of medicine, which, when presented with the amazing discoveries of kinesiology, merely ignored the information because it had no context, no paradigm of reality, with which to comprehend it. Medicine had forgotten that it was an art and that science was merely a tool of that art.

Within medicine, psychiatry had always been held at a

distance by traditionalists because in dealing with the immeasurables of human life it appeared less "scientific" from the Newtonian viewpoint. Academic psychiatry, in fact, has made major scientific breakthroughs in psychopharmacology since the 1950s. However, it remains the most nonlinear area of medicine, examining such subjects as intuition, decision-making and the whole phenomenon of life as *process*. Although in the academic psychiatric literature there is little mention of such things as love, meaning, value or will, the psychiatric discipline at least essays a somewhat larger view of man than other traditional medical fields.

Regardless what branch of inquiry one starts from—philosophy, political theory, theology—all avenues of investigation eventually converge at a common meeting point: the quest for an organized understanding of the nature of pure consciousness. But all of the major enterprises in human knowledge discussed above—even kinesiology and nonlinear dynamics—halted at this last great barrier to human knowledge, the investigation of the nature of consciousness itself. Some advanced thinkers, it is true, went beyond the parameters of their respective fields and began to ask questions about the relationship between the universe, science, and consciousness in its experience as mind.[7] We will refer to their theories and their impact on the advance of human understanding as we proceed.

The thesis of the present work derives from amalgamating these several scientific disciplines into a methodology both elegantly simple and rewarding. We have found thereby that consciousness can indeed be investigated. Although no road maps for such a study have thus far been available, research into the subject has produced its own design, and with it, the context needed to comprehend its findings.

Inasmuch as everything in the universe is connected with everything else,[8] it is not surprising that one of the primary

objectives of this study, a map of the energy fields of consciousness, would correlate with, and be corroborated by, all other
avenues of investigation, uniting the diversity of human experience and its expressions in an all-encompassing paradigm.[9]
Such an insight can bypass the artificial dichotomy between
subject and object, transcending the limited viewpoint that
creates the illusion of duality. The subjective and objective are,
in fact, one and the same,[10] as can be demonstrated without
resort to nonlinear equations or computer graphics.

By identifying subjective and objective as the same, we
are able to transcend the constraints of the concept of time,
which by its very definition is a major hindrance to comprehension of the nature of life, especially in its expression as
human experience. If in actuality the subjective and objective
are one and the same, then we can find the answers to all
questions by merely looking within man himself. By simply
recording observations, we can see a grand picture emerge, one
that predicates no limitations to the extent of further investigation.

All of us have available to us at all times a computer far
more advanced than the most elaborate artificial intelligence
machine—the human mind itself. The basic function of any
measuring device is simply to give a signal indicating the
detection by the instrument of slight change. In the experiments to be described, the reactions of the human body itself
provide such a signal of change in conditions. As will be seen,
the body can discern to the finest degree the difference
between that which is supportive of life and that which is not.

We should not be surprised at this. Living things all react
to what is life-supportive and what is not; this is the fundamental mechanism of survival. Inherent in all life forms is the
capacity to detect change and react correctively. Thus, trees
become smaller at higher elevations as the oxygen in the
atmosphere becomes scarcer. Human protoplasm is far more

sensitive than that of a tree.

The methodology, proceeding from the study of non-linear dynamics, which we employed in this work of developing a map of the fields of human consciousness, is known as *attractor research*. It is concerned with the identification of power ranges of energy fields utilizing *critical point analysis*.[11] (Critical point analysis is a technique derived from the fact that in any highly complex system there is a specific critical point at which the smallest input will result in the greatest change. The great gears of a windmill can be halted by lightly touching the right escape mechanism; it is possible to paralyze a giant locomotive if you know exactly where to put your finger.)

Nonlinear dynamics enables these significant patterns to be identified in complex presentations, even when they are obscured by incoherence or sheer mass of indecipherable data. It discovers the relevance in what the world discards as irrelevant, using an entirely different approach and totally different methods of problem resolution from the ones the world is used to.[12]

The world conventionally assumes that the processing of problems requires starting from the known (the question or conditions) and moving on to the unknown (the answer) in a time sequence following definite steps and logical progression. Nonlinear dynamics moves in the opposite direction: from the unknown (the non-deterministic data of the question) to the known (the answer)! It operates within a different paradigm of causality. The problem is seen as one of definition and access rather than of logical sequence (as in solving a problem by differential equations).[13]

But before we attempt defining the questions of this study further, let us examine some of the material we have introduced in greater detail.

Attractors

Attractor is the name given to an identifiable pattern that emerges from a seemingly unmeaningful mass of data. There is a hidden coherence in all that appears incoherent. This inner coherence was first demonstrated in nature by Lorenz in studying computer graphics derived from weather patterns over long courses of time. The attractor pattern he identified is now quite famous as "Lorenz's Butterfly."

Different types of attractors are denoted by different names, for instance, *strange attractors*. But most important to our research is the discovery that some patterns are very powerful and others are much weaker. There is a critical point which differentiates the two distinct classes. This phenomenon is parallel and corollary to the high and low energy bonds in the mathematics of the chemical bond.

Fields of Dominance

A field of dominance is exhibited by high energy patterns in their influence over weaker ones. This may be likened to the coexistence of a small magnetic field within the much larger field of a giant electromagnet. The phenomenological universe is the expression of the interaction of endless attractor patterns of varying strengths. The unending complexities of life are the reflections of the endless reverberations of the augmentations and diminutions of these fields, compounded by their harmonics and other interactions.

Critical Point Analysis

The traditional Newtonian concept of causality (see below) had excluded all such "non-deterministic" data because it did not fit into its paradigm. With the discoveries of Einstein, Heisenberg, Bell, Bohr and other great innovators, our model of the universe expanded rapidly. Advanced theoretical physics demonstrated that everything in the universe is subtly dependent upon everything else.[14]

The classic Newtonian four-dimensional universe is often described as a giant clockworks with the three dimensions of space manifesting linear processes in time. If we look at an even simpler clockworks we will notice that some gears move slowly and ponderously, while others move very rapidly, with tiny balances twirling about as escape mechanisms seesaw back and forth. To place pressure on one of the large moving gears would have no effect on the mechanism; however, somewhere there is a delicate balance mechanism at which the slightest touch stops the entire device. This is identified as the "critical point" where the least force exerts the greatest effect.

Causality

Within the observable world causality has conventionally been presumed to work in the following manner:

A→B→C

This is called a deterministic linear sequence—like billiard balls sequentially striking each other. The implicit presumption is that A causes B causes C.

But our own research indicates that causality operates in a completely different manner:

From this diagram we see that cause (ABC), which is unobservable, results in the sequence A→B→C, which is an observable phenomenon within the measurable three-dimensional world. The typical problems the world attempts to deal with exist on the observable level of A→B→C. But our work is to find the inherent attractor pattern, the ABC out of which the A→B→C arises.

In this simple diagram the operants transcend both the observable and the non-observable; we might picture them as a rainbow bridging the deterministic and the non-deterministic realms. (The existence of operants can be inferred by asking the question, "What encompasses both the possible and the impossible, the known and the unknown?"—i.e., what is the matrix of all possibility?)

This description of how the universe works is in accord with the theories of physicist David Bohm, who has described a holographic universe with an invisible *implicate* ("enfolded") and a manifest *explicate* ("unfolded") order.[15] But it is most important to note that this scientific insight corresponds with the view of reality experienced through history by enlightened sages who have evolved beyond consciousness to a state of pure awareness.[16] Bohm postulates a *source* that is beyond both the explicate and implicate realms, very much like the state of pure awareness described by the sages.[17]

The advent of artificial intelligence super-computers has allowed the application of the theories of nonlinear dynamics to be applied to the study of brain function through the technique of *neurophysiologic modeling*.[18] The function of memory, especially, is being studied by means of neural models among which attractor networks have been identified. Conclusions of current research are that the brain's neural networks act as a system of attractor patterns, and that stored memories act as attractors, so that the system does not behave in a random fashion overall, although each individual neuron may behave in random fashion.[19]

Neuron models of consciousness disclose a class of neural networks called "constraint satisfaction systems."[20] In these systems a network of interconnected neuron units operates within a series of limits and thus sets up attractor patterns, some of which are now being identified with psychopathology.[21] This kind of modeling correlates behavior with physiology and parallels the results of our kinesiologic muscle testing, demonstrating the connection between mind and body.

In terms derived from *chaos theory*, the clinical study described in the following pages has identified a *phase space*, encompassing the full range of the evolution of human consciousness. Within this range numerous attractor patterns of increasing power have been denoted. These patterns represent energy fields which are qualities of consciousness itself rather than of any particular individual, as is shown by their occurrence across large populations over long periods of time, independent of testers or subjects.

The evolution of consciousness and the development of human society can be depicted in the mathematical terms of nonlinear dynamics. Our study concerned itself with a limited set of parameters of consciousness which we calibrated from one to 1,000. The numbers represent the logarithm (to the base 10) of the power of the respective fields. The entire field or phase space of consciousness itself is unlimited, going on to infinity. The range of one to 600, representing the domain of the vast majority of human experience, is the primary scope of this study; the levels from 600 to 1,000, the realm of non-ordinary evolution—of enlightenment, sages, and the highest spiritual states—will also be described.

Within the total field studied, sequential patterns emerged identifying the progressive powers of attractor fields in which there were local variations, but global consistency. Strange attractors can be of either high or low energy, and the critical point in our data appeared to be the calibration range of 200, below which the power of attractors could be described as weak, or negative, above which as strong, or positive. By the time we reached the calibration of 600 they were enormously powerful.

An important element of chaos theory helpful in understanding this evolution of consciousness is the law of *sensitive dependence on initial conditions*.[22] This refers to the fact that a slight variation over a course of time can have the effect of producing a profound change,[23] much as a ship whose bearing is one degree off compass eventually finds itself hundreds of miles off course. This phenomenon, which we will refer to in more detail later, is an essential mechanism of all evolution and also underlies the potential of the creative process.

In overview, we can see that from time immemorial, man has tried to make sense of the enormous complexity and frequent unpredictability of human behavior. A multitude of systems has been constructed to try to make that which is incomprehensible comprehensible. To "make sense" has ordinarily meant to be definable in terms that are linear: logical and rational. But the process, and therefore the experience, of life itself is organic—that is to say, nonlinear by definition. This is the source of man's inescapable intellectual frustration.

In this study, however, test responses were independent of our subjects' belief systems or intellectual content. What emerged were patterns of energy Fields which were aspects of consciousness itself, irrespective of individual identities. In common left-brain/right-brain parlance we could say that the test subjects reacted globally to an attractor Field irrespective of the individual variation of their left-brain logic, reason or sequential thought systems. The results of the study indicate that profoundly powerful patterns organize human behavior.

We can intuit, then, an infinite domain of infinite potential, consciousness itself, within which there is an enormously powerful attractor Field organizing all of human behavior into what is innate to "humanness." Within the giant attractor Field are lesser Fields of progressively less energy and power. These Fields, in turn, dominate behavior, so that definable patterns are consistent across cultures and time throughout human history. The interactions of these variations within attractor Fields make up the history of civilization and mankind. (A side study not herein reported indicated that the animal and vegetable kingdoms as well are also controlled by attractor Fields of hierarchic power.)

Our study correlates well with Rupert Sheldrake's "morphogenetic Fields" hypothesis as well as Karl Pribram's holographic model of brain-mind function.[24] (Note that in a holographic universe the achievements of every individual contribute to the advancement and well-being of the whole.) Our study also correlates with the conclusions reached by Nobelist Sir John Eccles that the brain acts as a receiving set for energy patterns residing in the mind itself, which exist as consciousness expressed in the form of thought.[25] It is the vanity of the ego that claims thoughts as "mine." Genius, on the other hand, commonly attributes the source of creative leaps of awareness to that basis of all consciousness which has traditionally been called Divinity.

II
History and Methodology

THE BASIS OF THIS WORK is research done over a twenty-year period, involving millions of calibrations on thousands of test subjects of all ages and personality types, from all walks of life. By design, the study is clinical in method and thus has widespread pragmatic implications. Because the testing method is valid in application to all forms of human expression, calibrations have successfully been taken for literature, architecture, art, science, world events, and the complexities of human relationships. The test space for the determination of the data is the totality of the human experience throughout all time.

Mentally, test subjects ranged from what the world calls normal to severely ill psychiatric patients. Subjects were tested in Canada, the United States, Mexico and throughout South America and Northern Europe. They were of all nationalities, ethnic backgrounds, and religions, ranging in age from children to elders in their nineties, and covered a wide spectrum

of physical and emotional health. Subjects were tested individually and in groups by many different testers and groups of
testers. But in all cases, without exception, the results were
identical and entirely reproducible, fulfilling the fundamental
requirement of the scientific method: perfect experimental
replicability.[1]

Subjects were selected at random and tested in a wide
array of physical and behavioral settings: on top of mountains
and at the seashore, at holiday parties and during the course
of everyday work, in moments of joy and moments of sorrow.
None of these circumstances had any effect on test results,
which were found to be universally consistent irrespective of
any extraneous factor, with the singular exception of the
methodology of the testing procedure itself. Because of the
significance of this factor, the testing method will be described
in detail below.

Historical Background

In 1971, three physiotherapists published a definitive
study on muscle testing.[2] Dr. George Goodheart of Detroit,
Michigan, had studied muscle testing techniques extensively
in his clinical practice and made the breakthrough discovery
that the strength or weakness of every muscle was connected
to the health or pathology of a specific corresponding body
organ.[3] He further determined that each individual muscle was
associated with an acupuncture meridian and correlated his
work with that of the physician Felix Mann on the medical
significance of the acupuncture meridians.[4]

By 1976, Goodheart's book on applied kinesiology had
reached its twelfth edition; he began to teach the technique to
his colleagues and also published monthly research tapes. His
work was rapidly picked up by others, which led to the
formation of the International College of Kinesiology, many
members of which also belonged to the Academy of Preventive

Medicine. A thorough exposition of the development of the Field was detailed by David Walther in his extensive volume on Applied Kinesiology, also published in 1976.[5]

The most striking finding of kinesiology, initially, was a clear demonstration that muscles instantly become weak when the body is exposed to harmful stimuli. For instance, if a patient with hypoglycemia put sugar on his tongue, on muscle-testing the deltoid muscle (the one usually used as an indicator) instantly went weak. Accordingly, it was discovered that substances which were therapeutic to the body made the muscles instantly become strong.

Because the weakness of any particular muscle indicated the presence of a pathologic process in its corresponding organ (corroborated by diagnosis through acupuncture and physical or laboratory examination), it was a highly useful clinical tool to detect disease. Thousands of practitioners began to use the method and data rapidly accumulated showing kinesiology to be an important and reliable diagnostic technique which could accurately monitor a patient's response to treatment.

The technique found widespread acceptance among professionals from many disciplines, and although it never caught on in mainstream medicine, it was used extensively by holistically oriented physicians. One of these was Dr. John Diamond, a psychiatrist who began to use kinesiology in diagnosing and treating psychiatric patients. He labeled this extended use of kinesiology "Behavioral Kinesiology."[6]

While other investigators were researching the usefulness of the method in detecting allergies, nutritional disorders and response to medication, Dr. Diamond used the technique to research the beneficial or adverse effects of a great variety of psychological stimuli such as art forms, music, facial expression, voice modulation, and emotional stress. He was an excellent teacher, and his seminars attracted thousands of professionals who returned to their own practices with renewed interest and curiosity as they explored applications of the technique.

In addition to its inclusive applicability, the test was quick, simple, easy to perform and highly decisive; all researchers confirmed the absolute replicability of test results. For example, an artificial sweetener made every subject test weak, whether placed on the tongue, held in its package adjacent to the solar plexus or hidden in a plain envelope the contents of which neither the tester nor the subject knew.

That the body responded even when the mind was naïve was most impressive. Most practitioners did their own verification research, placing various substances in plain, numbered envelopes and having a naïve second person test a third. The overwhelming conclusion was that the body would indeed respond accurately, even when the conscious mind was unaware.

The reliability of the testing experience never ceased to amaze the public and patients—and, for that matter, the practitioners themselves. When this author was on the lecture circuit, for instance, in audiences of one thousand people, five hundred envelopes containing artificial sweetener would be passed out to the audience along with five hundred identical envelopes containing organic vitamin C. The audience would be divided up and would alternate testing each other. When the envelopes were opened, the audience reaction was always one of amazement and delight when they saw that all had gone weak in response to the artificial sweetener and strong in response to the vitamin C. The nutritional habits of thousands of families across the country were changed by this simple demonstration.

In the early 1970s, the medical profession in general, and psychiatry in particular, was highly resistant—if not forthrightly hostile—to the idea that nutrition had much to do with health at all, let alone emotional health or brain function. Publication of the book *Orthomolecular Psychiatry*, by this author and Nobelist Linus Pauling, received a favorable reception from a wide variety of audiences, but not from the medical establishment.[7] (Interestingly enough, twenty years later the concepts presented in the book are fundamental to current treatment of mental illness.)

The thrust of the book was that serious mental illnesses such as psychosis, as well as lesser ones such as emotional disorder, had a genetic basis involving an abnormal biochemical pathway in the brain, a molecular basis which could be corrected on the molecular level. Manic-depressive illness, schizophrenia, alcoholism and depression, therefore, could be affected by nutrition as well as medication. In 1973, when the book was published, the psychiatric establishment was still psychoanalytically oriented; the work was accepted primarily by holistic practitioners. The suggested treatment methods and results were frequently verified with kinesiology.

However, it was Dr. Diamond's demonstration that the body instantly went weak in response to unhealthy emotional attitudes or mental stresses which had the greatest ongoing clinical influence. His refinement of the muscle-testing technique, the one used by most practitioners, was used in this study over a period of fifteen years. It was universally observed by practitioners and researchers as well as this author that test responses were completely independent of the test subjects' belief systems, intellectual opinions, reason or logic. It was also observed that a test response where the subject went weak was accompanied by desynchronization of the cerebral hemispheres.[8]

The Testing Technique

Two persons are required. One acts as test subject by holding out one arm laterally, parallel to the ground. The second person then presses down with two fingers on the wrist of the extended arm and says, "resist." The subject then resists the downward pressure with all his strength. That is all there is to it.

A statement may be made by either party. While the subject holds it in mind, his arm's strength is tested by the tester's downward pressure. If the statement is negative or false, or reflects a calibration below 200 (see Map of Consciousness, Chapter 3), the test subject will "go weak." If the answer is yes or calibrates over 200, he will "go strong."

To demonstrate the procedure one might have the subject hold an image of Abraham Lincoln in mind while being tested, and then, for contrast, an image of Adolph Hitler. The same effect can be demonstrated by holding in mind someone who is loved in contrast to someone who is feared or hated or about whom there is some strong regret.

Once a numeric scale is elicited (see below) calibrations can be arrived at by stating, "This item" (e.g., this book, organization, this person's motive, etc.) is "over 100," then "over 200," then "over 300" until a negative response is obtained. The calibration can then be refined: "It is over 220? 225? 230?" etc. Tester and testee can trade places, and the same results will be obtained. Once one is familiar with the technique, it can be used to evaluate companies, movies, individuals, events in history, or for the diagnosis of current life problems.

The test procedure, the reader will note, is to use the muscle test to verify the truth or falsity of a *declarative statement*. Unreliable responses will be obtained if the question has not been put into this form. Nor can any reliable result be obtained from inquiry into the future; only statements regarding existent conditions or events will produce consistent answers.

It is necessary to be impersonal during the procedure to avoid transmitting positive or negative feelings. Accuracy is increased by having the test subject close his eyes; there should be no music in the background.

Because the test is so deceptively simple, it is well that an inquirer first verify its accuracy to his own satisfaction. Responses can be checked by cross-questioning, and everyone who becomes acquainted with the technique thinks of tricks to satisfy himself that it is reliable.[9] It will soon be found that the same response is observed in all subjects, that it is not necessary for them to have any knowledge of the matter in question, and that the response will always be independent of the test subject's personal opinions about the question.

Before presenting an inquiry we have found it instrumental to first test the statement, "I may ask this question." This is analogous to an entry requisite on a computer terminal, and will occasionally return a "no" answer. This indicates that one should leave that question alone or inquire into the reason for the "no." Perhaps the questioner might have experienced psychological distress from the answer or its implications at that time.[10]

In this study, test subjects were asked to focus on a specified thought, feeling, attitude, memory, relationship or life circumstance. The test was frequently done in large groups of people; for demonstration purposes we first established a baseline by asking the subjects, eyes closed, to hold in mind the memory of a time when they were angry, upset, jealous, depressed, guilty or fearful; at that point everyone universally went weak. We would then ask them to hold in mind a loving person or life situation, and all would go strong; typically a murmur of surprise rippled through the audience at the implications of what they had just discovered.

The next phenomenon demonstrated was that a mere image of a substance held in mind produced the same response as if the substance were in physical contact with the body. As an example, we would hold up an apple grown with pesticides and ask the audience to look directly at it while being tested; all would go weak. We would then hold up an organically grown apple, free of contaminants, and as the audience focused on it they would instantly go strong. Inasmuch as no one in the audience knew which apple was which, nor, for that matter, had any anticipation of the test, the reliability of the method was demonstrated to everyone's satisfaction.[11]

It should be remembered that people process experience differently: some primarily adopt a feeling mode, others are more auditory and still others, more visual. Therefore, test questions should avoid such phrasing as "How do you feel?" about a person, situation or experience or "How does it look?" or "How does it sound?" Customarily, if one says, "Hold the situation (or person, place, thing, or feeling) in mind," the subject will instinctively select his appropriate mode.[12]

Occasionally, in an effort, perhaps even unconscious, to disguise their response, subjects will select a mode which is not their customary mode of processing and give a false response. When the tester elicits such a response the question should be rephrased. For example, a patient who feels guilty about his anger toward his mother may hold in mind a photograph of her and test strong. However, if the tester were to rephrase the question to ask this subject to hold in mind his present attitude toward his mother, he would instantly go weak.

Other precautions to maintain the accuracy of the test include removing eyeglasses, especially if they have metal frames, and hats (synthetic materials on top of the head make everyone go weak). The testing arm should also be free of jewelry, especially quartz wristwatches. When an anomalous response does occur, further investigation should eventually reveal the cause—the tester, for instance, might be wearing a perfume to which the patient has an adverse reaction, producing false negative responses. If a tester experiences repeated failures in attempting to elicit an accurate response, the effect of this tester's voice on other test subjects should be evaluated;

some testers, at least at certain times, may express sufficient negative emotion in their voices to affect test results.[13]

Another factor to be considered in the face of a paradoxical response is the time frame of the memory or image involved. If a test subject is holding in mind a given person and their relationship, the response will depend on the period the memory or image represents. If he is remembering his relationship with his brother from childhood, he may have a different response than if he is holding in mind an image of the relationship as it is today. Questioning always has to be narrowed down quite specifically.[14]

One other cause for paradoxical test results is a physical condition of the test subject resulting from stress, or depression of thymus gland function from encountering a very negative energy field. The thymus gland is the central controller of the body's acupuncture energy system, and when its energy is low, test results are unpredictable. This can be easily remedied in a few seconds by a simple technique discovered by Dr. John Diamond, which he called the "Thymus Thump." The thymus gland is located directly behind the top of the breast bone. With clenched fist, pound over this area rhythmically several times while smiling and thinking of someone you love. At each thump say, "ha-ha-ha." Retesting will now show the resumption of thymic dominance, and test results will return to normal.[15]

Use of the Testing Procedure in this Study

The testing technique just described is that recommended by Dr. Diamond in *Behavioral Kinesiology*. The only variation introduced in our study was the correlation of responses with a logarithmic scale to calibrate the relative power of the energy of different attitudes, thoughts, feelings, situations and relationships. Because the test is rapid, actually taking less than ten seconds, it is possible to process an enormous amount of information about these matters in a short time.

The numerical scale, elicited spontaneously from test subjects, ranges from the value of mere physical existence at 1, to 600, the apex of ordinary consciousness, and then on to 1,000, comprehending advanced states of enlightenment. Responses in the form of simple yes-or-no answers determine the calibration of the subject. For example, "If just being alive is one, then the power of love is over 200?" (Subject goes strong, indicating a yes.) "Love is over 300?" (Subject still goes strong.) "Love is over 400?" (Subject stays strong.) "Love is 500 or over?" (Subject still strong.) In this case love calibrated at 500, and this figure proved reproducible regardless how many test subjects were tested. With repeated testing using individuals or groups of testers with individuals or groups of subjects, a consistent scale emerged which correlates well with human experience, history, and common opinion, as well as the findings of psychology, sociology, psychoanalysis, philosophy and medicine. It also correlates quite precisely with the perennial philosophy's strata of consciousness.[16]

The tester must be cautious, realizing that the answers to some questions may be quite disturbing to the subject. The technique must not be used irresponsibly and must always respect the subject's willingness to participate; it should never be used as a confrontational technique. In clinical situations a personal question is never posed to the test subject unless it is pertinent to a therapeutic purpose. It is possible, though, to pose a question which precludes personal involvement on the part of the test subject, who then functions merely as an indicator for the purposes of calibration.

The test response is independent of the subject's physical strength. It is frequently dumbfounding to well-muscled athletes when they go just as weak as anyone else in response to a noxious stimulus. The tester may well be a frail woman who weighs less than one hundred pounds, and the subject may be a professional football player who weighs more than two hundred, but the test results will be the same, as she puts down his powerful arm with a mere two fingers.

III
Test Results and Interpretation

A GOAL OF THIS STUDY is to generate a practical map of the energy fields of consciousness so as to delineate the range and general geography of an uncharted area of human investigation. In order to make this more easily apprehensible for the reader, the numerical designations arrived at for the various energy fields have been rounded to comparative figures.

As we look at the Map of Consciousness (following page), it becomes clear that the calibrated levels correlate with specific processes of consciousness—emotions, perceptions or attitudes, world-views and spiritual beliefs. If space permitted, the chart could be extended to include all areas of human behavior. Throughout, the research results were mutually corroborating; the more detailed and extensive the investigation, the greater was this corroboration.

MAP OF CONSCIOUSNESS

God-view	Life-view	Level	Log	Emotion	Process
Self	Is	Enlightenment ↑	700-1000	Ineffable	Pure Consciousness
All-Being	Perfect	Peace ↑	600	Bliss	Illumination
One	Complete	Joy ↑	540	Serenity	Transfiguration
Loving	Benign	Love ↑	500	Reverence	Revelation
Wise	Meaningful	Reason ↑	400	Understanding	Abstraction
Merciful	Harmonious	Acceptance ↑	350	Forgiveness	Transcendence
Inspiring	Hopeful	Willingness ↑	310	Optimism	Intention
Enabling	Satisfactory	Neutrality	250	Trust	Release

	Emotion				
200	Courage →	Permitting	Feasible	Affirmation	Empowerment
175	Pride →	Indifferent	Demanding	Scorn	Inflation
150	Anger →	Vengeful	Antagonistic	Hate	Aggression
125	Desire →	Denying	Disappointing	Craving	Enslavement
100	Fear →	Punitive	Frightening	Anxiety	Withdrawal
75	Grief →	Disdainful	Tragic	Regret	Despondency
50	Apathy →	Condemning	Hopeless	Despair	Abdication
30	Guilt →	Vindictive	Evil	Blame	Destruction
20	Shame	Despising	Miserable	Humiliation	Elimination

The critical response point in the scale of consciousness calibrates at about 200, the level associated with Courage. All attitudes, thoughts, feelings and associations below that level of calibration make a person go weak. Attitudes, thoughts, feelings, entities or historical figures which calibrate higher make subjects go strong. This is the balance point between weak and strong attractors, between negative and positive influence.

At the levels below 200, the primary impetus is survival, although at the very bottom of the scale, the zone of hopelessness and depression, even this motive is lacking. The levels of Fear and Anger higher are characterized by egocentric impulses arising from this drive for personal survival. At the level of Pride the survival motive may expand to comprehend the survival of others as well. As one crosses the demarcation between negative and positive influence into Courage, the well-being of others becomes increasingly important. By the 500 level, the happiness of others emerges as the essential motivating force. The high 500s are characterized by interest in spiritual awareness for both oneself and others, and by the 600s the good of mankind and the search for enlightenment are the primary goals. From 700 to 1,000 life is dedicated to the salvation of all of humanity.

Discussion

Reflection on this map can induce a profound expansion of one's empathy for life in its variety of expressions. If we examine ostensibly less "virtuous" emotional attitudes, we realize they are neither good nor bad; moralistic judgments are merely a function of the viewpoint from which they proceed.

We see, for instance, that a person in Grief, which calibrates at the low energy level of 75, will be in much better condition if he rises to Anger, which calibrates at 150. Anger, itself a destructive emotion, is still a low state of consciousness, but as social history shows, Apathy can imprison entire subcultures as well as individuals. If the hopeless can come to want something better (Desire, at 125) and then use the energy of Anger at 150 to develop Pride (175), they may then be able to take the step to Courage, which calibrates at 200, and proceed to ameliorate their individual or collective conditions.

Conversely, the person who has arrived at a habitual state of unconditional Love will experience anything less as unacceptable. As one advances in the evolution of his individual consciousness, the process becomes self-perpetuating and self-correcting, so that self-improvement becomes a way of life. This phenomenon can be commonly observed among members of twelve-step self-help groups who constantly work at overcoming such negative attitudes as self-pity or intolerance. People farther down on the scale of consciousness may find these same attitudes acceptable and even righteously defend them.

Throughout history all the world's great spiritual disciplines have been concerned with techniques to ascend through these levels of consciousness. Most have also implied or specifically stated that to move up this ladder is an arduous task; success depends on having a teacher or at least, teachings, to give specific instruction and inspiration to the aspirant, who might otherwise despair over his inability to achieve his goal unaided. Hopefully our chart may facilitate this ultimate human endeavor.

The epistemological effect of awareness of this schema is subtle, but can be far-reaching; implications of these findings have pragmatic applications to sports, medicine, psychiatry, psychology, personal relationships and the general quest for happiness. Contemplation of the Map of Consciousness can, for instance, transform one's understanding of causality. As perception itself evolves with one's level of consciousness, it becomes apparent that what the world calls the domain of causes is in fact the domain of effects. By taking responsibility for the consequences of his own perceptions, the observer can transcend the role of victim to an understanding that "nothing out there has power over you." It is not life's events, but how one reacts to them, the attitude that one has about them, which determines whether they have a positive or negative effect on one's life, whether they are experienced as opportunity or as stress.

Psychological stress is the net effect of a condition you are resisting or wish to escape, but the condition does not have any power in itself. Nothing has the power to "create" stress. The loud music that raises the blood pressure of one person can be a source of delight to another. A divorce may be traumatic if it is unwanted or a release into freedom if it is desired.

The Map of Consciousness also casts a new light on the progress of history. A most important distinction for the purposes of this study is that between force and true power. We can, for example, investigate a historical epoch such as the end of British colonialism in India. If we calibrate the position of the British Empire at the time, one of self-interest and exploitation, we find that it was well below the critical level of 200 on the scale of consciousness. The motivation of Mahatma Gandhi (calibrated at 700) was very near the top of the range of normal human consciousness. Gandhi won in this struggle because his position was one of far greater power. The British Empire represented force (calibrated at 175), and when force meets power, force is eventually defeated.

We may observe how throughout history society has tried to "treat" social problems by legislative action, warfare, market manipulation, laws and prohibitions—all manifestations of force—only to see these problems persist or recur despite the treatment. Although governments, or individuals, proceeding from positions of force are myopic, to the sensitive observer it eventually becomes obvious that conditions of social conflict will not disappear until the underlying etiology has been exposed and "healed."

The difference between treating and healing is that in the former the context remains the same, whereas in the latter the clinical response is elicited by a change of context, so as to bring about an absolute removal of the cause of the condition rather than mere recovery from its symptoms. It is one thing to prescribe an anti-hypertensive medication for high blood pressure. It is quite another to expand the patient's context of life so that he stops being angry and repressive.

The empathy derived from contemplating this Map of Consciousness will hopefully make it a shorter step to Joy. The key to joy is the unconditional kindness to all life, including one's own, that we refer to as compassion.[1] Without compassion little of any significance is ever accomplished in human endeavor. We may generalize to the greater social context from individual therapies, wherein the patient cannot be truly cured or fundamentally healed until he invokes the power of compassion both for himself and others. At that point the healed may become a healer.

IV
Levels of Human Consciousness

MILLIONS OF CALIBRATIONS over the years of this study have defined a range of values accurately corresponding to well-recognized sets of attitudes and emotions, localized by specific attractor energy fields, much as electromagnetic fields gather iron filings. We have adopted the following classification of these energy fields to be easily comprehensible as well as clinically accurate.

It is very important to remember that the calibration figures do not represent an arithmetic but a *logarithmic* progression. Thus, the level 300 is *not* twice the amplitude of 150; it is 300 to the tenth power (10^{300}). An increase of even a few points therefore represents a major advance in power; the rate of increase in power as we move up the scale is enormous.

The ways the various levels of human consciousness express themselves are profound and far-reaching; their effects are both gross and subtle. All levels below 200 are destructive of life in both the individual and society at large; all levels above 200 are constructive expressions of power. The decisive level of 200 is the fulcrum that divides the general areas of force and power.

In describing the emotional correlates of the energy fields of consciousness, it is well to remember that they rarely are manifested as pure states in an individual. Levels of consciousness are always mixed; a person may operate on one level in a given area of life and on quite another level in another area. An individual's overall level of consciousness is the sum total effect of these various levels.

Energy Level 20: Shame

The level of Shame is perilously proximate to death, which may be chosen out of Shame as conscious suicide or more subtly elected by failure to take steps to prolong life. Death by avoidable accident is common here. We all have some awareness of the pain of "losing face," becoming discredited, a non-person. In Shame we hang our heads and slink away, wishing we were invisible. Banishment is a traditional accompaniment of shame, and in the primitive societies from which we all originate, banishment is equivalent to death.

Early life experiences such as sexual abuse, which lead to Shame, warp the personality for a lifetime unless these issues are resolved by therapy. Shame, as Freud determined, produces neurosis. It is destructive to emotional and psychological health and, as a consequence of low self-esteem, makes one prone to the development of physical illness. The Shame-based personality is shy, withdrawn and introverted.

Shame is used as a tool of cruelty, and its victims often become themselves cruel. Shamed children are cruel to animals and cruel to each other. The behavior of people whose consciousness is only in the 20s is dangerous. They are prone to hallucinations of an accusatory nature, as well as paranoia; some become psychotic or commit bizarre crimes.

Some Shame-based individuals compensate by perfectionism and rigidity and become driven and intolerant. Notorious examples of this are the moral extremists who form vigilante groups, projecting their own unconscious shame onto others whom they then feel justified in righteously attacking. Serial killers have often acted out of sexual moralism with the justification of punishing "bad" women.

Because it pulls down the whole level of personality, Shame results in a vulnerability to the other negative emotions and, therefore, often produces false pride, anger and guilt.

Energy Level 30: Guilt

Guilt, so commonly used in our society to manipulate and punish, manifests itself in a variety of expressions such as remorse, self-recrimination, masochism, and the whole gamut of symptoms of victimhood. Unconscious guilt results in psychosomatic disease, accident-proneness and suicidal behaviors. Many people struggle with guilt their entire lives, while others desperately attempt escape by amorally denying guilt altogether.

Guilt-domination results in a preoccupation with "sin," an unforgiving emotional attitude frequently exploited by religious demagogues, who use it for coercion and control. Such "sin-and-salvation" merchants, obsessed with punishment, are likely either acting out their own guilt or projecting it onto others.

Subcultures displaying the aberration of self-flagellation often manifest other endemic forms of cruelty, such as the public ritual killing of animals. Guilt provokes rage, and killing frequently is its expression. Capital punishment is an example of how killing gratifies a guilt-ridden populace. Our unforgiving American society, for instance, pillories its victims in the press and metes out punishments which have never been demonstrated to have any deterrent or corrective value.

Energy Level 50: Apathy

This level is characterized by poverty, despair, and hopelessness. The world and the future look bleak; pathos is the theme of life. It is a state of helplessness; its victims, needy in every way, lack not only resources, but the energy to avail themselves of what may be available. Unless external energy is supplied by care-givers, death through passive suicide can result. Without will to live, the hopeless stare blankly, unresponsive to stimuli, until eyes stop tracking and there is not enough energy left to even swallow proffered food.

This is the level of the homeless and the derelicts of society. It is also the fate of many of the aged and others who become isolated by chronic or progressive diseases. The apathetic are dependent; people in Apathy are "heavy" and are felt as a burden by those around them.

Too often society lacks sufficient motivation to be of any real help to cultures, as well as individuals, at this level, who are seen as drains of resources. This is the level of the streets of Calcutta where only the saintly such as Mother Teresa and her followers dare to tread. It is the level of the abandonment of hope, and few have the courage to really look in its face.

Energy Level 75: Grief

This is the level of sadness, loss, and despondency. Most of us have experienced it for periods of time, but those who remain at this level live a life of constant regret and depression. This is the level of mourning, bereavement and remorse about the past. It is also the level of habitual losers and those chronic gamblers who accept failure as part of their life style, often resulting in loss of jobs, friends, family, and opportunity, as well as money and health.

Major losses in early life make one later vulnerable to passive acceptance of grief as though sorrow were the price of life. In Grief one sees sadness everywhere: the sadness of little children, the sadness of world conditions, the sadness of life itself. This level colors one's entire vision of existence. Part of the syndrome of loss is the notion of the irreplaceablity of what is lost or that which it symbolized. There is a generalization from the particular, so that the loss of a loved one is equated with the loss of love itself. At this level, such emotional losses may trigger a serious depression or death.

Though Grief is the cemetery of life, it still has more energy to it than does Apathy. Thus, when a traumatized apathetic patient begins to cry, we know he is getting better. Once he starts to cry, he will eat again.

Energy Level 100: Fear

At the level of 100 there is a lot more life energy available; fear of danger is healthy. Fear runs much of the world, spurring on endless activity. Fear of enemies, fear of old age or death, fear of rejection and a multitude of social fears are basic motivators in most people's lives.

From the viewpoint of this level, the world looks hazardous, full of traps and threats. Fear is the favored official tool for control by oppressive totalitarian agencies, and insecurity is the stock-in-trade of major manipulators of the marketplace. The media and advertising play to Fear to increase market share.

The proliferation of fears is as limitless as the human imagination; once Fear is one's focus, the endless fearful events of the world feed it. Fear becomes obsessive and may take any form: fear of loss of relationship leads to jealousy and a chronically high stress level. Fearful thinking can balloon into paranoia or generate neurotic defensive structures and, because it is contagious, become a dominant social trend.

Fear limits growth of the personality and leads to inhibition. Because it takes energy to rise above Fear, the oppressed are unable to reach a higher level unaided. Thus, the fearful seek strong leaders who appear to have conquered their fear to lead them out of its slavery.

Energy Level 125: Desire

There is yet more energy available at this level; Desire motivates vast areas of human activity, including the economy. Advertisers play on desires to program us with needs linked to instinctual drives. Desire moves us to expend great effort to achieve goals or obtain rewards. The desire for money, prestige or power runs the lives of many of those who have risen above Fear as their predominant life motif.

Desire is also the level of addictions, wherein desire becomes a craving more important than life itself. The victim of Desire may actually be unaware of the basis of his motives. Some people become addicted to the desire for attention and drive others away by their constant demands. The desire for sexual approval has produced an entire cosmetics and fashion industry.

Desire has to do with accumulation and greed. But Desire is insatiable because it is an ongoing energy field, so that satisfaction of one desire is merely replaced by unsatisfied desire for something else. Multimillionaires remain obsessed with acquiring more and more money.

Desire is a much higher state than apathy or grief, obviously. In order "to get," you have to first have the energy to "want." TV has had a major influence on many oppressed people, inculcating wants and energizing their desires to the degree that they move out of Apathy and begin to seek a better life. Want can start us on the road to achievement. Desire can, therefore, become a springboard to yet higher levels of awareness.

Energy Level 150: Anger

Although Anger may lead to homicide and war, as an energy level it is farther removed from death than those below it. Anger can lead to either constructive or destructive action. As people move out of Apathy and Grief to overcome Fear as a way of life, they begin to want; Desire leads to frustration which in turn leads to Anger. Thus, Anger can be a fulcrum by which the oppressed are eventually catapulted to freedom. Anger over social injustice, victimization and inequality has created great movements that led to major changes in the structure of society.

But Anger expresses itself most often as resentment and revenge and is, therefore, volatile and dangerous. Anger as a life style is exemplified by irritable, explosive people who are oversensitive to slights and become "injustice collectors," quarrelsome, belligerent or litigious.

As Anger stems from frustrated want, it is based on the energy field below it. Frustration results from exaggerating the importance of desires. The angry person may, like the frustrated infant, go into rage. Anger leads easily to hatred, which has an erosive effect on all areas of a person's life.

Energy Level 175: Pride

Pride, which calibrates at 175, has enough energy to run the United States Marine Corps. It is the level aspired to by the majority of our kind today. People feel positive as they reach this level, in contrast to the lower energy fields. This rise in self-esteem is a balm to all the pain experienced at lower levels of consciousness. Pride looks good and knows it; it struts its stuff in the parade of life.

Pride is at a far enough remove from Shame, Guilt or Fear that to rise, for instance, out of the despair of the ghetto to the pride of being a Marine is an enormous jump. Pride as such generally has a good reputation and is socially encouraged; yet, as we see from the chart of the levels of consciousness, it is sufficiently negative to remain below the critical level of 200. This is why Pride feels good *only* in contrast to the lower levels.

The problem, as we all know, is that "Pride goeth before a fall." Pride is defensive and vulnerable because it is dependent upon external conditions, without which it can suddenly revert to a lower level. The inflated ego is vulnerable to attack. Pride remains weak because it can be knocked off its pedestal into Shame, which is the threat that fires the fear of loss of pride.

Pride is divisive and gives rise to factionalism; the consequences are costly. Man has habitually died for Pride—armies still regularly slaughter each other for that aspect of Pride called nationalism. Religious wars, political terrorism and zealotry, the ghastly history of the Middle East and Central Europe, are all the price of Pride, which all of society pays.

The downside of Pride is arrogance and denial. These characteristics block growth; in Pride, recovery from addictions is impossible, because emotional problems or character defects are denied. The whole problem of denial is one of Pride. Thus Pride is a very sizable block to the acquisition of real power, which displaces Pride with true stature and prestige.

Energy Level 200: Courage

At the 200 level power first appears. When we test subjects at all the energy levels below 200, we find, as can be readily verified, that all go weak. Everyone goes strong in response to the life-supportive fields above 200. This is the critical line that distinguishes the positive and negative influences of life. At the level of Courage an attainment of true power occurs; therefore, it is also the level of empowerment. This is the zone of exploration, accomplishment, fortitude and determination. At the lower levels the world is seen as hopeless, sad, frightening, or frustrating; but at the level of Courage, life is seen to be exciting, challenging and stimulating.

Courage implies the willingness to try new things and deal with the vicissitudes of life. At this level of empowerment one is able to cope with and handle effectively the opportunities of life. At 200, for instance, there is the energy to learn new job skills. Growth and education become attainable goals. There is the capacity to face fears or character defects and to grow despite them, and anxiety does not cripple endeavor as it would at lower stages of evolution. Obstacles which defeat people whose consciousness is below 200 act as stimulants to those who have evolved into the first level of true power.

People at this level put back into the world as much energy as they take; at lower levels populations as well as individuals drain energy from society without reciprocating. Because accomplishment results in positive feedback, self-reward and esteem become progressively self-reinforcing. This is where productivity begins.

The collective level of consciousness of mankind remained at 190 for many centuries and, curiously, only jumped to its current level of 204 within the last decade.

Energy Level 250: Neutrality

Energy becomes very positive as we get to the level which we have termed Neutral because it is epitomized by release from the positionality which typifies lower levels. Below 250 consciousness tends to see dichotomies and take on rigid positions, an impediment in a world which is complex and multifactoral rather than black and white.

Taking such positions creates polarization, and polarization in turn creates opposition and division. As in the martial arts, a rigid position becomes a point of vulnerability; that which does not bend is liable to break. Rising above barriers or oppositions which dissipate one's energies, the Neutral condition allows for flexibility and non-judgmental, realistic appraisal of problems. To be Neutral means to be relatively unattached to outcomes; not getting one's way is no longer experienced as defeating, frightening or frustrating.

At the Neutral level a person can say, "Well, if I don't get this job, then I'll get another." This is the beginning of inner confidence; sensing one's power, one is not easily intimidated. One is not driven to prove anything. The expectation that life, with its ups and downs, will be basically okay if one can roll with the punches is a 250-level attitude.

People at Neutrality have a sense of well-being; the mark of this level is confident capability to live in the world. This is the level of safety. People at the Neutral level are easy to get along with, safe to be around and associate with, because they are not interested in conflict, competition or guilt. They are comfortable and basically undisturbed emotionally. This attitude is non-judgmental and does not lead to any need to control other people's behaviors. Correspondingly, because Neutral folk value freedom, they are hard to control.

Energy Level 310: Willingness

This very positive level of energy may be seen as the gateway to the higher levels. Whereas jobs, for instance, are done adequately at the Neutral level, at the level of Willingness work is done well and success in all endeavors is common. Growth is rapid here; these are people chosen for advancement. Willingness implies that one has overcome inner resistance to life and is committed to participation. Below the 200 calibration people tend to be close-minded, but by level 310 a great opening occurs. At this level people become genuinely friendly, and social and economic success seem to follow automatically. The willing are not troubled by unemployment; they will take any job when they have to, or create a career or self-employment for themselves. They do not feel demeaned by service jobs or by starting at the bottom. They are helpful to others and contribute to the good of society. They are also willing to face inner issues and do not have major learning blocks.

At this level self-esteem is high and is reinforced by positive feedback from society in the forms of recognition, appreciation and reward. Willingness is sympathetic and responsive to the needs of others. Willing people are builders of and contributors to society. With their capacity to bounce back from adversity and learn from experience, they tend to become self-correcting. Having let go of Pride, they are willing to look at their defects and learn from others. At the level of Willingness, people become excellent students. They are easily trainable and represent a considerable source of power for society.

Energy Level 350: Acceptance

At this level of awareness a major transformation takes place with the understanding that one is oneself the source and creator of the experience of one's life. Taking such responsibility is distinctive of this degree of evolution, characterized by the capacity to live harmoniously with the forces of life.

All people at levels below 200 tend to be powerless and see themselves as victims, at the mercy of life. This stems from a belief that the source of one's happiness or the cause of one's problems is "out there." An enormous jump, taking back one's own power, is completed at this level with the realization that the source of happiness is within oneself. At this more evolved stage, nothing "out there" has the capacity to make one happy, and love is not something that is given or taken away by another, but is created from within.

Acceptance is not to be confused with passivity, which is a symptom of apathy. This form of acceptance allows engagement in life on life's own terms, without trying to make it conform to an agenda. With acceptance, there is emotional calm and perception is widened as denial is transcended. One now sees things without distortion or misinterpretation; the context of experience is expanded so that one is capable of "seeing the whole picture." Acceptance has to do essentially with balance, proportion and appropriateness.

The individual at the level of Acceptance is not interested in determining right or wrong, but instead is dedicated to resolving issues and finding out what to do about problems. Tough jobs do not cause discomfort or dismay. Long-term goals take precedence over short-term ones; self-discipline and mastery are prominent.

At the level of Acceptance we are not polarized by conflict or opposition; we see that other people have the same rights as we do and we honor equality. While lower levels are characterized by rigidity, at this level social plurality begins to emerge as a form of resolution of problems. Therefore this level is free of discrimination or intolerance. There is an awareness that equality does not preclude diversity; Acceptance includes rather than rejects.

Energy Level 400: Reason

Intelligence and rationality rise to the forefront when the emotionalism of the lower levels is transcended. Reason is capable of handling large, complex amounts of data and making rapid, correct decisions; of understanding the intricacies of relationships, gradations and fine distinctions; and of expert manipulation of symbols as abstract concepts become increasingly important. This is the level of science, medicine and of generally increased capacity for conceptualization and comprehension. Knowledge and education are here sought as capital. Understanding and information are the main tools of accomplishment, which is the hallmark of the 400 level. This is the level of Nobel Prize winners, great statesmen, Supreme Court justices. Einstein, Freud and many other important figures in the history of thought calibrate here.

The shortcomings of this level are failure to clearly distinguish the difference between symbols and what they represent, and confusion between the objective and subjective worlds that limits the understanding of causality. At this level it is easy to lose sight of the forest for the trees, to become infatuated with concepts and theories and end up missing the essential point. Intellectualizing can become an end in itself. Reason is limited in that it does not afford the capacity for the discernment of essence or of the critical point of a complex issue.

Reason does not of itself provide a guide to truth. It produces massive amounts of information and documentation, but lacks the capability to resolve discrepancies in data and conclusions. All philosophical arguments sound convincing on their own. Although Reason is highly effective in a technical world where the methodologies of logic dominate, Reason itself, paradoxically, is the major block to reaching higher levels of consciousness. Transcending this level is relatively uncommon in our society.

Energy Level 500: Love

Love as depicted in the mass media is not what this level is about. What the world generally refers to as love is an intense emotionality combining physical attraction, possessiveness, control, addiction, eroticism and novelty. It is usually evanescent and fluctuating, waxing and waning with varying conditions. When frustrated, this emotion often reveals an underlying anger and dependency that it had masked. That love can turn to hate is a common concept, but what is being spoken about then, rather than Love, is likely an addictive sentimentality. Hate stems from Pride, not Love; there probably never was actual love in such a relationship.

The 500 level is characterized by the development of a love which is unconditional, unchanging and permanent. It does not fluctuate because its source within the person who loves is not dependent on external factors. Loving is a state of being. It is a way of relating to the world which is forgiving, nurturing and supportive. Love is not intellectual and does not proceed from the mind; love emanates from the heart. It has the capacity to lift others and accomplish great feats because of its purity of motive.

At this level of development the capacity to discern essence becomes predominant; the core of an issue becomes the center of focus. As reason is bypassed there arises the capacity for instantaneous recognition of the totality of a problem and a major expansion of context, especially regarding time and process. Reason deals only with particulars, whereas love deals with wholes. This ability, often ascribed to intuition, is the capacity for instantaneous understanding without resort to sequential symbol processing. This apparently abstract phenomenon is, in fact, quite concrete; it is accompanied by a measurable release of endorphins in the brain.

Love takes no position and thus is global, rising above the separation of positionality. It is then possible to be "one with another" as there are no longer any barriers. Love is therefore inclusive and expands the sense of self progressively. Love focuses on the goodness of life in all its expressions and augments that which is positive. It dissolves negativity by recontextualizing it rather than by attacking it.

This is the level of true happiness, but although the world is fascinated with the subject of love, and all viable religions calibrate at 500 or over, it is interesting to note that only 0.4% of the world's population ever reaches this level of evolution of consciousness.

Energy Level 540: Joy

As Love becomes more and more unconditional it begins to be experienced as inner Joy. This is not the sudden joy of a pleasurable turn of events; it is a constant accompaniment to all activities. Joy arises from within each moment of existence rather than from any outer source. 540 is also the level of healing and of spiritually based self-help groups.

From level 540 up is the domain of saints, spiritual healers and advanced spiritual students. Characteristic of this energy field is a capacity for enormous patience and the persistence of a positive attitude in the face of prolonged adversity. The hallmark of this state is compassion. People who have attained this level have a notable effect on others. They are capable of prolonged open visual gaze which induces a state of love and peace.

At the high 500s the world one sees is illuminated by the exquisite beauty and perfection of creation. Everything happens effortlessly, by synchronicity, and the world and everything in it is seen to be an expression of love and divinity. Individual will merges into divine will. A Presence is felt whose power facilitates phenomena outside conventional expectations of reality, termed miraculous by the ordinary observer. These phenomena represent the power of the energy field, not the individual.

One's sense of responsibility for others at this level is of a different quality from that shown at the lower levels. There is a desire to use one's state of consciousness for the benefit of life itself rather than for particular individuals. This capacity to love many people simultaneously is accompanied by the discovery that the more one loves, the more one can love.

Near-death experiences, characteristically transformative in their effect, frequently have allowed people to experience the energy level between 540 and 600.

Energy Level 600: Peace

This energy field is associated with the experience designated by such terms as transcendence, self-realization and God-consciousness. It is extremely rare, attained by only one in ten million people. When this state is reached the distinction between subject and object disappears, and there is no specific focal point of perception. Not uncommonly, individuals at this level remove themselves from the world, as the state of bliss that ensues precludes ordinary activity. Some become spiritual teachers; others work anonymously for the betterment of mankind. A few become great geniuses in their respective fields and make major contributions to society. These people are saintly and may eventually be designated officially as saints, though at this level formal religion is commonly transcended, to be replaced by the pure spirituality out of which all religion originates.

Perception at the level of 600 and above is sometimes reported as occurring in slow-motion, suspended in time and space—though nothing is stationary; all is alive and radiant. Although this world is the same world seen by others, it has become continuously flowing, evolving in an exquisitely coordinated evolutionary dance in which significance and source are overwhelming. This awesome revelation takes place nonrationally so that there is an infinite silence in the mind, which has stopped conceptualizing. That which is witnessing and that which is witnessed take on the same identity; the observer dissolves into the landscape and becomes equally the observed. Everything is connected to everything else by a Presence whose power is infinite, exquisitely gentle, yet rock-solid.

Great works of art, music and architecture which calibrate between 600 and 700 can transport us temporarily to higher levels of consciousness and are universally recognized as inspirational and timeless.

Energy Levels 700-1,000: Enlightenment

This is the level of the Great Ones of history who originated the spiritual patterns which multitudes have followed through the ages. All are associated with divinity, with which they are often identified. It is the level of powerful inspiration; these beings set in place attractor energy fields which influence all of mankind. At this level there is no longer the experience of an individual personal self separate from others; rather, there is an identification of Self with Consciousness and Divinity. The Unmanifest is experienced as Self beyond mind. This transcendence of the ego also serves by example to teach others how this can eventually be accomplished. This is the peak of the evolution of consciousness in the human realm.

Great teachings uplift the masses and raise the level of awareness of all of humanity. To have such vision is called grace, and the gift it brings is infinite peace, described as ineffable, beyond words.[1] At this level of realization the sense of one's existence transcends all time and all individuality. There is no longer any identification with the physical body as "me," and therefore its fate is of no concern. The body is seen as merely a tool of consciousness through the intervention of mind, its prime value that of communication. The self merges back into the Self. This is the level of non-duality, or complete Oneness. There is no localization of consciousness; awareness is everywhere equally present.[2]

Great works of art depicting individuals who have reached the level of Enlightenment characteristically show the teacher with a specific hand position, called *mudra*, wherein the palm of the hand radiates benediction. This is the act of the transmission of this energy field to the consciousness of mankind. This level of divine grace calibrates up to 1,000, the highest level attained by any persons who have lived in recorded history—to wit, the Great Avatars to whom the title "Lord" is appropriate: Lord Krishna, Lord Buddha and Lord Jesus Christ.

V
Social Distribution of Consciousness Levels

GENERAL DESCRIPTION
A graphic representation of the distribution of the respective energy levels among the world's population would resemble the shape of a pagoda roof, in that 85% of the race is below the critical level of 200, while the overall average level of human consciousness today is approximately 204.[1] The power of the relatively few individuals near the top counterbalances the weakness of the masses toward the bottom to achieve this overall average. As mentioned, only 0.4% of the world's population calibrates at an energy field of 500 or over; a level of consciousness calibrating at 600 or over is reached by only one in ten million.

At first glance these figures may seem improbable, but if we examine world conditions, we will quickly be reminded that the populations of whole subcontinents live at a bare subsistence level. Famine and disease are commonplace, frequently accompanied by political oppression and paucity of social resources. Many of such people live in a state of hopelessness calibrating at the level of Apathy, in resignation to their abject poverty. We must also realize that much of the remainder of the world's population, civilized as well as primitive, lives primarily in Fear; the majority of humans spend their lives in a quest for one form or another of security. Those whose lifestyles transcend the imperative of survival to allow discretionary options become grist for the Desire-driven world economic mill, and success in attainment of desires leads at best to Pride.

Any meaningful human satisfaction cannot even commence until about the level of 250, where some degree of self-confidence begins to emerge as a basis for positive life experiences in the evolution of consciousness.

Cultural Correlations

The energy fields below 200 are most common in extremely primitive conditions where people eke out bare subsistence. Clothing is sparse, illiteracy is the rule, infant mortality is high, disease and malnutrition are wide-spread, and there is a vacuum of social power. Skills are rudimentary and center around fuel and food gathering and shelter preparation, and there is total dependence on the vagaries of the immediate environment. This is the stone-age cultural level, little more than animal existence.

Populations characterized by the low 200s are typified by unskilled labor, rudimentary trade, the building of simple artifacts such as dug-out canoes and temporary housing. Mobility begins to express itself in the nomadic lifestyle, and in populations that average a somewhat higher consciousness, agriculture appears and barter evolves into the use of token currency.

The mid-200s are associated with semi-skilled labor. Simple but life-sustaining housing and food economy become dependably available; clothing is adequate and elementary education begins.

The high 200s are represented by skilled labor, blue-collar workers, tradesmen, retail commerce and industries. At lower levels, for example, fishing is an individual or a tribe activity, but above the mid-200s, it becomes an industry.

At the level of 300 we find technicians, skilled and advanced craftsmen, routine managers and a more sophisticated business structure. Completion of secondary education becomes customary. There is an interest in style, sport and public entertainment; television is the great pastime at this level.

In the mid-300s we find upper management, artisans and educators, with an informed awareness of public events and a world view that extends beyond the tribe, neighborhood, or city to the nation at large and its welfare. Social dialogue becomes a meaningful matter of interest. Survival has been assured by the acquisition of skills and information adequate to function as a civilized society. There is social mobility and flexibility and resources which enable a limited amount of travel and other stimulating recreation.

The 400s are the level of the awakening of the intellect, the locus of true literacy, higher education, the professional class, executives and scientists. The home, devoid of reading material at the lower levels, here exhibits magazines, periodicals and full bookcases. There is an interest in educational broadcast channels and a more sophisticated political awareness. Great communication adeptness, intellectual preoccupation and artistic creativity are common. Recreational activities take the form of chess, travel, theater and concerts. Civic enterprises intended to enhance the social milieu receive serious attention. Supreme Court justices, presidents, statesmen, inventors and leaders of industry occupy this general range.

Because education is the underpinning of this level, individuals tend to gather in metropolitan areas where they have access to sources of information and instruction such as the great universities. Some aspire to faculty status; others become lawyers or members of the other professional classes. The welfare of one's fellow man is a common concern, though not yet a driving force. The high 400s are associated with leaders in their respective fields and with high social prestige, accomplishment and corresponding social trappings. Both Einstein and Freud calibrate at 499. But while the 400s are the level of universities and doctorates, they are also the source of the limited and limiting Newtonian vision of the universe and of the Cartesian split between mind and body (Newton and Descartes also calibrate at 499).

Just as the level 200 demarcates a critical change of consciousness, 500 is a point at which awareness makes another giant leap. Although survival of the individual is still important, the motivation of love begins to color all activities, and creativity comes into full expression, accompanied by commitment, dedication and expressions of charisma. Here excellence is common in every field of human endeavor, from sport to scientific investigation. Altruism becomes a motivating factor, along with dedication to principles. Leadership is accepted rather than sought. From this level emerges great music, art and architecture and the capacity to uplift others by one's mere presence.

In the upper 500s are found inspirational leaders who set an example for the rest of society and, in their respective fields, create new paradigms with far-reaching implications for all of mankind. Although well aware themselves that they still have defects and limitations, people on this level are often seen by the general public as out of the ordinary and may be recognized with emblems of distinction. Many in the mid-500s begin to have spiritual experiences of profound import and become immersed in spiritual pursuit. Some astonish their friends and families by sudden breakthroughs into new subjective contexts of reality. Consciousness at this level can be described as vision and may focus on uplifting society as a whole. From this level a few make the great leap to the region which calibrates at 600. At this point an individual's life may become legendary. The signature of the 600s is compassion, pervading all motivation and activity.

Progression of Consciousness

Although the levels we have described span great variation, it is not common for individuals to move from one level to another during their lifetimes. The energy field which is calibrated for an individual at birth only increases, on the average, by about five points. That an individual's level of consciousness is already in effect at birth is a sobering idea with profound implications. Consciousness itself, in its expression as human civilization, evolves slowly indeed, through innumerable generations.

The majority of people utilize their life experiences to elaborate and express the variations of their native energy field; it is the rare individual who manages to move beyond it, although many may make considerable internal improvement. The reason for this is more easily understandable when we see that what defines one's level is motivation. Motivation proceeds from meaning, and meaning, in turn, is an expression of context. Thus, achievement is bounded by context, which, when correspondingly aligned with motivation, determines the individual's relative power.

The average advance of a mere five points in a lifetime is, of course, a statistical figure, produced by, among other things, the unfortunate fact that people's cumulative life choices not uncommonly result in a net *lowering* of their level of consciousness. As will be enumerated in detail later (see Chapter XXIII, p. 234), the influence of a very few individuals of advanced consciousness counterbalances whole populations at the lower levels. But, conversely, the extreme negativity of a few perverse individuals can sway entire cultures and produce a global drag on the general level of consciousness, as history illustrates too well. Kinesiological testing indicates that a mere 2.6% of the human population, identifiable by an abnormal kinesiological polarity (testing strong to negative attractors and weak to positive attractors), account for 72% of society's problems.

Nonetheless, it is possible for isolated individuals to make sudden positive jumps, even of hundreds of points. If one can truly escape the egocentric entrainment of sub-200 attractor fields, consciously choosing a friendly, earnest, kind and forgiving approach to life, and eventually making charity towards others one's primary focus, higher levels can certainly be attained—at least in theory; in practice, great will is required.

Thus, though it is not ordinary to move out of one energy field into another during one's lifetime, the opportunity still exists. It remains for motivation to activate that potential; without the exercise of choice no progression will occur. It is well to re-emphasize that the progression of the calibrated power levels is logarithmic; thus, individual choice can have a mighty effect. The difference in power level, for instance, between 361.0 and 361.1 is very significant and capable of transforming both one's life and one's effect on the world at large.

VI
New Horizons in Research

OUR CONCERN THUS FAR has been primarily to elucidate the structure of the anatomy of consciousness, with some reference to the mechanisms of force and power. But ours is in no sense a purely theoretical subject. The unique nature of the research method described herein allows exploration of hitherto inaccessible areas of potential knowledge. It is as applicable to the most prosaic practical questions as to the most advanced theoretical explorations. Let us investigate a few general examples.

Social Problems

Drug and alcohol addiction is a crucial social concern which feeds parallel problems of crime, poverty and welfare. Addiction has proved an intractable social and clinical problem, thus far not understood beyond the most basic description. By the term "addiction" we mean clinical addiction in the classical sense of continued dependence on alcohol or a drug despite serious consequences, a condition exceeding the capacity of the addicted person to discontinue use of the substance unaided, because the will itself has been rendered ineffective. But what is the essential nature of addiction, and to what is the addict really addicted?

The common belief is that it is the addictive substance itself to which the victim has become addicted, because of that substance's power to create a high state of euphoria. But if we re-examine the nature of addiction through the methodology outlined herein, a different formulation of the process emerges. Alcohol or drugs do not in themselves have the power to create a "high" at all; they calibrate at only 100 (the level of vegetables). The so-called "high" that the drug or alcohol user experiences can calibrate from 350 up to 600. The actual effect of drugs is merely to suppress the lower energy fields, thereby allowing the user to experience exclusively the higher ones. It is as though a filter screened out all the lower tones coming from an orchestra, so that all that could be heard were the high notes. The suppression of the low notes does not create the high ones, it merely reveals them.

Within the levels of consciousness, the higher frequencies are extremely powerful, and few people routinely experience these as pure states because they are masked by lower energy fields of anxiety, fear, anger, resentment, etc. Rarely does the average person get to experience, for instance, love without fear, or pure joy, much less ecstasy. But these higher states are so powerful that once experienced, they are never forgotten and are sought ever after.

It is to this experience of higher states that people become addicted.[1] A good illustration is presented in the classic movie, *Lost Horizon*. Shangri-La (the movie's metaphor for unconditional love and beauty) calibrates as a concept at 600. Once experienced, it reprograms the experiencer so that he is never content with ordinary consciousness again. The hero of the movie discovers this fact when he is unable to find happiness again in the ordinary world after returning from Shangri-La. He then gives up everything in order to seek out and return to that state of consciousness, spending years in a struggle, which almost costs him his life, to find Shangri-La again.

This same reprogramming process occurs in people who have reached high states of consciousness by other means, such as the experience of Samadhi through meditation, or near-death experiences. Such individuals are frequently observed to have changed forever. It is not uncommon for them to leave all that the material world represents and become seekers after truth. Many who had transcendental experiences with LSD in the 1960s did the same thing. Such higher states are also attained through the experiences of love or religion, classical music or art, or through the practice of spiritual disciplines.

The high state which people seek, by whatever means, is in fact the experience field of their own consciousness (Self). If they are spiritually unsophisticated and lack a context with which to comprehend the experience, they believe it is created from something "out there" (i.e., a guru, the music, the drug, the lover, etc.). All that has actually happened is that, under special circumstances, they have experienced what is, in reality, "in here." The majority of people are so divorced from their own states of pure consciousness that they do not recognize them when they experience them, because they identify with their lower ego states, with their own lowest common denominator. A negative self-image blots out the joyous brilliance that is the true essence of their identities, which therefore goes unrecognized. That this joyous, peaceful, fulfilling state is really one's own essence has been a basic tenet of every great spiritual teacher (e.g., "the kingdom of God is within you").[2]

A "high" is any state of consciousness above one's customary level of awareness. Therefore, to a person who lives in

Fear, moving up to Courage is a high. To people who live in hopeless Apathy, Anger is a high (for instance, rioters in third-world ghettos). Fear feels at least better than Despair, and Pride feels far better than Fear. Acceptance is much more comfortable than Courage; Love makes any lower state seem comparatively unattractive. While Joy surpasses all lesser human emotions, ecstasy is a rarely-felt emotion in a class by itself. The most sublime experience of all is the state of infinite Peace so exquisite that it belies all attempts at description.

The higher the attainment of each of these states, the greater is its power to reprogram the subject's entire life. Just one instant in a very high state can completely change a person's orientation in life, his goals and values. It can be said that the individual who was, is no more, and a new person is born out of the experience. Through hard-won progress on a dedicated spiritual path, this is the very mechanism of spiritual evolution.

The permanent high-state experience that may be legitimately attained only through a lifetime of dedicated inner work can, however, be reached temporarily by artificial means. But the balance of nature dictates that to artificially acquire that state without having earned it creates a debt, and the negative imbalance results in negative consequences. The cost of such stolen pleasure is the desperation of addiction, and finally both the addict and society pay the price.

Ours is a society which idealizes the pleasureless—hard work, stoicism, self-sacrifice, restraint, etc.—and condemns pleasure in most of its simpler forms, frequently even declaring these illegal. (Politicians, whether secular or ecclesiastic, understand this phenomenon well. Part of the standard repertoire of local politicians to gain headlines today is the public announcement of intent to prohibit *Playboy Magazine* in the prisons, for instance, or deny the inmates tobacco or TV.)[3] In our society, unfulfilled promise and enticement are legitimized, but satisfaction is denied. Commercialized sexual allure, for instance, is used to sell products endlessly, but the enjoyment of actual commercial sex is forbidden as immoral.

Historically, all ruling classes have achieved status and wealth by controlling society through some form of puritanical ethic. The harder underlings work and the more meager their pleasures, the richer will be the ruling system, whether that be a theocracy, aristocracy, oligarchy or corporate industrial barony. Such power is built upon the forfeited pleasure of workers. Experientially, as we have seen, pleasure is merely high energy. The energies of the masses have been co-opted over the centuries to produce for the overclasses the very wealth of pleasures denied the underclasses.

In truth, the pleasure of the life energy is mankind's basic capital; robbing man of this has resulted in the wide division between "haves" and multitudes of "have-nots." What working classes envy in the lives of upper classes is, appropriately, their pleasures, from the pleasures of the exercise of power in its varied forms to the beautiful trophies of self-indulgence. The realization that the pleasures denied oneself are being enjoyed by others begets the outrage of revolution or, sublimated, the repression of restrictive laws against the pleasures of one's peers.

The moral code thus functions as a rationalized exploitation of the life energy of the masses through a calculated distortion of values. The illusion proffered is that the more hellish one's life, the more heavenly will be one's reward. This distorted coupling of pleasure with suffering has produced a morally perverse social milieu, in which pain becomes associated with pleasure. In this atmosphere the insane alternation of suffering and euphoria that typifies addiction becomes at least provisionally tenable, in a deadly antisocial game of winning and losing the forbidden high.

From the same life-view arises society's current method of "treating the problem" by playing the other half of the game:

denying the substance of abuse. By doing so, we have created a marketplace that is so highly lucrative and easily entered that a whole criminal industry flourishes as a result, corrupting life on multiple levels. The arrest of a drug kingpin, for instance, has no effect at all on the drug problem; before he is even jailed he will have been replaced by a new incarnation. In the recent demise of the South American drug lord Escobar, he was instantly replaced by three new kingpins, so the hydra now had three heads instead of one.[4]

Society's drug problem requires a social approach calibrating at 350, and society's current anti-drug program calibrates at only 150. It is therefore ineffective and the money spent on it is wasted.

Industrial and Scientific Research

The diagnostic method we have described quickly tracks fruitful areas for research and development in science and industry. Historical examples illustrate how the use of this method could save years of effort and millions of dollars.

Materials Research. Thomas Edison tested over 1,600 substances before he arrived at tungsten as the most suitable element to be used for his historic development of the incandescent light bulb.[5] An easier way to detect the best material would be to divide the possible alternatives into two groups and ask, "The material is in this group." (Y/N?) After this determination, the group is again subdivided, and so on. By this method an answer can be derived in a matter of minutes rather than years.

Product Development. RJR Nabisco Corporation wasted approximately $350 million to research and produce a smokeless cigarette[6] on the mistaken assumption that smoking is primarily an oral habit (in fact, it has since been discovered that when people go blind, they tend to stop smoking—smoking has multiple bases of which oral gratification is only one).[7]

A kinesiolocicalal test of the market viability of any potential product, including this one, can arrive at clear conclusions regarding public acceptance and feasibility of marketing in less than a minute. Product acceptability and profitability can be ascertained very accurately if questions are phrased with precision and all contingencies are investigated, including timing, markets, advertising and subpopulations to be addressed.

Scientific Inquiry. Science provides a Field of kinesiolocicalal exploration that offers a group of inquirers excitement eclipsing any parlor game. (It is also fascinating for a group to compare what they have discovered with the discoveries of other groups using the same method.) In a more general application, avenues for fruitful research can be identified quickly, and it will be discovered that often the most valuable insights to be obtained have to do with the range and dimension of that research. Because this method bypasses limitations of context, one of its most valuable uses is as a check on the process itself—whether or not it is a correct direction to take. We may thus confirm that basic premises from which inquiries originate have validity.

For instance, our current search for life elsewhere in the universe takes the form of broadcasting into space the mathematical symbol π . Implicit herein is the assumption that no civilization could develop radio reception unless it could understand that mathematical concept. But it is enormously presumptuous to assume that life elsewhere is even three-dimensional or detectable by human senses at all, let alone composed of discrete life units that solve problems by use of an intellect and employ symbols to communicate across space and time.

Medical Science. Kinesiolocical diagnosis is a science in its own right, governed by the International College of Applied Kinesiology. Each organ of the body has its corresponding detector muscle whose weakness signals pathology in the corresponding organ. Kinesiology is already widely used to confirm both diagnosis and the efficacy of a probable therapy. The right dose of the right medicine can also be determined by the patient's kinesiologic response. Similarly, allergies can be detected, and the need for nutritional supplements may be determined.

Research in Theology, Epistemology and Philosophy

Though the validity of its application may vary with the capacity for awareness of the observer, the technique of using kinesiology to ascertain truth itself calibrates at a level of 600. This means that the method described has a degree of reliability which is beyond duality, or the realm of ordinary consciousness as we know it in daily life. The level of truth of this book as a whole is approximately 750. To maintain that level throughout, the truth of every chapter, page, paragraph and sentence has been examined by use of the method described, and all statements and conclusions have been similarly verified.

The confusion surrounding the nature of truth can be mitigated if we calibrate the level of truth of our questions as well as our answers. Paradoxes and ambiguities arise from confusing levels of consciousness; an answer is true only at its own level of consciousness. Thus, we may find that an answer is "correct" but simultaneously "invalid," like a musical note that is correctly played but at the wrong place in the score. All observations are reflections of specific levels of consciousness and are valid only on their own level. Every means of approaching a subject therefore has its own built-in limitations.

A statement may be true at a high level of understanding but be incomprehensible to the average mind. Its value may therefore be corrupted when the statement is distorted by the limitations of the listener. This has been the fate of religions throughout the ages, when pronouncements originating from high levels of awareness were later misinterpreted by followers vested with authority. Such distortion can be seen to an extreme degree in fundamentalist sects of any religion. The fundamentalist's interpretation of religious teachings, proceeding always from negativity, is removed by this negativity from truth. The lowest depictions of deity are of a god who is jealous, vengeful and angry, a god of death far removed from the God of mercy and love. The god of righteous negativity represents a glorification of the negative, and provides for his followers a disavowal of responsibility through justification of human cruelty and mayhem. Pain and suffering in general increase as one nears the bottom levels of consciousness.

The truth of each level of consciousness is self-verifying in that each level has its native range of perception which confirms what is already believed to be true. Thus, everyone feels justified in the viewpoints which underlie his actions and beliefs. That is the inherent danger of all "righteousness." Anyone can be righteous, from the killer who justifies his rage to ecclesiastic demagogues and political extremists of all persuasions. By distorting context, it is possible to rationalize and justify virtually any human behavior.

The human dialogue is awesome in its enormity and subtlety, reflecting the kaleidoscopic interactions of the powerful attractor energy fields constituting man's consciousness. The brilliance of the world's great philosophers through twenty-five centuries has been staggering in its scope and complexity. Yet, overall there are few areas of agreement as to the nature of truth. Without an objective yardstick, every individual who has ever lived has had to sift through the changing reflections of life to discern his own truth; this seems a never-ending struggle to which man is condemned by virtue of his own mental design.

This design predicates that any statement will be true only within a given context, despite the fact that the definitions and derivations of that context are invisible and unstated. It is as though every individual is exploring life with a compass that has a unique setting. That any meaningful dialogue at all is possible bespeaks man's enormous compassion for his own condition and attests that giving cohesion to the whole is an all-inclusive, overarching attractor Field that facilitates the manifestation of the possible into the actual.

Concordance emerges from the organizing patterns hidden behind apparent chaos; thus the evolution of mankind progresses despite the apparently aberrant signals of individuals at any given moment. Chaos is only a limited perception. Everything is part of a larger whole; everyone is involved in the evolution of the all-inclusive attractor Field of consciousness itself. It is this evolution, innate to the overall Field of consciousness, which guarantees the salvation of mankind, and with it, of all life. The nobility of man is in his constant struggle with his own unasked-for existence in a world which is a house of mirrors—his sole support, his faith in the process of life itself.

VII
Everyday Critical Point Analysis

THE POTENTIAL APPLICATIONS for research we have described thus far give some suggestion of the limitless uses to which this method lends itself. As the interaction of attractor fields of energy with human consciousness reveals itself in an interaction of mind and body, the basic level of available energy in any enterprise can be calibrated by anyone, anywhere, any time. All that is required is to have two people, one of whom is familiar with the muscle-testing technique described in this study. The practical implications are staggering; this tool can be as germinal in the continuing evolution of society as any of the major discoveries of the physical sciences to date. Let us spell out in more pragmatic detail what this could mean in everyday life.

Inasmuch as the calibrated power of an identified attractor pattern is directly related to its degree of veracity, or level of truth, it is possible to cleanly distinguish true from false, constructive from destructive, the practical and efficient from the unworkable and wasteful. We can identify motive, agenda and goal in any project or in individuals themselves. Sheep's clothing need no longer hide the wolf.

As we have seen, consciousness reacts decisively to the difference between truth and falsehood. You may instantly reconfirm this by stating your true age (let us say that you are forty-three years old), "I am forty-three years old," and having someone press down on your extended arm. You will stay strong. Now say, "I am forty-five years old," and you will instantly go weak. Like a computer, consciousness simply answers 0 or 1, true or false. (Any ambiguities in the process are introduced by the questioning method, not the answering mechanism. See Appendix B, Chapter II, and below.)

We can identify the level of truth of any statement, belief system or body of knowledge. We may accurately measure the truth of any sentence, paragraph, chapter, or entire book, including this one.[1] We can reliably identify our own level of consciousness or motive in any enterprise. We now have available a perspective on social movements and history never before possible. Political research is not confined to the present. We can look back into history to make calibrations, for instance, to compare Gorbachev with Stalin, Trotsky with Lenin, and so on.

In all of these exercises kinesiology reveals the hidden implicit order by making it explicit, disclosing its true nature. The use of the system is self-educative and self-directing. Each answer, it will be discovered, leads to the next question—happily, in an upward and beneficial direction. We discover the truth about ourselves because our questions themselves are merely the reflections of our own motives, goals and levels of awareness. It is always informative to calibrate not the answer, but the question.

In discussing the process, we must emphasize again, more specifically, some aspects of the form of questioning. *Precision in wording is of paramount importance.* The question might be posed, for instance, "Is this decision a good one?" But what do we mean by "good"? Good for whom, and in what time frame? Questions have to be very carefully defined. What we think is good or bad is merely subjective; what the universe "thinks" about it may be quite something else.

Motive in questioning is highly significant. Always ask first, "I may ask this question?" Never ask a question unless you are prepared for the answer; the facts may be quite different from what you currently believe. Though there is a potential for emotional upset through the unwise use of this method, experience has shown that continuing the line of inquiry will enlarge the context and heal the disturbance. Let us say a young woman asks, "My boyfriend is honest?" "He is good for my life?" and the answers are negative. She is disappointed to find his love is selfish and his interest exploitative. But further questions provide a resolution: "This relationship would end in emotional pain?" (Yes.) "I am saving myself a lot of misery now by knowing this?" (Yes.) "I can learn from this experience?" (Yes.)

On a more mundane level, the same technique can determine whether an investment is an honest one or not, or whether an institution can be trusted. We can accurately predict the potential of new developments, not only in marketing, but in medical research or engineering. We can check the safety precautions being used on great oil tankers. We can judge in advance the advisability of military strategy. We can ascertain who is fit to govern and distinguish the statesman from the mere politician. In the case of a media event, we can instantly tell whether the interviewer or the interviewee is telling the truth, and, if he is, what level of truth is being expressed. (If you try this during a network news hour you may have a shocking revelation; on many occasions *all* the public figures are lying.)

Want to tell if that's a good used car to buy? Easy. If a salesman is telling the truth? Simple. Your new romantic interest a good bet? This a reliable product? That employee trustworthy? What is the degree of safety of a new device; will it be successful or a flop? What is the integrity, skill and competence level of a particular doctor or lawyer? Who is the best available therapist, teacher, coach, repairman, mechanic or dentist? What levels of consciousness are required to properly discharge the duties of specific public offices, and what are the levels of the incumbents?

This capacity to instantly differentiate truth from falsehood is of such extraordinary potential value to society that we have felt it appropriate in our research to document and verify some explicit practical applications.

Current and Historic Events

Because the technique immediately distinguishes true from false evidence, it can resolve factual disputes—the identity of perpetrators, for instance, or the whereabouts of missing persons. The truth underlying major news events can be revealed, whether the guilt or innocence of contemporary victims and accusers, the validity of historic conspiracy theories or unsolved mysteries, such as the Amelia Earhart story, the Lindbergh kidnapping, etc. Testimony before Senate hearings and media reports of events are verifiable in a matter of seconds. By use of this technique, for instance, it will be discovered that a major sports figure who recently served a prison term is innocent, and his accuser was lying. In another recent prominent case, the accuser is telling the truth, and the accused is still holding a high office.

Health Research

The failure to eradicate certain diseases or find their cure is often due to the fact that reason is its own limitation. False answers often preclude searching for true causes. For instance, it is currently dogma that tobacco causes cancer; our research, however, revealed that organically grown tobacco tests kinesiolocicalally strong, whereas commercial tobacco tests weak. Tobacco was not noted as a carcinogen before 1957 and it does so now as the result of chemicals introduced into its manufacture at that time. There are other solutions to smokers" lung cancer. Research reported in *Science* in 1995 indicates that one gram per day of Vitamin C prevents cell damage from smoking. But the real solution is to identify and remove the carcinogenic chemicals from the manufacturing process.

Criminal Justice and Police Work

To know whether a witness is lying is of obvious importance in any case under investigation. But it is equally significant to discover whether the prosecution is withholding evidence or if a jury has been tampered with (or, for that matter, is even capable of understanding the evidence).

One of the most interesting applications of the technique is in crimes where there are no witnesses, and it is the word of the accuser against that of the accused. The rash of allegations of sexual crimes against prominent people is an obvious example. Public figures are easy targets for politically motivated character assassination, and in a society where defendants are treated by the media as if proven guilty merely by virtue of having been accused, they need public protection as much as the accusers.

Statistics and Methodology: Time Saving

Great amounts of money and time are spent gathering data to document what could be discerned in minutes. For instance, to "prove" the validity of the kinesiolocical method itself to the skeptical, the following procedures had to be followed: 15 different small groups totaling 360 subjects were tested with both positive and negative stimuli (statistical analysis revealed p ≤ .001) 2) 7 large groups totaling 3,293 volunteers were similarly tested (p ≤ .001) 3) 325 subjects were tested individually (p ≤ .001) 4) 616 psychiatric patients were tested in groups and individually (p ≤ .01). The conclusion from all the above was that the null hypothesis was rejected. Traditional methodologies are inefficient.

Politics and Government

Are our leaders telling us the truth? Is a political figure upholding the Constitution of the United States or subverting it for personal gain? Does a particular candidate have the unique capacity to rise to the demands of the office he or she seeks? Are facts being misrepresented by a government agency or spokesperson? Will a proposed policy actually solve the problem for which it is designed? Such practical issues can now be addressed with more certitude. Political debates and public addresses can be analyzed for factuality, and proposed legislation can be assessed from a clearer perspective. Programs that are worthwhile can be definitely identified, and ineffective programs can be dropped.

Commerce

It is possible to diagnose an ailing business or industry and solve its problems without risking financial resources on experiments. Complete analysis of a business starts with calibrating the current and past levels of collective motivation and the abilities of all concerned in its operation. Next, one may calibrate what level needs to be reached by the various departments to succeed. Then policies, personnel, products, supplies, advertising, marketing and hiring procedures can be similarly assessed. Various market strategies can then be investigated without investment in expensive market analysis, preserving capital while saving enormous amounts of time and energy.

It is wise to remember that in the conventions of commerce, like those of politics, truth has an ambiguous status. There is a universally accepted implicit understanding that things said to gain advantage are not held to any standard of personal honesty. A convenient conscience regarding the exaggerated claim, the bluff, the white lie, is as much a part of the garb of the marketplace as the business suit and tie. (In fact, intriguingly, kinesiological analysis commonly tells us to no longer believe an erstwhile trustworthy person once he has donned a suit and tie!) Therefore, numerous applications arise in everyday business—for instance, to determine whether a bill or invoice is accurate. A padded account will make any investigator's arm go weak as will inferior quality or workmanship. Fraud and bogus imitations are easily detectable; the technique can quickly differentiate a bad check from a good one, a false diamond from a true gem.

Science and Research

The level of truth of any scientific paper, experiment or theory is easily determinable, a great potential asset to the scientific community and the public at large. The benefits to be derived from a given direction of investigation can be ascertained in advance, as can the value of alternate avenues of research. Examination of the economics of research projects and the capabilities of investigators and equipment is also of practical value.

Critical factor analysis can detect the point in a system at which the least effort is capable of producing the greatest result. Computer simulation, with all its complex and uncertain variables, is the present state-of-the-art technique for predicting developments and exploring alternative proposals. The built-in limitations of logic circuits, however, can be transcended by the kinesiologic use of the world's most advanced computer, the human nervous system. Quantum nonlocality guarantees that the answers to every question are everywhere present, but this in itself can be confusing to a conventional computer.

Clinical Work

In medicine, the accuracy of diagnoses as well as the efficacy of a prescribed treatment can be tested. The technique is also valuable in psychological issues where the etiology of a disorder can be quickly ascertained. One currently controversial subject of investigation that obviously suggests itself is the area of so-called repressed childhood memories of alleged sexual abuse. Facts can be quickly differentiated from false "memories" elicited in response to suggestion. Freud concluded that most reports of childhood incest he encountered were of hysterical origin, and he finally stopped believing them.

Kinesiologic testing can be used to back up clinical judgments as well as scientifically controlled investigation, because it can transcend the built-in design limitation of double-blind research, which can of itself create the very error it is supposed to prevent. Statistics are no substitute for truth and in the complexity of bio-behavioral phenomena, proximal antecedents can too easily become classified as ostensible causes. The real "cause" may well be the pull of the future through a hidden attractor field.

Education

A profoundly telling exercise may be performed by evaluating the books in one's library. Simply hold them over the solar plexus and have somebody test your muscle strength. As you do this, your books will end up in two piles; reflection on the differences between the two can produce a revelation—

many testers have found it one of the most valuable experiences of their lives. (Some left the two piles there for a period of time to let the lesson sink in.)

It is equally informative to try the same procedure with one's music collection. The negative group will include violent, sexist rap music and heavy metal rock. The positive pile will contain classical music, classic rock (the Beatles included), much Country Western (surprisingly, it calibrates generally at 520—the problems of the heart), Reggae, popular ballads, etc.

Spirituality

Though this chapter has dealt primarily with secular uses of this tool, it should be pointed out that applications of the technique can be profoundly spiritual. We may, for instance, test the contrasting statements: "I am a body," and "I have a body." Appropriate questions proceeding from this point can resolve one's most basic fears. All limiting self-definitions create fear because they create vulnerability. Our perceptions are essentially distorted by our own self-definition, which in turn is qualified by identifying with our limitations. Error occurs when we cling to the belief that I *am* "that." Truth is unveiled when we see that one *has* "that," or *does* "that," instead of *is* "that."

There is great freedom in the realization that I "have" a body and a mind, rather than I "am" my mind or body. Once the fear of death is transcended, life becomes a transformed experience because that particular fear underlies all others. Few people know what it is to live without fear. But beyond fear lies joy, as the meaning and purpose of existence become transparent. Once this realization occurs, life becomes effortless and the sources of suffering dissolve; suffering is only the price we pay for our attachments.

Empirical issues, however, are involved even in spiritual quests. In the matter of spiritual teachers, Americans are extremely naïve, partly because spiritual pursuit does not have a long tradition here as it does in older cultures. That the world abounds with false gurus is well known in India, but such cynicism does not come readily to Americans. Fakes repeatedly come out of India with impressive presentations and hoodwink naïve Western spiritual aspirants who, in childlike trust, leave home and hearth, sell their belongings, and follow the charismatic spiritual con man down a path to eventual disillusionment. The acumen of some of these "gurus" can be dazzling, and their capacity to mimic a convincing sincerity is amazing; they often take in even sophisticated spiritual seekers. This is spiritual seduction. A mixture of truth and falsehood blended in a slick package, the teachings sound valid if one cannot see that their truth has been distorted by a false context.

Such spiritual exploitation is routinely exposed in India where these media-hungry frauds are held in low regard and often confined to their quarters by the government should they return home. Such "teachers" can inflict terrible suffering and tragedy. The most catastrophic depressions in clinical practice occur in people who have discovered that they have been spiritually deceived. Such disillusionment and pain is far more severe than that which results from other losses in life, and recovery has not always been possible.

The charm of all false prophets is persuasiveness. But use of the testing method herein described provides a foolproof safeguard against such deception. It is informative to watch TV evangelists with the sound turned off and have somebody test you. False gurus also make everyone go weak in a dramatic fashion. It is as though the universe considers spiritual rape a specially grave error.

What of a true teacher? In the first place, a universal hallmark is that the true teacher never controls anyone's life in any way, instead merely explaining how to advance consciousness. If we do test, though, we will find, for instance, that Mother Teresa, recognized by the world through the Nobel Prize, calibrates at 700, as does the acknowledged Indian spiritual saint, Ramana Maharshi, who died in 1956. (He went into a state of enlightenment at age sixteen, never left the mountain where he lived and led a life of humble simplicity, eschewing money, prestige and followers, and would have remained unknown had not a well-known American writer's description of Ramana's enlightened state brought seekers from all over the world.)[2]

Nowhere is spiritual fraud more prevalent than in the world of channelers and psychics. It is informative to check out the level of truth these mediums express as well as the level of the "source" on the "other side." Sometimes a surprisingly high level of truth is in fact being taught. A level of truth which calibrates at 500 is worth listening to regardless of its origin, because the inability to love is at the root of most human problems. Beyond the level of 500, material possessions and worldly needs become irrelevant, which is why true teachers neither seek nor desire material gain.

Appropriate use of the system will always lead to self-discovery and growth. Eventually it can lead us to compassion for everyone, when we see how we all must struggle with the downside of human nature. Everyone is crippled in some area, and everyone is somewhere on the path of evolution, some ahead of us and some behind. In the steps we have walked are the old lessons of life, and before us are new teachings.

There is nothing to feel guilty about and nothing to blame. There is no one to hate, but there is that which is better avoided, and such blind alleys will become increasingly apparent. Everyone has chosen his own level of consciousness, yet nobody could have done otherwise at any given point in time. We can only get "there" from "here." Every leap has to have a platform from which to originate. Pain exists to promote evolution; its cumulative effect finally forces us in a new direction, though the mechanism may be very slow. How many times is it necessary to hit bottom before a lesson is learned? Perhaps thousands, which may account for the sheer quantity of human suffering, so vast as to be incomprehensible. Slowly, by inches, does civilization advance.

It is an interesting exercise to use our technique to reassess our society's scapegoats—for example, to calibrate the current power level of the United Nations and then ask what level would be required to successfully do the job for which it was designed. When we see such discrepancies spelled out in plain numbers we may stop berating individuals and institutions, realizing they often simply do not have the requisite power to accomplish their tasks. Condemnation disappears with understanding, as does guilt. All judgment reveals itself to be self-judgment in the end, and when this is understood a larger comprehension of the nature of life takes its place.

That which is injurious loses its capacity to harm when it is brought into the light. And now nothing need remain hidden. Every thought, action, decision or feeling creates an eddy in the interlocking, interbalancing, ever-moving energy fields of life, leaving a permanent record for all of time. This realization can be intimidating when it first dawns on us, but it becomes a springboard for rapid evolution.

In this interconnected universe, every improvement we make in our private world improves the world at large for everyone. We all float on the collective level of consciousness of mankind, so that any increment we add comes back to us. We all add to our common buoyancy by our efforts to benefit life. What we do to benefit life automatically benefits all of us because we are all included in that which is life. We *are* life. It is a scientific fact that "what is good for you is good for me".

Simple kindness to one's self and all that lives is the most powerful transformational force of all. It produces no backlash, has no downside, and never leads to loss or despair. It increases one's own true power without exacting any toll. But to reach maximum power such kindness can permit *no* exceptions, nor can it be practiced with the expectation of some selfish reward. And its effect is as far reaching as it is subtle.

In a universe where "like goes to like" and "birds of a feather fly together," we attract to us that which we emanate. Consequences may come in an unsuspected way. We are kind to the elevator man, and a year later a helpful stranger gives us a hand on a deserted highway. An observable "this" does not *cause* an observable "that." Instead, in reality, a shift in motive or behavior acts on a field which then produces an increased likelihood of responding in a positive way. Our inner work is like building up a bank account, but one from which we cannot draw at will. The disposition of the funds is determined by a subtle energy field which awaits a trigger to release this power back into our own lives.

Dickens' *A Christmas Carol* is the story of all our lives. We all are Scrooge. We are all Tiny Tim. All of us are both selfish and lame in some areas. We are all victims like Bob Cratchit, and we are all as indignantly moralistic as Mrs. Cratchit refusing to toast Scrooge. The Ghost of Christmas Past haunts all of our lives; the Spirit of Christmases to come beckons us all to make the choices that will enhance both our own existence and that of others. (If we calibrate the energy level of Christmas, by the way, it becomes obvious that power resides within the human heart itself.)

All avenues of questioning lead to the same ultimate answer. The discovery that nothing is hidden and truth stands everywhere revealed is the key to enlightenment about the simplest practical affairs and the destiny of mankind. In the process of examining our everyday lives we can find that all our fears have been based on falsehood. The displacement of the false by the true is the essence of the healing of all things visible and invisible.

And always a final question will eventually arise for every questioner—the biggest question of all: "Who am I?"

VIII
The Source of Power

THE ULTIMATE OBJECT of our investigation is a practical rather than an academic or philosophical understanding, although certain philosophical conclusions can immediately be drawn from even a brief analysis of power and force. From a practical viewpoint, before proceeding we need to know what is the intrinsic source of power and how it operates. What accounts for its greater strengths? Why is it that force always eventually succumbs to power?

In this respect the Constitution of the United States can provide a rewarding study. This document calibrates at about 700. If one goes through it sentence by sentence, the source of its power appears: it is the concept that all men are equal by virtue of the divinity of their creation, and human rights are intrinsic to human creation and therefore inalienable. Interestingly enough, this is the very concept that was the source of Mahatma Gandhi's power.

On examination we will see that power arises from meaning. It has to do with motive and it has to do with principle. Power is always associated with that which supports the significance of life itself. It appeals to that in human nature which we call noble, in contrast to force, which appeals to that which we call crass. Power appeals to that which uplifts and dignifies—ennobles. Force must always be justified, whereas power requires no justification. Force is associated with the partial, power with the whole.

If we analyze the nature of force it becomes readily apparent why it must always succumb to power; this is in accordance with one of the basic laws of physics. Because force automatically creates counter-force, its effect is limited by definition. We could say that force is a movement. It goes from here to there, or tries to go from here to there against opposition. Power, on the other hand, is still. It is like a standing field that does not move. Gravity itself, for instance, does not move against anything. Its power moves all objects within its field, but the gravity field itself does not move.

Force always moves against something, whereas power does not move against anything. Force is incomplete and therefore has to constantly be fed energy. Power is total and complete in itself and requires nothing from outside itself. It makes no demands; it has no needs. Because force has an insatiable appetite, it constantly consumes. Power, in contrast, energizes, gives forth, supplies and supports. Power gives life and energy. Force takes these away. We notice that power is associated with compassion and makes us feel positively about ourselves. Force is associated with judgment and makes us feel badly about ourselves.

Force always creates counter-force; its effect is to polarize rather than unify. Polarization always implies conflict; its cost, therefore, is always high. Because force incites polarization, it inevitably produces a win/lose dichotomy; and because somebody always loses, enemies are always created. Constantly faced with enemies, force requires constant defense. Defensiveness is costly, invariably, whether in the marketplace, politics or international affairs.

In looking for the source of power we have noted that it is associated with meaning, and this meaning has to do with the significance of life itself. Force is concrete, literal and arguable. It requires proof and support. The sources of power, however, are inarguable and are not subject to proof. The self-evident is not arguable. That health is more important than disease, that life is more important than death, that honor is preferable to dishonor, that faith and trust are preferable to doubt and cynicism, that the constructive is preferable the destructive—all are self-evident statements not subject to proof. Ultimately, the only thing we can say about a source of power is that it just "is."

Every civilization is characterized by native principles. If the principles of a civilization are noble, it succeeds; if they are selfish, it falls. As a term, "principles" may sound abstract, but the consequences of principle are quite concrete. If we examine principles we will see that they reside in an invisible realm within consciousness itself. Although we can point out examples of honesty in the world, honesty itself as an organizing principle central to civilization is nowhere independently existent in the external world. True power, then, emanates from consciousness itself; what we see is a visible manifestation of the invisible.

Pride, nobility of purpose, sacrifice for quality of life—all such things are considered inspirational, giving life significance. But what actually inspires us in the physical world are things that symbolize concepts with powerful meanings for us. Such symbols realign our motives with abstract principle. A symbol can marshal great power because of the principle which already resides within our consciousness.

Meaning is so important that when life loses meaning, suicide commonly ensues. When life loses meaning, we first go into depression; when life becomes sufficiently meaningless, we leave it. Force has transient goals; when those goals are reached there remains the emptiness of meaninglessness. Power, on the other hand, motivates us endlessly. If our lives are dedicated, for instance, to enhancing the welfare of everyone we contact, our lives can never lose meaning. If the purpose of our life, on the other hand, is financial success, what happens after it is attained? This is one of the primary etiologies of depression in middle-aged men and women.

The disillusionment of emptiness comes from failing to align one's life with the principles from which power emanates. A good illustration of this phenomenon can be seen in the lives of great musicians, composers and conductors of our own times. How frequently they continue productive careers into their eighties and nineties, often having children and living vigorously until a ripe old age![1] Their lives have been dedicated to the creation and embodiment of beauty; beauty incorporates and expresses enormous power. We know clinically that alignment with beauty is associated with longevity and vigor. Because beauty is a function of creativity, such longevity is common in all creative occupations.

The philosophic position of positivism, based on the premise that nothing is real except as it is quantifiable, is endemic to the sciences. The sources of power, however, are invisible and intangible. The sophistry of logical empiricism is clear from its essential premise. To say that nothing is real unless it is measurable is already an abstract position, is it not? This proposition itself is nowhere tangible, visible or measurable; the argument of tangibility is itself created from the intangible.

Even were such a position valid, who would want to live without pride, without honor, without love, compassion or value? Despite the pathetic implications of this argument, let us nevertheless address it.

Does power have any tangible basis? Does it proceed exclusively from the undefinable, the mystical, philosophic, spiritual or abstract? Is there anything more we can know about power that would make sense to those who are oriented only to that left-brain world which, regardless of its computerized sophistication, remains only a system of mechanical measurements?

Before we proceed, let us remind ourselves that the most advanced artificial intelligence machines in the world are unable to feel joy or happiness. Force can bring satisfaction, but only power brings joy. Victory over others brings us satisfaction, but victory over ourselves brings us joy. But as previous chapters have shown, not only can these qualities now be measured, they can be accurately calibrated. To make this fact more comprehensible to reason, let us continue our tour through some easily understood concepts from advanced theoretical physics.

We need not be intimidated by these concepts; to the contrary, their implications for daily life, though profound, are quite simple. We don't have to understand the molecular structure of rubber in order to benefit from having tires on our cars. Though their proofs may be complex, Einstein's Theory of Relativity, Bell's Theorem, and so on, can all be stated in a few easily understandable sentences.

Several recently defined concepts have relevance in understanding of the nature of power. One is physicist David Bohm's theory that states there is both a visible and an invisible universe.[2] This idea should not be daunting; many things with which we have a daily familiarity—x-rays, radio and TV waves—are not visible either. An "enfolded" universe runs parallel to the visible, "unfolded" universe, which is itself merely a manifestation of that enfolded, invisible universe.

Thus, for instance, did the idea of building the world's tallest building marshal support and eventually result in an invisible concept becoming the Empire State Building in the visible world. The enfolded universe is connected with human consciousness, as inspiration arises in the mind of a creator. Bohm says meaning links mind and matter like opposite sides of a coin.[3]

Another useful concept is Rupert Sheldrake's notion of morphogenetic fields, or M-fields.[4] These invisible organizing patterns act like energy templates to establish forms on various levels of life. It is because of the discreteness of M-fields that identical representations of a species are produced. Something similar to M-fields also exists in the energy fields of consciousness, underlying thought patterns and images—a phenomenon termed "formative causation." The idea that M-fields assist learning has been verified by wide-scale experimentation.[5]

When Roger Bannister broke the four-minute mile, he created a new M-Field. The belief system prevailing in human consciousness had been that the four-minute mile was a limit of human possibility. Once the new M-Field was created, many runners suddenly began to run sub-four-minute miles. This occurs every time mankind breaks into a new paradigm, whether it is the capacity to fly, an M-Field created by the Wright Brothers, or the capacity to recover from alcoholism, an M-Field created by Bill W., the founder of AA. Once an M-Field is created, everyone who repeats the accomplishment reinforces the power of that M-Field.

We are all familiar with the fact that new ideas often seem to arise in the minds of several far removed people at the same time. Somehow the M-Field acts as an organizing principle, like a sort of general magnetic attraction. An M-Field does not have to move anywhere. It is a standing energy field which is everywhere present. Once it is created it exists as a universally available pattern throughout the invisible universe.

The next concept we need to consider in more detail is chaos theory (nonlinear dynamics). Its first application was in the prediction of weather, the study of which, over the centuries, had established the consensus that there was no definable, predictable mathematical pattern to weather (just as it had also been determined that there was no mathematical way to prove when a dripping faucet will drip, or even to explain how a droplet is formed). Chaos merely means a mass of apparently meaningless data—for instance, dots—in which one cannot see any inherent organizing pattern. With the advent of advanced computer technology, it was discovered that inner organizing patterns could be found by computer analysis in what looked disorganized: that which appears to be incoherent actually has an inner coherence.

Such analysis revealed patterns which often look like the figure eight folded back upon itself, frequently with a funnel effect, so that the graphic itself has a repeatable geometric configuration. What science has realized is what mystics have claimed throughout the centuries: that the universe is indeed coherent, unified and organized around unifying patterns.[6]

Nonlinear dynamics has verified that there really is no chaos in the universe; the appearance of disorder is merely a function of limits of perception. This came as a disturbing revelation to left-brain people, but seemed self-evident to right-brain types. Creative people merely write, paint, sculpt or design what they already see within their own minds. We don't dance from logic, we dance from feeling patterns. We make our choices from values, and values are associated with intrinsic patterns.

The accepted chain of causality as commonly understood in the basic sciences occurs as the sequence $A \rightarrow B \rightarrow C$. In this scheme of material determinism nothing is inherently free, but only the result of something else. It is thereby limited; what this system really defines is the world of force. Force A results in Force B and is transmitted to Force C with consequence D. D in turn becomes the beginning of another series of chain reactions, *ad infinitum*. This is the left-brain world, mundane and predictable. It is the limited paradigm from which the conventional sciences operate: chartable, familiar, controllable, but uncreative—determined, and therefore limited, by the past. It is not the world of genius, but to many it feels safe. It is the world of productivity and practicality. To creative people, though, it seems pedestrian, prosaic and uninspiring.

It is one thing to conceive of the Empire State Building, but something else to make it happen. To make a thing happen requires motivation. Motivation is derived from meaning. Therefore, the visible and invisible worlds are linked together, as we have already diagrammed it:

Here we see that the concept ABC, which is within the invisible, enfolded universe will activate emergence into the visible world to result in A→B→C. Thus the visible world is created from the invisible world, and is therefore influenced by the future.[7] The capacity of the invisible concept to materialize is based on the power of the original concept itself. We might say that the right brain "gets the pattern" and the left brain "makes it visible." An ABC may be either a high energy attractor or a low energy attractor. Certain concepts and values apparently have much greater power than others. (Thus far science has only defined that attractors may have either high energy or low energy.)

Simply stated, powerful attractor patterns make us go strong, and weak patterns make us go weak. Some ideas are so weakening that merely holding them in mind makes a test subject unable to keep up his arm at all. Other concepts are so powerful that when they are held in mind it is impossible to force down the subject's arm with any amount of exertion. This is a universal clinical observation. Powerful patterns are associated with health; weak patterns are associated with sickness, disease and death. If you hold forgiveness in mind, your arm will be very strong. If you hold revenge in mind, your arm will go weak.

For our purposes it is really only necessary to recognize that power is that which makes you go strong. Force makes you go weak. Love, compassion and forgiveness, which may by some be mistakenly thought of as submissive, are, in fact, profoundly empowering. Revenge, judgmentalism, and condemnation, on the other hand, inevitably make you go weak. Therefore, regardless of moral righteousness, it is a simple clinical fact that in the long run the weak cannot prevail against the strong. That which is weak falls of its own accord.

Individuals of great power throughout human history have been those who have totally aligned themselves with powerful attractors. Again and again they have stated that the power they manifested was not of themselves. Each has attributed the source of the power to something greater than himself.

All of the Great Teachers throughout the history of our species have merely taught one thing, over and over, in whatever language, at whatever time. All have said, simply: Give up weak attractors for strong attractors.

In examining these attractors we will notice that some weak patterns tend to imitate (in form only) more powerful patterns. These we will call "imitators." Thus, the German people under the Third Reich were deceived by patriotism because they thought it was Patriotism. The demagogue or the zealot tries to sell us imitators as the real thing. Demagogues, to this end, always put forth a great deal of rhetoric. Those who move from power need say very little.

PART TWO:
WORK

IX
Power Patterns in Human Attitudes

THE ABILITY TO DIFFERENTIATE between high- and low-energy patterns is a matter of perception and discrimination that most of us learn by painful trial and error. Failure, suffering and eventual sickness result from the influence of weak patterns; success, happiness and health proceed from powerful attractor patterns. Therefore, it is well worth taking a few minutes to scan the list of contrasting patterns below, which have been researched and calibrated to determine their respective criteria. This exhaustive listing is an educational tool operating from the principle of closure. Reflection on the many contrasting pairs of qualities can initiate a consciousness-raising process, so that one gradually becomes aware of patterns operating in relationships, business affairs and all the various interactions that make up the fabric of life. On the left are adjectives describing powerful (positive) patterns, which calibrate above 200; on the right, weak (negative) patterns, which calibrate below 200.

Abundant....	Excessive	Detached	Removed
Accepting....	Rejecting	Determined ..	Stubborn
Admitting....	Denying	Devoted	Possessive
Aesthetic	Artsy	Diplomatic ...	Deceptive
Agreeable....	Condescending	Doing	Getting
Allowing.....	Controlling	Educating	Persuading
Appreciative..	Envious	Egalitarian....	Elitist
Approving ...	Critical	Empathetic...	Pitying
Attractive	Seductive	Encouraging..	Promoting
Authoritative .	Dogmatic	Energetic.....	Agitated
Aware.......	Preoccupied	Enlivening....	Exhausting
Balanced	Extreme	Envisioning...	Picturing
Beautiful.....	Glamorous	Equal........	Superior
Being	Having	Erotic	Lustful
Believing.....	Insisting	Essential	Apparent
Brilliant......	Clever	Eternal.......	Temporal
Candid	Calculating	Ethical.......	Equivocal
Carefree	Frivolous	Excellent.....	Adequate
Challenged...	Impeded	Experienced ..	Cynical
Charitable....	Prodigal	Fair	Scrupulous
Cheerful.....	Manic	Fertile	Luxuriant
Cherishing ...	Prizing	Flexible......	Rigid
Choosing-to ..	Having-to	Forgiving.....	Resenting
Civil	Formal	Free.........	Regulated
Concerned...	Judgmental	Generous	Petty
Conciliatory ..	Inflexible	Gentle.......	Rough
Confident....	Arrogant	Gifted	Lucky
Confronting ..	Harassing	Giving.......	Taking
Conscious ...	Unaware	Global.......	Local
Considerate ..	Indulgent	Gracious.....	Decorous
Constructive..	Destructive	Grateful	Indebted
Contending ..	Competing	Harmonious..	Disruptive
Courageous ..	Reckless	Healing......	Irritating
Defending ...	Attacking	Helpful	Meddling
Democratic ..	Dictatorial	Holistic	Analytic

Honest	Legal		Principled	Expedient
Honoring	Enshrining		Privileged	Entitled
Humble	Diffident		Prolific	Barren
Humorous . . .	Somber		Purposeful . . .	Desirous
Impartial.	Righteous		Receiving	Grasping
Ingenious	Scheming		Releasing	Tenacious
Inspired	Mundane		Reliant.	Dependent
Intentional . . .	Calculating		Requesting . . .	Demanding
Intuitive	Literal		Respectful . . .	Demeaning
Inventive.	Prosaic		Responsible . .	Guilty
Inviting	Urging		Satisfied	Sated
Involved	Obsessed		Selective	Exclusive
Joyful	Pleasurable		Serene	Dull
Just	Punitive		Serving	Ambitious
Kind	Cruel		Sharing	Hoarding
Leading.	Coercing		Significant. . . .	Important
Liberating	Restricting		Sober	Intoxicated
Long-term. . . .	Immediate		Spontaneous .	Impulsive
Loyal.	Chauvinistic		Spiritual	Materialistic
Merciful	Permissive		Steadfast.	Faltering
Modest.	Haughty		Striving	Struggling
Natural	Artificial		Surrendering. .	Worrying
Noble.	Pompous		Tender	Hard
Nurturing	Draining		Thoughtful . . .	Pedantic
Observant . . .	Suspicious		Thrifty	Cheap
Open	Secretive		Timeless	Faddish
Optimistic . . .	Pessimistic		Tolerant	Prejudiced
Orderly.	Confused		Tractable.	Contrary
Outgoing	Reserved		Trusting.	Gullible
Patient	Avid		Truthful	False
Patriotic	Nationalistic		Unifying	Dividing
Peaceful	Belligerent		Unselfish.	Selfish
Polite	Obsequious		Valuing	Exploitive
Powerful.	Forceful		Virtuous	Celebrated
Praising.	Flattering		Warm	Feverish

Simply having read over this list, you are no longer the same person; merely to become acquainted with the differences between these poles begins to increase one's inner power. With these distinctions in mind we will start to notice things we never observed before. Such revelations occur because, as the reader will discover, the universe favors power.

Moreover, the universe does not forget. There are many sides to the question of karma, but every choice of who and how to be is a choice of great consequence. All our choices reverberate through the ages. Thousands of reports of near-death experiences, as reflected in such best-sellers as Brinkley's *Saved by the Light* or B. J. Eadie's *Embraced by the Light*—the latter of which calibrates at 595—confirm that we shall eventually have to accept responsibility for every thought, word and deed we beget and re-experience exactly whatever suffering we have caused. It is in this sense that we each create our own heaven or hell.

The universe holds its breath as we choose, instant by instant, which pathway to follow; for the universe, the very essence of life itself, is highly conscious. Every act, thought and choice adds to a permanent mosaic; our decisions ripple through the universe of consciousness to affect the lives of all. Lest this idea be considered either merely mystical or fanciful, let us remember that fundamental tenet of the new theoretical physics: everything in the universe is connected with everything else.[1]

Our choices reinforce the formation of powerful M-Fields, which are the attractor patterns that influence others.[2] Even if one sits isolated in a cave, his thoughts influence others whether he wishes it or not. Every act or decision you make that supports life supports all life, including your own. The ripples we create return to us. This, which may once have seemed a metaphysical statement, is now established as a scientific fact.[3]

Everything in the universe constantly gives off an energy pattern of a specific frequency which remains for all time and can be read by those who know how. Every word, deed and intention creates a permanent record. Every thought is known and recorded forever. There are no secrets; nothing is hidden, nor can it be. Our spirits stand naked in time for all to see. Everyone's life, finally, is accountable to the universe.

X
Power in Politics

TO BETTER UNDERSTAND the critical difference between force and power and the implications of this
distinction for our own lives, it is helpful to examine human
endeavor on a larger scale—the interactions of men and governments provide many clear illustrations.

Looking at history from our unique perspective, we will,
of course, be reminded of the powerful example set by the
American Revolution which first formally established freedom
as an inalienable right, setting a precedent for centuries to
come. Principles which calibrate as high as 700 affect mankind
over great courses of time. The pen is indeed mightier than
the sword, because power originates from the mind, whereas
force is rooted in the material world.

A related pivotal event in global history, to which we have
already referred and will again, came about in this century
through the power of a solitary man: Mahatma Gandhi, a
ninety-pound "colored," who single-handedly overcame the

British Empire, then the greatest force in the world, ruling two-thirds of the face of the globe.[1]

Gandhi not only brought the British Empire to its knees; he effectively rang down the curtain on the centuries-old drama of colonialism, and he did it by simply standing for a principle: the intrinsic dignity of man and his right to freedom, sovereignty and self-determination.[2] Fundamental to this principle, in Gandhi's view, was the fact that such rights derive to man by virtue of the divinity of his creation. Gandhi believed that human rights are not granted by any earthly power, but are inherent in the nature of man himself because they are inherent in his creation.[3]

Violence is force; because Gandhi was aligned with power, rather than force, he forbade all use of violence in his cause.[4] And because he expressed universal principles (which calibrate at 700) he was able to unite the will of the people. When the will of the people is so united by and aligned with universal principle, it is virtually unconquerable. Colonialism (calibrated at 175) is founded in the self-interest of the ruling country. Gandhi demonstrated, for the world to witness, the power of selflessness versus the force of self-interest.[5] The same principle has now been demonstrated quite dramatically in South Africa by Nelson Mandela.[6]

Power accomplishes with ease that which force is unable to accomplish even with extreme effort; thus, in our own time we have seen the almost effortless toppling of communism as a governmental form, after half a century of the most ominous—and ultimately ineffectual—military confrontation of history. The political naïveté of the Russian people, long used to the tyrannical rule of czars, did not allow them the civic wisdom to understand that in the name of communism a totalitarian dictatorship was being established. Similarly, the German people were deceived by Hitler, who rose to power in the name of national socialism only to establish a virtual tyranny. A distinctive characteristic of force in politics is that it cannot tolerate dissent. Both rules depended on the pervasive use of force through secret police; Stalin, who also put millions to death, relied on his KGB, as Hitler his Gestapo.

Adolph Hitler assembled the greatest military machine the world had ever seen. On the simple level of force, his military was unbeatable; yet he could not defeat a tiny island across the English Channel because of the power expressed by Winston Churchill, who unified the will of his people through principles of freedom and selfless sacrifice. Churchill stood for power, Hitler for force.[7] When the two meet, power always eventually succeeds; in the long run, if it is deeply founded in the will of the people, power is immune to force.

Force is seductive because it emanates a certain glamour, whether that glamour is manifested in the guise of false patriotism, prestige or dominance, while true power very often is quite unglamorous. What could be more glamorous than the Luftwaffe and Waffen SS of Nazi Germany during the Second World War? These elite branches embodied romance, privilege and style and certainly had at their disposal enormous force—the most advanced weapons of the day and an *esprit de corps* that cemented their might. Such is the glamour of the formidable.

The weak are attracted to and will even die for the glamour of force. How else could something so outrageous as war even occur? Force often seizes the upper hand temporarily, and the weak are attracted by those who seem to have overcome weakness. How else could dictatorship be possible?

One characteristic of force is arrogance; power is characterized by humility. Force is pompous; it has all the answers. Power is unassuming. Stalin, who strutted military autocracy, has gone down in history as an arch-criminal.[8] The humble Mikhail Gorbachev, who wore a plain suit and easily admitted to faults, has been awarded the Nobel Prize for Peace.

Many political systems and social movements begin with true power, but as time goes on become co-opted by self-seekers and end up relying increasingly on force until they finally fall in disgrace. The history of civilization demonstrates this repeatedly. It is easy to forget that the initial appeal of communism was idealistic humanitarianism, as was that of the union movement in the United States until it became a refuge of petty politicians.[9]

To fully comprehend the dichotomy we are discussing, it is necessary to consider the difference between a politician and a statesman. The politician, operating out of expediency, rules by force after gaining his position through the force of persuasion—he often calibrates at a level less than 200. Statesmen represent true power, ruling by inspiration, teaching by example and standing for self-evident principle. The statesman invokes the nobility which resides within all men and unifies them through what can best be termed the heart. Though the intellect is easily fooled, the heart recognizes truth. Where the intellect is limited, the heart is unlimited; where the intellect is intrigued by the temporary, the heart is only concerned with the permanent.

Force often relies upon rhetoric, propaganda and specious argument to garner support and disguise underlying motivations. One characteristic of truth, though, is that it needs no defense; it is self-evident. That "all men are created equal" requires no justification or rhetorical persuasion. That it is wrong to gas people to death in concentration camps is self-evident; it requires no argument. The principles upon which true power is based never require vindication, as force inevitably does—there are always endless arguments about whether force is "justified" or not.

It is clear that power is associated with that which supports life, and force is associated with that which exploits life for the gain of an individual or an organization. Force is divisive and, through that divisiveness, weakens, whereas power unifies. Force polarizes. The jingoism that has such obvious internal appeal to a militaristic nation just as obviously alienates the rest of the world.

Power attracts, whereas force repels. Because power unifies, it has no true enemies, though its manifestations may be opposed by opportunists whose ends it does not serve. Power serves others, whereas force is self-serving. The true statesman serves the people;[10] the politician exploits people to serve his own ambitions. The statesman sacrifices himself to serve others; the politician sacrifices others to serve himself. Power appeals to our higher nature, force to our lower nature. Force is limited, whereas power is unlimited.

Through its insistence that the end justifies the means, force sells out freedom for expediency. Force offers quick, easy solutions. In power, the means and end are the same, but ends require greater maturity, discipline and patience to be brought to fruition. Great leaders inspire us to have faith and confidence because of the power of their absolute integrity and alignment with inviolate principles. Such figures understand that you cannot compromise principle and still retain your power. Winston Churchill never needed to use force with the British people; Gorbachev brought about total revolution in the largest political monolith in the world without firing a shot; Gandhi defeated the British Empire without raising a hand in anger. And we might note that the seemingly endless Middle Eastern conflict finally appears to be approaching resolution, not through violence, but communication, at long last, between the adversaries.

Democracy and the United States of America

Democracy is eventually being acknowledged universally as the superior form of government. Around the globe there is a rising call for freedom; many nations with a heritage of repression are learning the lessons necessary for the establishment of liberty. Following conventional science, historians usually try to explain such sequences of political events through an A→B→C causality; this, however, is merely the apparent sequential unfolding of something with a much greater power, the ABC attractor pattern out of which a society evolves.

The power of the United States, or any other democracy, arises from the principles upon which it is founded. Thus we can find the basis of power by examining such documents as the Constitution of the United States, the Bill of Rights, the Declaration of Independence and such acknowledged expressions of the spirit of democracy as the Gettysburg Address.

If we calibrate the relative power of each line of these documents, we find the highest attractor pattern of all, out of which the power of the entire United States government emanates, in the Declaration of Independence: "We hold these truths to be self-evident, that all men are created equal, that they are endowed by their Creator with certain unalienable Rights, that among these are Life, Liberty and the pursuit of Happiness." (calibrated at 700). These sentiments are echoed in the Gettysburg Address where Lincoln reminds us that this nation was conceived in Liberty and "...dedicated to the proposition that all men are created equal" and that "this nation, under God, shall have a new birth of freedom—and that government of the people, by the people, for the people, shall not perish from the earth." (also 700).

If we examine the actions and statements of Lincoln himself during the trying years of the Civil War, we will find with absolute certainty that he was devoid of all hatred. He had compassion rather than malice for the South, for he understood better than anyone else that the battle was really between man's higher and lower natures. He therefore represented the "self-evident truths" he referred to, and personally mourned the price that he knew had to be paid.[11]

The Declaration of Independence states, "We hold these truths to be self-evident"—that human rights are endowed by nature of man's creation and are inalienable; they do not derive as a fiat from force, nor are they granted by any temporal ruler. Democracy recognizes the divine right of the ruled, rather than the ruler. It is not a right by virtue of title, wealth or military superiority, but instead is a profound statement of the essence of man's nature, defining principles intrinsic to human life itself: liberty and the pursuit of happiness. (Mahatma Gandhi's power base calibrates identically with the power base of the Declaration of Independence and the Constitution; all are essentially concerned with freedom, liberty and the equality of all men by virtue of endowment by a divine higher power.)[12]

Interestingly, if we calibrate the power of the attractor field of theocracy, we find it consistently lower than that of any democracy which also recognizes the Creator as the ultimate authority. The makers of the Declaration of Independence were astute in drawing a very clear distinction between that which is spiritual and that which is religious. And they must have intuitively, if not rationally, known the marked difference between the power of the two. Religion is often associated with force, sometimes disastrously so, historically and today; whereas spiritual concepts such as loyalty, freedom and peace do not create strife or conflict, much less war. Spirituality is always associated with non-violence.

If we examine the application of the Bill of Rights today, however, we find that its power in several areas has dwindled. The right to freedom from unreasonable search and seizure, as well as freedom from cruel and unusual punishment, have both been eroded over the years by expediency. The spirit of the United States Constitution has become sufficiently dimmed that laws which are blatantly unconstitutional are frequently proposed and often passed without a murmur of protest. Pockets of totalitarianism exist within government itself; our society routinely tolerates totalitarian tactics by both federal and local agencies, manifested in the conspicuous use of intimidation. Unfortunately, we have gotten so used to an atmosphere of fear and violence that it comes as a surprise to Americans abroad that the threat of government intrusion or police force does not even exist in many foreign countries.

It is most important to remember that to violate principle for practical expediency is to relinquish enormous power. The rationalization that the execution of criminals deters crime, for instance, does not hold up under study; and the end does *not* justify the means. The consequence of this violation of principle is reflected in the crime statistics of the United States, where murder is so common it does not even make the front pages.

Because we fail to differentiate principle from expediency, the average person lacks the discernment to understand the difference between *patriotism* and *Patriotism*, between *americanism* and *Americanism*, between *god* and *God*, between *freedom* and *Freedom*, between *liberty* and *Liberty*. Thus, "Americanism" is used as a justification by white supremacy groups (calibrated at 150) and lynch mobs, just as war mongering throughout history has been conducted in the name of "God." The misinterpretation of liberty as license tells us that many people do not know the difference between *freedom* and *Freedom*.

Learning the difference between principles and their imitators requires experience and educated judgment. The exercise of such discretion is necessary for moral survival in the modern world in general, but is imperative in those grayest of areas, where ethical ambiguity has been elevated from convention to art form: the political arena and the marketplace of daily commerce.

XI
Power in the Marketplace

MAN HAS FREEDOM OF CHOICE, without which there would be no accountability or responsibility. The ultimate choice, really, is whether to align with a high energy attractor field or a low energy attractor field. The same weak attractor patterns that have brought down governments, social movements and entire civilizations routinely destroy organizations and careers. One makes one's choice and then takes the consequences.

Nowhere are these consequences more dramatically visible than in the realm of business. Nowhere else, however, could failure be more easily avoided if a few basic concepts were clearly understood. Attractor fields can be quickly calibrated, whether in a product, a company or an employee. In our research, the differences between businesses that have failed and businesses that have succeeded have proved so marked that excellent predictive accuracy can be expected.

All too often the "buyer"—who can be a voter, investor or truth-seeker, as well as a purchaser—is captured by the glamour of an imitator pattern which on the surface appears to be a high energy attractor pattern. People are dazzled by superficial style and slick presentation, like those naïve investors who recently bought silver only to find that the entire commodity market had been manipulated. Our notorious savings-and-loan fiascoes and their perpetrators could easily have been identified long before the scandals surfaced. Similar disasters can be avoided by simply examining whether a business endeavor is associated with a high or a low attractor pattern. This identification can become almost instinctive once one understands the difference between the operation of force and power in commerce.

Sam Walton, the founder of Wal-Mart, provides a model of how power comes from aligning with high energy attractor patterns. The ABC which he conceived has resulted in the A→B→C that is the rapidly growing Wal-Mart colossus. The basic principles involved are spelled out in the book *Sam Walton* by Vance Trimble.[1]

In the aisles of many of today's giant stores there seem to be no employees whatsoever; the gross indifference to customer goodwill is shocking. Wal-Mart's employees, in contrast, are trained to be accommodating, warm and energetic, to reflect a humane energy field in their workplace. Their jobs have meaning and value because they are aligned with Service, a commitment to the support of life and human value. All Wal-Marts feature an area where you can rest your feet and decide about purchases. Such allocation of space to meet simple human needs would not pass the scrutiny of scientific management calculations in terms of gross sales per square footage. But such efficiency expertise has discarded, along with human compassion, the market allegiance of millions of customers. Computers don't feel; more attention would be paid to feelings if it was realized that *feelings determine purchases.*

A commercial factor of great, though often unrecognized, importance is the "family" feeling of employees—their loyalty to their organization. This is a very prominent quality in successful companies. Employees who feel nurtured and supported are those who smile genuinely at customers. Another characteristic of such an environment is low employee turnover, whereas cold and impersonal companies have very rapid employee turnover. Employee shortage is always an expression of a low attractor energy pattern. Critical factor analysis of a large cut-rate drug chain that had just gone Chapter Eleven revealed that the few dollars saved by not having extra employees at the checkout counter regularly cost thousands of dollars in sales; such shortsightedness is common in businesses dominated by low energy fields.

To be a success it is necessary to embrace and operate from the principles that produce success, not just imitate the actions of successful people. To really do what they do, it is necessary to *be like they are*. Companies that have imitated some of Wal-Mart's features in hopes of regaining market share have not been successful because they merely imitated the A→B→C instead of aligning with the ABC from which those features emanated.

Our research on attractor patterns correlates closely with the conclusions arrived at by Peters and Waterman in their work, *In Search of Excellence*, a detailed analysis of several great companies.[2] They concluded that successful companies were those which had "heart," as opposed to strictly left-brain, scientifically managed companies. In reading this study, one cannot help but be struck by the inadequacy of many marketing survey procedures: the statisticians simply don't know what questions to ask.

In addition to counting the millions that companies make, analysts might well assess the multimillions that they do not make. A good example is the recent decline in the U.S.

auto industry. One would think it would be apparent from the success of the Rolls Royce or the Volkswagen Beetle that espousing a philosophy of planned obsolescence rather than enduring quality demonstrates a gross miscalculation. Our research indicated years ago that by following the high energy attractor patterns we have already identified Detroit could reclaim the auto market. Truly creative innovation is required in order to recapture the imagination of the public, and enduring quality must supplant planned obsolescence, as the price of a new car approaches twenty thousand dollars.

Sensibly enough, not many Americans are happy to lay out such sums in full knowledge that that investment will shortly be lost to obsolescence. Obviously, what the depreciating car loses is not any real, innate value. The inflated price of glamour and novelty does not reflect any actual worth. People will gladly pay fifty thousand dollars or more for a used Rolls Royce knowing that twenty years from now it will still be classic in style and mechanically sound, with high resale value.

Our research indicates that Americans would willingly pay such high prices for cars if their intrinsic worth were equivalent to their purchase price, so as to protect the investment, and if they would run well and maintain value a long time, ideally a lifetime. (For instance, a modular car in which the motor, drive train, etc., were easily removable and replaceable—with a lifetime guarantee—would be a sure winner.) Attractor research tells us that customers are willing to pay for quality, and that good products would sell themselves without slick advertising gimmicks. Integrity and excellence speak for themselves, because they are aligned with power.

One of the most profitable and simple applications of critical factor analysis is in the field of advertising. The use of the simple kinesiologic technique we have described can instantly reveal whether an advertising campaign or given commercial is weak or strong.

Companies pay enormous sums to reach the greatest possible audience but this strategy can backfire when a widely viewed commercial that makes viewers go weak damages the company's image. An ad that makes people go strong will always produce a positive feeling about the product rather than an aversion. Similarly, advertisers who buy time during TV programs that make people go weak will find their product unconsciously associated with these negative feelings. By analyzing a commercial in detail one can ascertain the elements that have a weakening, negative effect—the voice of the announcer, the mannerisms of an actor, or the use of certain words, concepts or symbols. That some companies repeatedly produce tasteless and even embarrassing commercials reflects low attractor fields prevalent in their advertising and marketing departments.

Beyond the surface world of commerce, society provides numerous other marketplaces where fulfillment of human needs is sought, bartered, stolen, coerced and denied. It is a simple fact of life that satisfaction of needs brings contentment; frustration breeds violence, crime and emotional turmoil. If the mission of government regulatory institutions were realigned to support the fulfillment of human needs, rather than mounting moralistic, black-and-white campaigns to stamp out "social problems," these institutions could become powerful forces for human betterment.

Perceptual fields are limited by the attractor patterns with which they are associated. This means that the capacity to recognize significant factors in a given situation is limited by the context that arises from the level of consciousness of the observer. The motive of the viewer automatically determines what is seen; causality is, therefore, ascribed to factors that are in fact a function of the biases of the observer and are not at all instrumental in the situation itself. The concept of "situational ethics" tells us that the right or wrong of behavior cannot be determined without reference to context. As each conditioning factor colors the picture, shades of gray are introduced that alter the significance of the whole scenario.

One indication of a low energy attractor field is a struggle of opposites. Whereas power always results in a win-win solution, force produces win-lose situations; the consequent struggle indicates that the correct solution has not been found, as when the assertion of one group's interests violates those of another, or the rights of the accused conflict with those of the victim. The way to finesse a high energy attractor field solution is to seek the answer which will make all sides happy and still be practical. Such solutions involve utilization of both the ameliorative right brain as well as the judgmental left brain.

One basic principle has the power to resolve the problems of the social marketplace; it may be stated: Support the solution instead of attacking the supposed causes. Attack is in itself inherently a very weak attractor pattern (150) leading through fear to intimidation, coercion and, eventually, moral corruption. The "vice squad" becomes just that, turning city streets into jungles of crime.

Objective examination reveals that most intractable "social problems" appear unsolvable due to the persistence of either sentimentality or juvenile moralizing. Neither of these positions is based in truth, and, therefore, all approaches proceeding from them are weak. Falsehood makes us go weak; acting from false positions typically results in the use of force. Force is the universal substitute for truth. The gun and the nightstick are evidence of weakness; the need to control others stems from lack of power, just as vanity stems from lack of self-esteem. Punishment is a form of violence, an ineffectual substitute for power. When, as in our society, the punishment rarely fits the crime anyway, it can hardly be effectual; punishment is based on revenge at the weak energy level of 150.

Supporting the solution of human needs, on the other hand, creates a no-cost resolution that brings serenity; attacking the artificially created "problem" is always expensive, in addition to criminalizing society. Only the childish proceed from the assumption that human behavior can be explained in black and white terms. Denying basic biologic needs and instinctual drives is futile. Blocking normal sexual outlets merely results in the creation of abnormal sexual outlets. The solutions that have power are the ones realistically based at the level of acceptance (350) rather than condemnation (150). In Amsterdam one section of the city is traditionally designated as a red-light district, quiet and serene with a pastoral atmosphere; its streets are safe. In Buenos Aires parts of parks are set aside for lovers. The police patrol these areas to protect rather than harass, and all is peaceful.

Another example is the previously cited government inability to solve the problem of drug use. Again, the mistake is in looking at the problem moralistically and acting out of force in a punitive role. The original critical error was the failure to differentiate between hard drugs and soft drugs. Hard drugs (narcotics) are addicting, with severe withdrawal effects, and have been traditionally associated with crime. Soft drugs (recreational) are non-addicting, do not induce withdrawal and are usually initially handled by amateurs. By criminalizing soft drugs, the government created a new criminal syndicate, wealthy and international in scope. When interdiction was effective, shortages of cheap, relatively harmless recreational material on the streets were quickly filled by hard-drug merchants, and the peaceful, largely innocuous drug culture became criminalized and vicious.

Successful solutions are based on the powerful principle that resolution occurs not by attacking the negative, but by fostering the positive. Recovery from alcoholism cannot be accomplished by fighting intoxication, but, rather, only by choosing sobriety. The "war to end all wars" did no such thing nor could it possibly have done so. Wars, including wars on "vice," "drugs" or any of the human needs regularly traded for in the great hidden social marketplace that underlies conventional commerce, can only be won by choosing peace.

XII
Power and Sports

THE THEORETICAL UNDERSTANDING at which we have arrived in our study of consciousness provides a context which may be applied to any field of human activity. This can be illustrated by an examination of sports, a good example because sport is so widely observed and extensively documented. Great heroes of sports have been celebrated throughout history at least as much as great figures in science, the arts or any other area of cultural achievement. Sports figures symbolize for all of us the possibilities of excellence, and, at the level of the champion, mastery.

What is it in athletics that brings a crowd to its feet and commands wildly enthusiastic loyalty? At first we might think it is pride, a fascination with competition and triumph. But while these motives may produce pleasure and excitement, they cannot account for the far greater emotions of respect and awe elicited by a display of athletic excellence. What animates the crowd is an intuitive recognition of the heroic striving required to overcome human limitation and achieve new levels of prowess.

High states of consciousness, also, are frequently experienced by athletes. It is well documented that long-distance runners frequently attain sublime states of peace and joy. This very elevation of consciousness, in fact, often inspires the prolonged transcendence of pain and exhaustion necessary to achieve higher levels of performance. This phenomenon is commonly described in terms of pushing oneself to the point where one suddenly breaks through a performance barrier and the activity becomes effortless; the body then seems to move with grace and ease of its own accord, as though animated by some invisible force. The accompanying state of joy is quite distinct from the thrill of success; it is a joy of peace and oneness with all that lives.

It is notable that this transcendence of the personal self and surrender to the very essence or spirit of life often occurs at a point just beyond the apparent limit of the athlete's ability. The seeming barrier is predicated by the paradigm of one's own past accomplishments or of what has been recognized as theoretically possible, such as the historic "four-minute mile." Until Roger Bannister broke the four-minute mile, it was universally accepted that it was not humanly possible to run any faster; Bannister's greatness was not just in breaking the record, but in breaking through that paradigm to a new model of human possibility. This breakthrough to new levels of potential has correspondences in every field of human endeavor; in many diverse enterprises, those who have achieved greatness have given parallel accounts of the circumstances surrounding their accomplishments.

We have made calibrations of various kinds of records of athletic achievement, including movies. Of all of the movies about sport studied, the French film *The Big Blue* produced the highest calibration.[1] This is the story of the world's deep-sea diving champion, Jacques Mayol, the Frenchman who for many years, until very recently, held the world record. The movie calibrates at the extraordinary energy level of 700 (universal truth). The movie itself has the capacity to put viewers into a high state of consciousness; the manager of one movie-house which showed it described audiences wandering out of the theater lost in silence or crying with a joy which they could not describe.

The movie achieves an accurate depiction of the world's greatest deep-sea diver in elevated states of consciousness through the use of slow-motion photography. A subjective sensation of slow-motion, beauty and grace is frequently noted in higher states; time seems to stop and there is an inner silence despite the noise of the world.

We see throughout the film that Jacques Mayol maintains this state by the intensity of his concentration, which keeps him in an almost constant meditative condition. In this mode he transcends ordinary human limitations, enabled to achieve great feats through altered physiology; the deeper he dives, the slower is his heartbeat, and his blood distribution concentrates almost entirely in his brain (as does that of the porpoise). His best friend, himself a highly evolved athlete, dies in an attempt to match Mayol's feat because he has not reached the level of consciousness required to transcend the normal limits of the body.

The subjective experience of effortless bliss also occurs in other types of exceptional physical performance, such as that of the world-famous Sufi dancers known as whirling dervishes, who, through discipline and exhausting practice, become able to move effortlessly through space over long periods of time with dazzling precision.

The most highly developed martial arts clearly demonstrate how motive and principle are of ultimate importance in extraordinary athletic achievement.[2] The most frequently heard admonition to trainees is "stop trying to use force."[3] Schools devoted to these arts produce masters whose overriding concern is victory of the higher self over the lower self through control, training and commitment to goals aligned with true power.[4] Alignment with these high power attractor patterns is not limited to the exercise of the discipline itself but becomes an entire lifestyle. Thus, when the power of the principle is transferred to the practitioner, the results begin to be manifested everywhere in his life.

The hallmark of true greatness in athletic achievement is always humility, such as that exhibited by Pablo Morales after winning his Gold Medals in the 1992 Summer Olympics. Such athletes express gratitude, inner awe and an awareness that their performance was not merely the result of a personal effort—that maximum personal effort brought them to the breakthrough point from which they were then transported by a power greater than that of the individual self. This typically is expressed as the discovery of some aspect of the self hitherto unknown, or unexperienced in its pure form.

Through kinesiology we can demonstrate that if one is motivated by any of the energy fields below courage, one goes weak. The notorious Achilles heel that brings down not just athletes but the potentially great in all areas of human achievement is pride. Pride, calibrated at 175, not only makes the performer go weak, but cannot provide the motivational power of love, honor or dedication to a higher principle (or even to excellence itself). If we ask a powerful athlete to hold in mind the hope of defeating his opponent, or becoming a star, or making a lot of money, we will see that he goes weak and we can put down his trained, muscular arm with minimal effort. The same athlete holding in mind the honor of his country or his sport, or the dedication of his performance to someone he loves, or even the sheer joy of maximum effort for the sake of excellence, goes powerfully strong, and we cannot push down his arm with even the greatest effort.

Thus the competitor motivated by pride or greed, or interested primarily in defeating an opponent, will go weak at the moment of the starting gun and be unable to achieve the maximum continued effort necessary for great achievement. At times we see an athlete start badly for such reasons, but, as the contest progresses and selfish goals are forgotten, improve his performance. We also see the opposite happen when an athlete starts well because he is competing for the honor of his country, his team, or of the sport itself, and then falters as he nears the goal and the anticipation of personal glory or triumph over a rival makes him lose strength and form.

One unfortunate sequence of consciousness occurs when an athlete sets a new record during qualifying trials, arousing new personal ambitions, and then during the final competition goes to pieces to the puzzlement of the audience. If top performers are imbued with the belief that their excellence is not a personal accomplishment but a gift belonging to all of mankind as a demonstration of man's potential, they will go strong and remain so through any event.

The scale of consciousness may be seen in one aspect as a scale of ego, with the level of 200 being the fulcrum at which selfishness begins to turn to selflessness. At the rarefied plane of Olympic competition, the disastrous consequences, both in private and in public life, of motivations emanating from levels below 200 are all too clearly illustrated by the recent debacle of figure skater Tonya Harding. This athlete's excessive zeal to capture an Olympic medal and defeat her rival Nancy Kerrigan by any means available led her to abandon the power of ethical principle and descend to the grossest level of force. There could hardly be a more telling example of how submission to a negative attractor field can produce a rapid collapse of an otherwise promising athletic career.

Where higher motivations toward excellence give access to the realm of grace and power, self-centered motivations of personal gain draw one almost magnetically into the realm of force. The reaping of recognition—even in the symbolic form of a medal, let alone the financial reward that may accompany it—has little to do with true athletic greatness, which proceeds from an attainment of stature of the spirit; it is this that we laud in the champion. Even if the competitor does not surrender to the lust for wealth and fame so prominent in the case just cited, the drive to attain dominance in one's sport, rather than to simply manifest all the excellence of which one is capable, has its own corrupting egocentric effect, entrainment by the negative forces associated with the level of Pride.

There is nothing intrinsically wrong with some manifestations of pride. We all may well be proud when we take the America's Cup or our Olympians win medals, but that is a different kind of pride. It is an honoring of human achievement that transcends personal pride. We honor the endeavor, not the personal accomplishment, which is only the occasion and expression of something greater, universal and innate in the human heart. The Olympics, one of the greatest dramas of human striving, and one which captures everyone's imagination, provides a context which should counteract personal pride. The whole setting inspires the competitor to move from personal pride to an esteem which is an expression of unconditional love, and which honors one's opponents, as well, for their dedication to the same lofty principles.

The media tend to evoke the downside of sports and undermine the athlete, because celebrity status either consciously or unconsciously elicits this egotism. Great athletes need to gird themselves against this source of contamination. Humility and gratitude seem to be the only effective shield against the onslaughts of media exploitation. Athletes in the traditional martial arts employ specific exercises to overcome any tendency towards egotism. The dedication of one's skill, performance or career to a higher principle provides the only absolute protection.

True athletic power is characterized by grace, sensitivity, inner quiet and, paradoxically, gentleness in the non-competitive lives of even fierce competitors. We celebrate the champion because we recognize that he has overcome personal ambition through sacrifice and dedication to higher principles. The great become legendary when they teach by example. It is not what they have, nor what they do, but what they have become that inspires all of mankind, and it is that which we honor in them. We should seek to protect their humility from the forces of exploitation that accompany acclaim in the everyday world. We need to educate the public that the abilities of these athletes and their great performances are gifts to mankind to be respected and defended from the abuse of the media and corporate commerce.

The Olympic spirit resides within the heart of every man and woman. Great athletes can, by example, awaken awareness of that principle in all people. These heroes and their spokesmen have a potentially powerful influence on all of mankind, literally the power to lift the world on their shoulders. The nurturing of excellence and recognition of its value is the responsibility of all men, because the quest for excellence in any area of human endeavor inspires us all toward the actualization of every form of man's yet unrealized greatness.

XIII
Social Power
and the Human Spirit

WHEN WE CHEER THE SPIRIT of the true athlete, what we applaud is a demonstration of all the significances the word "spirit" entails for us: courage, tenacity, commitment, alignment with principle, demonstration of excellence, honor, respect and humility.[1] To inspire implies filling with spirit; dispirited means dejected, hopeless, defeated. But what exactly does the term "spirit" signify? The collective totality of human experience can be comprehended by *spirit* in phrases such as "team spirit" or when we exhort people to "get into the spirit." That spirit is a highly pragmatic factor which can determine the difference between victory and defeat is well known by military commanders, coaches and CEOs. An employee or other group member who doesn't enter into the spirit of the group enterprise soon finds himself without a job or group.

From all the above it is clear that the term "spirit" refers to an unseen essence, and that although its expression varies from one situation to another, the essence itself never changes.[2] This essence is vital; when we lose our spirit, we die—we expire from lack of that which inspires.

Clinically speaking, then, we can say that Spirit equates with Life; the energy of life itself can be termed spirit. Spirit is the alive-ness that accompanies and is an expression of alignment with life energy. The power of high energy attractor patterns is anabolic, sustaining life; their opposites are catabolic, eventually leading to death. True power equals life equals spirit, whereas force equals weakness equals death. When an individual has lost or lacks those qualities we term spiritual, he becomes devoid of humanity, love and self-respect, perhaps selfish and violent. When a nation veers from its alignment with the spirit of man, it can become an international criminal.

It is a common error to identify spirituality with religion. We have noted that the United States Constitution, the Bill of Rights and the Declaration of Independence clearly differentiate between the spiritual and the religious. Government is forbidden to establish any religion, lest it impair the freedom of the people; yet these same documents presume that government's authority derives from spiritual principles.[3]

In fact, the founders of the world's great religions would be shocked at the profoundly unspiritual deeds wrought in their names through history, much that would make a heathen shudder. Force always distorts truth for its own self-serving purposes. Over time, the spiritual principles upon which religions are based become distorted for expedient ends such as power, money, and other worldliness. Whereas the spiritual is tolerant, religiosity is commonly intolerant. The former leads to peace, the latter to strife, bloodshed and pious criminality. There remains, however, buried within every religion, the spiritual foundation from which it originated.[4] Like religions, entire cultures are weakened when the principles upon which they are based are obscured or contaminated by false interpretation.

To more fully understand the nature of spirit in power and how it originates and operates as a social movement, we will do well to study a contemporary spiritual organization of enormous power and influence about which everything is of public record, one which is avowedly aligned with the spirit of man and yet flatly states that it is not religious. That is the fifty-five-year-old organization known as Alcoholics Anonymous.

We all know something about AA, because it has become woven into the very fabric of modern society, and its adherents number in the millions. It and its offshoot organizations have been estimated to affect in one way or another the lives of about fifty percent of Americans at this time. Even where the twelve-step-based self-help groups do not enter lives directly, they affect everyone indirectly because they reinforce certain values by example. Let us study the power principles upon which Alcoholics Anonymous is based and how this foundation came about historically, and examine the impact these principles have within the general population as well as among members. We can look at what AA is and also what it is not, and learn from both.

AA is, according to its preamble, "Not allied with any sect, denomination, politics, or organization." In addition, it has "no opinion on outside matters." It is neither for nor against any other approach to the problem of alcoholism. It has no dues or fees, no ceremonies, no trappings, no officers, no laws. It owns no property, has no edifices. Not only are all members equal, but all AA groups are autonomous and self-supporting.[5] Even the twelve basic steps by which members recover are specified as only "suggestions." The use of coercion of any kind is avoided and this is emphasized by slogans such as, "Easy does it," "First things first," and, most importantly, "Live and let live."[6]

Alcoholics Anonymous respects freedom, in that it leaves choice up to the individual. Its identifiable power patterns are those of honesty, responsibility, humility, service, and the practice of tolerance, goodwill and brotherhood. AA does not subscribe to any particular ethic, has no code of right and wrong or good and bad and avoids moral judgments. AA does not try to control anyone, including its own members. What it does instead is to chart a path. It merely says to its members, "If you practice these principles in all your affairs, you will recover from this grave and progressive fatal illness, and regain your health, self-respect and the capacity to live a fruitful and fulfilling life for yourself and others."[7]

AA is the original example of the power of these principles to cure hopeless disease and change the destructive personality patterns of members. From this paradigm came all subsequent forms of group therapy, through the discovery that groups of people coming together on a formal basis to address their mutual problems have enormous power: Al-Anon for the spouses of AA members, then Al-Ateen for their children, then Gamblers Anonymous, Narcotics Anonymous, Parents Anonymous, Overeaters Anonymous, and so on. There are now close to 300 anonymous twelve-step self-help organizations dealing with every form of human suffering. Americans, as a result of all this, have now largely turned from condemning self-destructive behaviors to recognizing that these conditions are indeed curable diseases.

From a practical viewpoint the sizable impact of self-help organizations on society can be counted not only in the relief of human suffering and the reconstitution of families, but in savings of billions of dollars. Absenteeism, automobile insurance rates, welfare, health care and penal system costs are all

greatly moderated by the widespread behavioral change produced by this movement. The cost of state-provided counseling
and group therapy alone for the millions of troubled individuals served would be staggering.

The members of these organizations, by the millions,
unanimously agree that admitting the limitations of their
individual egos allowed them to experience a true power and
that it is that power which brought about their recovery—which
hitherto nothing on earth, including medicine, psychiatry or
any branch of modern science, had been able to effect.

We can make some important observations from the
story of how the prototype organization, AA, came into
existence. Back in the 1930s alcoholism was accepted, as it had
been over the centuries, as a hopeless progressive disease
which had baffled medical science and religion as well. (In fact,
the prevalence of alcoholism amongst the clergy itself was
alarmingly high.) All forms of drug addiction were thought to
be incurable, and when they reached a certain stage, victims
were "put away."

In the early 1930s a prominent American businessman
known to us as Rowland H., who had sought every cure for
his alcoholism without avail, went to see the famous Swiss
psychoanalyst Carl Jung. Jung treated Rowland H. for approximately a year, by which time he had achieved some degree of
sobriety. Rowland returned to the United States full of hope,
only to fall ill again with active alcoholism.

Rowland went back to Switzerland to see Jung again and
ask for further treatment. Jung humbly told him that neither
his science nor art could help him further, but that throughout
man's history—rarely, but from time to time— some who had
abandoned themselves completely to some spiritual organization and surrendered to God for help had recovered.[8]

Rowland returned to the United States dejected, but he
followed Jung's advice and sought out an organization of that

time called the Oxford Groups. These were groups of individuals who met regularly to discuss living life according to spiritual
principles very much like those adopted later by AA. Through
this means Rowland in fact recovered, and his recovery was a
source of astonishment to another concerned party named
Edwin T., or "Ebby," also an alcoholic hopeless beyond all
help. When Rowland told Ebby of how he had recovered, Ebby
followed suit and also got sober. The pattern of one person
helping another with the same problem then extended from
Ebby to his friend Bill W., who had been hospitalized frequently for hopeless, incurable alcoholism and whose condition was medically grave. Ebby told Bill that his recovery was
based on service to others, moral housecleaning, anonymity,
humility and surrendering to a power greater than oneself.[9]

Bill W. was an atheist and found the idea of surrendering
to a higher power unappealing to say the least. The whole idea
of surrender was abhorrent to Bill's pride; he sank into
absolute black despair. He had a mental obsession with and a
physical allergy to alcohol that condemned him to sickness,
insanity and death, a prognosis which had been clearly spelled
out to him and his wife Lois. Ultimately, Bill gave up completely, at which point he had a profound experience of an
infinite Presence and Light and felt a great sense of Peace. That
night he was finally able to sleep, and when he awoke the next
day he felt as though he had been transformed in some
indescribable way.[10]

The efficacy of his experience was confirmed by Dr.
William D. Silkworth, his physician at what was then Town's
Hospital on the west side of New York City. Silkworth had
treated ten thousand alcoholics and in the process acquired
enough wisdom to recognize the profound importance of Bill's
experience. It was he who later introduced Bill to the great
psychologist William James's classic, *The Varieties of Religious
Experience*.

Bill wanted to pass his gift on to others, and as he himself said, "Spent the next few months trying to sober up drunks, but without success." Eventually he discovered that it was necessary to convince the subject of the hopelessness of his condition—in modern psychological terms, to overcome his denial. Bill's first success was with a surgeon from Akron, Ohio, Dr. Bob, who turned out to have a great aptitude for the spiritual and became a co-founder of AA. He never took another drink until his death in 1956 (nor did Bill W. until he died in 1980).[11] The enormous power which was realized through Bill W.'s inner experience has manifested itself externally in the millions of lives which have been transformed because of it. In *Life's* listing of the one hundred greatest Americans who ever lived, Bill W. is credited with being the originator of the entire self-help movement.[12]

The story of Bill W. is typical of individuals who have been channels of great power: the principles they convey in a brief career reorder the lives of millions over long periods of time. Jesus Christ, for instance, taught for only three short years, and yet his teachings transformed all of Western society for the generations since; man's encounter with these teachings lies at the center of Western history for the last two thousand years. The highest calibrations of attractor power fields which we have discovered have invariably been associated with the teachings of the great spiritual masters of history.

There is always a diminution from the calibrated power of the energy field of the original teachings of the great masters to their current practice in the form of organized religion (see Chapter 23). Yet the original principles themselves retain their innate attractor power pattern; it is merely their expression which has become weaker. The teachings themselves have the same profound power they always did.

The power of a principle remains unchanged throughout time. Whether we fully understand them or not, these principles are the ideals for which mankind strives. From our own struggles to better ourselves we learn compassion for those still in the grip of inner conflict; out of this grows a wisdom including compassion for the entire human condition.

If we refer to the principles of advanced theoretical physics and the results of our own attractor research, it will be obvious that in a universe in which everything is connected with everything else, unseen power accomplishes for us things that we could never do by ourselves. As we have said before, we cannot see electricity, x-rays or radio waves, but we know of their intrinsic power by virtue of their effects. Similarly, we constantly observe the effects of power in the world of thoughts and feelings, although until now it had not been considered possible to measure a thought.

When we discuss high power attractor fields, we frequently can allude to them only by means of symbols. National flags are just dyed patterns on pieces of material, from a physical viewpoint, but men are willing to die for what they symbolize. Empowerment, as we have said, comes from meaning. Those things which have the greatest meaning to us arise from the spiritual, not the material world.

Thus far, we have seen that alignment with the principles associated with high power attractor energy fields can result in Olympic achievement, success in commerce, political victory on an international level and recovery from hopeless progressive diseases. These same attractor patterns are responsible for the finest music ever written. They are the basis of the eminent religious teachings, the world's grand art and architecture and the wellspring of all creativity and genius.

XIV
Power in the Arts

THE GREAT WORKS OF ART, music and architecture
which have come down to us through the centuries
are enduring representations of the effect of high attractor
patterns. In them we see a reflection of the commitment of
the master artists of our civilization to perfection and grace,
and thereby to the ennoblement of humanity. The fine arts
have always provided the venue for man's highest spiritual
strivings in the secular realm. As far back as the time of the
sculptor Phidias in ancient Greece, it has been the role of the
arts to realize, in physical media, ideals about what man could
and should be, to set down in tangible form, accessible to all,
a distilled expression of the human spirit.

Great art bodies forth the ordered essence not only of
human experience but of the world we live in, too. It is this
that we call beauty. Like the theoretical physicist, the artist
finds order in apparent chaos. Where there was only a block
of meaningless marble, Michelangelo sees the *David* or *Pieta*

and with his chisel removes the senseless stone to liberate that perfected image. Contemplating the random patterns of a meaningless plaster wall in the Sistine Chapel, he conceives through the inspiration of Art a wondrous ABC, and then through the technique of art, he actualizes the A→B→C we know as *The Last Judgment.*

The bequest of the arts to man is internal, too; in beholding realized beauty, a sensitivity to the beautiful is inculcated in us, enabling us to discover—and create—our own aesthetic rewards in the apparently disordered jumble of existence. Art and Love are man's greatest gifts to hmself.

There is no art without love. Art is always the making of the soul, the craft of man's touch, whether that touch is corporeal or the touch of the mind and spirit; so it has been since Neanderthal times, and so it will always be. Thus we find that computer-generated art and even great photographs never calibrate as highly as original paintings. A most interesting kinesiolocicalal experiment, which anyone can reduplicate, is to test the strength of a person who is looking at an original painting iand then looking at a mechanical reproduction of that painting. When a person looks at something that has been hand-crafted, he goes strong; when he looks at a reproduction, he goes weak, and this is true regardless of pictorial content. An original of a disturbing subject will make the subject go stronger than a copy of a pleasant subject. Dedicated artists put love into their work. There is great power in both the human touch and human originality. Therefore kinesiology provides a fail-safe detector of art forgery.

The great psychoanalyst Carl Jung emphasized over and over again the relation of art to the dignity of man and the importance of the human spirit in art. Jung himself and his work calibrate highest of all the famous psychoanalysts of history. (Many of the others, aligned with such attractor patterns as material determinism, produced much lower scores.)

Music is in some ways the most subtle, in that it is the least concrete, of the arts. However, in bypassing left-brain rationality to appeal directly to our subconscious right-brain sense of pattern, it is at the same time the most visceral and emotional. It also provides the easiest example of how attractor patterns order reality: if you wish to comprehend the difference between chaos and meaning, thereby attaining an effective definition of Art, simply contemplate the difference between noise and music.

A description of the creative process by the contemporary Estonian composer Arvo Pärt, whose work is often described as transcendental or mystical, condenses much of what we have observed regarding the crucial role of artistic genius in the unfoldment of attractor patterns:

> To write I must prepare myself for a long time. Sometimes it takes five years....In my life, my music, my work, in my dark hours, I have the certain feeling that everything outside this one thing has no meaning. The complex and many-faceted only confuses me, and I must search for unity. What is it, this one thing, and how do I find my way to it? Traces of this thing appear in many guises and everything that is unimportant falls away....Here I am alone with silence. I have discovered that it is enough when a single note is beautifully played....That is my goal. Time and timelessness are connected. This instant and eternity are struggling within us.[1]

Amongst the arts it is music that most readily brings tears to our eyes, or brings us to our feet, or inspires us to pinnacles of love and creativity. We have already noted that longevity seems to be a corollary of association with the attractor fields of classical music whether as performer, conductor or composer. Classical music often demonstrates extremely high inherent power patterns.

But of all the arts, architecture is the most tangible and influential in the lives of men everywhere. We shop, go to work and seek our entertainment in buildings; thus the form of the structure itself, because its influence is a background to so much human activity, deserves the utmost attention.

Among all world architecture, the great cathedrals elicit a special awe. Their energy patterns have calibrated the highest among architectural forms. This appears to be the result of several factors. Our experience of cathedrals can combine a number of arts simultaneously: music, sculpture, painting, as well as spatial design. Moreover, these edifices are dedicated to the divine; that which is begotten in the name of the Creator is aligned with the highest attractor patterns of all. The cathedral not only inspires, but unifies, teaches, symbolizes and serves all that is noblest in man.

Beauty in architecture, however, need not be expansive nor grand in scale. There are few architectural settings more charming than the little thatched cottages dotting the Irish countryside, each one more quaint and picturesque than the last. Innate appreciation for the aesthetic allows in much traditional domestic architecture elegant statements of beauty and simplicity.

Well conceived public architecture speaks with historical authenticity of the beauty of line combined with utility. Function and beauty are impressively joined in the great subway stations of Russia and in the design and layout of many new high-rise apartment buildings in Canada. Older cultures seem always to have known the practicality of beauty: that that which is designed without beauty quickly deteriorates. An architecturally ugly neighborhood becomes part of a feedback loop of blight and violence; the sleazy, dehumanized housing projects of urban ghettos manifest their weak power patterns as a matrix for squalor and crime—although it must be remembered that depending on which attractor pattern one aligns with, the destitution of the ghetto can be an excuse for depravity or the inspiration to rise above it. (It is not the facts of one's environment but one's attitude towards them that determines whether they will be the occasion for defeat or the inspiration to victory.)

Grace is the expression of the power of aesthetic sensitivity, and power is always manifested with grace, whether in beauty of line or style of expression. We associate grace with elegance, refinement and economy of effort. We marvel at the grace of the Olympic athlete, just as we are uplifted by the grace of the Gothic vault. Gracious power patterns acknowledge and support life, respect and uphold the dignity of others; grace is an aspect of unconditional love. Graciousness also implies generosity—not merely material generosity but generosity of spirit, such as the willingness to express thanks or acknowledge the importance of others in our lives. Grace is associated with modesty and humility. Power does not need to flaunt itself, though force always must because it originates in self-doubt. Great artists are thankful for their power, whatever its expression, because they know it is a gift for the good of mankind, entailing responsibility to others.

Beauty has expressed itself in so many different forms in different cultures throughout various periods of time, that we have good reason to say it is in the eye of the beholder. However, we should note that it is only the vehicle of beauty that changes; the essence of beauty does not change, only the form in which it is perceived. It is interesting that people of advanced consciousness are able to see beauty in all forms. To them not only is all life sacred, but all form is beauty.

XV
Genius and the Power of Creativity

CREATIVITY AND GENIUS are the loci of powerful high energy attractors. No human talents are more germane to the creation of new M-fields or the unfoldment of the enfolded universe; in fact, these are the explicit domain of creativity and genius. Yet these closely allied processes remain shrouded in mystery; there is a paucity of information about the essential nature of either creativity or genius.

Human history is the record of man's struggle to comprehend truths which to those of genius appear obvious. Genius is by definition a style of consciousness characterized by the ability to access high energy attractor patterns. It is not a personality characteristic. It is not something that a person "has," nor even something that someone "is." Those in whom we recognize genius commonly disclaim it. A universal characteristic of genius is humility. The genius has always attributed his insights to some higher influence.

The process of animating genius most commonly involves first formulating a question, and waiting an indefinite interval for consciousness to work with the problem; then suddenly the answer appears in a flash, in a form which is characteristically non-verbal. Great musicians throughout history have stated that they did not plan their music, but rather wrote down what they heard, finished, within their own minds.[1] The father of organic chemistry, Kukule, saw the pattern of the carbon ring organic nucleus in a dream. In an illuminated moment, Einstein had the revolutionary insight which then took him years to translate into provable mathematics.[2] Indeed, one of the main problems of genius is how to transform that which is perceived in one's private understanding into a visible expression comprehensible to others. The revelation itself is usually complete and self-explanatory to him who receives it, but to make it so to others may take a lifetime.[3]

Genius thus seems to proceed from sudden revelation rather than conceptualization, but there is an unseen process involved. Although the genius's mind may appear stalled, frustrated with the problem, what it really is doing is preparing the field. There is a struggle with reason which eventually leads, like a Zen Koan, to a rational impasse from which the only way forward is by a leap from a lower to a higher attractor energy pattern.

Attractor energy patterns have harmonics, as do musical tones. The higher frequency the harmonic, the higher the power. What the genius arrives at is a new harmonic. Every advance in human consciousness has come through a leap from a lower attractor pattern to its higher harmonic. Posing the original question activates an attractor; the answer lies within its harmonic. This is why it is said that the question and the answer are merely two sides of one coin, and that one cannot pose a question unless the answer already exists—otherwise there would be no pattern from which the question could be formulated.[4]

Recognized geniuses may be rare, but Genius resides within all of us. There is no such thing as luck or accident in this universe. And not only is everything connected to everything else, but no one is excluded from the universe. We are all members. Consciousness is a universal quality, like the quality of physicality. Because genius is a characteristic of consciousness, genius also is universal. That which is universal is available to every man.

The processes of creativity and genius are inherent in human consciousness. Inasmuch as every human has within himself the same essence of consciousness, genius is a potential that resides within everyone. It awaits only the right circumstance to express itself. Each of us has had moments of genius in our lifetimes, perhaps only known to ourselves or to those close to us. We suddenly make a brilliant move or decision, or say exactly the right thing at the right moment, without quite knowing why. Sometimes we would like to congratulate ourselves for these fortuitous events, but in truth we really do not know from whence they come.

Genius often is expressed through a change of perception—a change of context or paradigm. The mind struggles with an insoluble problem, poses a question, and is open to receive an answer. The source from which this answer comes has been given many names, varying from culture to culture and time to time; in the arts of Western civilization it has traditionally been identified with the Greek goddesses of inspiration called the Muses. Those who are humble and grateful for illumination received continue to have the capacity to access genius. Those who arrogate the inspiration to their own ego soon lose this capacity, or are destroyed by their success. High power, like high voltage, must be handled with respect.

Genius and creativity, then, are subjectively experienced as a witnessing. It is a phenomenon which bypasses the individual self, or ego. The capacity to finesse genius can be learned, though often only through painful surrender, when the phoenix of genius arises out of the ashes of despair after a fruitless struggle with the unsolvable. Out of defeat comes victory, out of failure, success, and out of humbling, true self-esteem.

One of the problems in attempting to understand genius is that it takes near-genius to recognize it. The world frequently fails to identify genius altogether; society often gives acclaim to the work of genius without noting the intrinsic genius of its creation itself. Until one acknowledges the genius within oneself, one will have great difficulty recognizing it in others— we can only see without that which we realize within. In recent times, as an example, Mikhail Gorbachev has been the subject of enormous world-wide attention, but the world does not really acknowledge his *genius*. Single-handed, in only a few short years, he completely revolutionized one of the greatest empires on earth, his only sources of power his inspiration and vision. (Had the communist regime been based on power, nothing could have overturned it; because it was based on force it was destined to come to an end under the hand of a charismatic leader aligned with power.)[5]

Genius is one of the greatest untapped resources of our society. It is no more specific than it is personal. People of great gifts not infrequently have multiple talents. A genius may be a genius in different realms and might have answers to a diversity of problems. Society suffers a great loss because it does not know how to nurture its geniuses. They don't cost much to maintain—the source of genius is impersonal and true genius is seldom interested in money or fame. But society, in fact, is often either indifferent or hostile to genius.

The lifestyle of those whom we term genius is typically simple. Genius is characterized by an appreciation for resources and the economy of ingenuity because the genius values life and sees the intrinsic worth of all its expressions. Inasmuch as time and resources are precious, doing more than necessary is viewed as a waste; therefore people of genius often lead very quiet lives and reluctantly sally forth only when there is a cause that must be supported. There is no need to "get" when you already "have." Genius, because it is in touch with an endless source of supply, experiences only a minimum of need. (Such simplicity seems a common characteristic of true success in general.) The basis of this non-materiality, this seeming naïveté, is a radical understanding of the nature of the universe itself: that which supports life is supported by life; survival is thus effortless, and giving and receiving are one and the same thing.

Genius is notoriously interpreted as unconventionality or eccentricity. It is true that persons of genius, because of their alignment with high energy attractors, have a different perspective on life; therefore, things have a different significance for them. The genius is frequently inspired to intense activity by insights beyond our understanding.

Genius is not stardom. Those of genius who attain prominence are a very small minority. There remains a legion of geniuses who achieve no such status; many appear in no way noteworthy and may, in fact, have never had formal higher education. What characterizes this type is the capacity to utilize exhaustively what experience they have and to capitalize on it by the dedication necessary to reach a high degree of mastery. Many productive geniuses are not recognized until years after they are dead. In fact, the gift—or curse—of genius often brings about unfortunate consequences during an individual's lifetime.

One characteristic of genius is the capacity for great intensity, often expressed in cyclic form. When inspired, the person of genius may work twenty hours a day to realize a solution while it is still fresh in mind. These periods of intense activity are interspersed with periods of apparent stasis which are in actuality intervals of fermentation, a necessary part of the creative process. Therefore, the personality of the genius sometimes seems to incorporate polar extremes. Geniuses understand the need for creating a space for ideas to crystallize. The stage is often set by complete distraction. Creativity occurs under appropriate inner, not outer circumstances. We all know stories of people who have gotten the answers to complex problems while sitting in traffic on the freeway.

A primary reason so many people fail to recognize and therefore empower their own genius is because in the popular mind genius is confused with high IQ. This is a gross misunderstanding. It would be more helpful to see genius as simply an extraordinarily high degree of savvy in a given area of human activity. The misconception about IQ has arisen from the fact that many celebrated geniuses in the fields of mathematics and physics indeed have high IQs; however, in those fields the IQ necessary to comprehend the work is a prerequisite. There are droves of non-cerebral artistic geniuses, musical geniuses, designers and inventors, geniuses in many fields whose talent is that of innovative creativity within a certain limited area.

Let us remember that IQ is merely a measure of academic capacity for logically comprehending symbols and words. The values that one lives by are more definitive of genius than IQ. From our studies it appears that the alignment of one's goals and values with high energy attractors is more closely associated with genius than anything else. Genius can be more accurately identified by perseverance, courage, concentration, enormous drive and absolute integrity. Talent alone is not enough. Dedication of an unusual degree is required to achieve mastery, and in the simplest definition, one could say that genius is the capacity for an extraordinary degree of mastery in one's calling. A formula followed by all geniuses, prominent or not, is: Do what you like to do best, and do it to the very best of your ability.

XVI
Surviving Success

THE TRAGIC CAREERS of many individuals of genius subsequent to being discovered and celebrated by the public illustrate that there is success, and then there is Success. The former frequently jeopardizes life, while the latter enhances it. True Success enlivens and supports the spirit; it has not to do with isolated attainments, but being successful as a total person, attaining a successful lifestyle that benefits not only yourself but everyone around you. Successful people's lives are empowered throughout by the context of their accomplishments.

In contradistinction, that which the tabloid world calls success often erodes the "successful" person's health and relationships; spiritual collapse is commonplace in the lives of the rich and famous. But what the world calls success is merely celebrity, and the capacity of celebrity to destroy is documented daily. Famous people constantly succumb to failed marriages, addiction, alcoholism and suicide or other untimely death. If we listed the names of all the celebrities whose careers were blighted by such tragedies, it would fill a score of pages—the movie stars (Judy Garland, Marilyn Monroe, James Dean); the pop stars (Elvis Presley, Janis Joplin, Jimi Hendrix); the writers (Poe, London, Hemingway, F. Scott Fitzgerald)—the list goes on and on. In addition to such notorious examples of the price of celebrity are the uncounted thousands of less famous "successful" lives ruined by drug problems or the twisting of personality whereby formerly decent folk become vain, cruel, self-centered and inordinately self-indulgent.

It is not just that such people have gotten too much wealth, too much fame, or too much attention, but that these influences distorted their egos and reinforced what might be called the small self instead of the big Self. The small self is the part of us that is vulnerable to flattery; the Self is an aspect of our more evolved nature which is humble and grateful for success. The self aligns with weak attractor patterns; the Self is aligned with high power energy fields.

Whether it uplifts or destroys us depends not upon success itself, but how it is integrated into our personalities. Whether we are proud or humble, whether we are egotistic or grateful, whether we deem ourselves better than others because of our talents or consider them a gift for which we are thankful—these are the determining factors. We all know people for whom even a bit of success is corrupting, who become arrogant, officious and controlling when given a little authority. And we all know people of much greater authority who are cordial, sensitive and caring.

When we come to know the powerful men of the world, captains of industry, presidents of banking firms, Nobel Prize winners and members of legendary American families, it is striking to see how many are open, warm, sincere and view success as a responsibility, *noblesse oblige*. These are truly successful people, notably courteous and considerate to all, whether visiting potentates or servants, *treating everyone as an equal.* The truly successful have no inclination to act arrogantly because they consider themselves not better but more fortunate than others. They see their position as a *stewardship*, a responsibility to exercise their influence for the greatest benefit of all.

What allows the truly successful to be so gracious, open and giving can be explained through our formula of causality:

The truly successful identify with the ABC. They realize that they are a channel acted through to create success in the outer world. Inasmuch as they identify with the source of success, they have no anxiety about losing it. But a person who views his success in the realm of A→B→C will always be insecure because its source is "out there." Solid confidence comes from the knowledge that the source of success is "in here." By believing that the source of power lies outside oneself, one becomes powerless and vulnerable and, therefore, defensive and possessive. True success originates within, independent of external circumstances.

The ladder of success seems to have three main steps. Initially, it is what we "have" that counts; status depends upon visible signs of material wealth. As one progresses, status is afforded by what one "does," rather than has. At this level on the ladder, one's position and activities bring significant social status. But the attraction of social roles loses glamour as one achieves mastery and matures; it is what one has accomplished that is important. Finally, one is concerned only with what one has become as a result of life's experiences. Such people have a charismatic "presence" that is the outer manifestation of the grace of their inner power. In their company we feel the effect of the powerful attractor energy patterns with which they are aligned and which they reflect. Success comes as the automatic consequence of aligning one's life with high power energy patterns.

Why is true success so relatively effortless? It might be likened to the magnetic field created by an electric current running through a wire. The higher the power of the current, the greater the magnetic field that it generates. And the magnetic field itself then influences everything in its presence. There are very few at the top. The world of the mediocre, however, is one of intense competition, and the bottom of the pyramid is crowded. Charismatic winners are sought out; losers have to strive to be accepted. People who are loving, kind and thoughtful of others have more friends than they can count; success in every area of life is a reflex to those who are aligned with successful patterns. And the capacity to be able to discern the difference between the strong patterns of success and the weak patterns leading to failure is now available to each of us.

XVII
Physical Health and Power

W E BECOME HEALTHY as well as wealthy by being wise. But what is wisdom? According to our research, it is the result of alignment with high power attractor patterns. Although in the average life we find a mixture of energy fields, the pattern with the highest power dominates. We have now explored sufficient material to be able to introduce a basic dictum of nonlinear dynamics and attractor research: *attractors create context*. In essence, this means that one's motive, which arises from the principles to which one is committed, determines one's capacity to understand and, thereby, give significance to one's actions.

The effect of alignment with principle is nowhere more striking than in its physiological consequences. Alignment with high energy attractor patterns results in health; with weak ones, in disease. This syndrome is specific and predictable. That high energy patterns can be proven to strengthen and low energy patterns to weaken through a demonstration meeting the scientific criterion of one-hundred-percent replicability is a fact with which the reader is by now thoroughly familiar.

The human central nervous system clearly has an exquisitely sensitive capacity to differentiate between life-supportive and life-destructive patterns. High power attractor energy patterns which make the body go strong release brain endorphins and have a tonic effect on all the organs, whereas adverse stimuli, which release adrenaline, suppress immune response and instantaneously cause both weakness and enervation of specific organs, depending on the nature of the stimulus.

It is this clinical phenomenon upon which treatment modalities such as chiropractic, acupuncture, reflexology and many others are based. All of these treatments, however, are designed to correct the results of an energy imbalance; unless the basic attitude which is causing the energy imbalance is corrected, the illness tends to return. People by the millions in self-help groups have demonstrated that health and recovery from a whole gamut of human behavioral problems and illnesses comes as a consequence of adopting attitudes correlated with high energy attractor patterns.

Generally speaking, physical and mental health are attendant upon positive attitudes, whereas ill health, both physical and mental, is associated with such negative attitudes as resentment, jealousy, hostility, self-pity, fear, anxiety, etc. In the field of psychoanalysis, these positive attitudes are called welfare emotions, and the negative ones are called emergency emotions. Chronic immersion in emergency emotions results in physical or mental ill health and a gross weakening of one's personal power.

How does one overcome negative attitudes so as to avoid this atrophy of power and health? Clinical observation indicates that the patient must reach a decision point. A sincere desire for change allows one to seek higher attractor energy patterns in their various expressions.

One does not get over pessimism by associating with cynics; the popular idea that you are defined by the company you keep has some clinical basis. Attractor patterns tend to dominate any field in which they are received; thus, all that is really necessary is to expose oneself to a high energy field and one's inner attitudes will spontaneously begin to change. This is a phenomenon well known among self-help groups—as reflected in the saying, "Just bring the body to the meeting." If you merely expose yourself to the influence of higher patterns, they begin to "rub off," as it is said, "You get it by osmosis."

It is generally held by traditional medicine that stress is the cause of many human disorders and illnesses. The problem with this diagnosis is that it does not accurately address the source of the stress. It looks to blame external circumstances, without realizing that *all stress is internally generated by one's attitudes.* It is not life's events, but one's reaction to them that activates the symptoms of stress. A divorce, as we have said, can bring agony or relief. Challenges on the job can result in stimulation or anxiety, depending on whether one's supervisor is seen as a teacher or an ogre.

Our attitudes stem from our positions, and our positionality has to do with motive and, therefore, context. According to the overall way in which we interpret the meaning of events, the same situation may be tragic or comic. Physiologically speaking, in choice of attitude one chooses between anabolic endorphins or catabolic adrenaline.

It would be foolish to claim that the only impacts on our health are those originating internally. Impersonal elements of the physical world can also increase or decrease our strength. Here, too, kinesiological testing is valuable. It will clearly show that synthetics, plastics, artificial coloring, preservatives, insecticides, and artificial sweeteners, to mention a few, make the body go weak, whereas substances which are pure, organic or made by human hands tend to make us go strong. If we experiment with vitamin C, for example, we find that organic vitamin C is far superior to chemically produced vitamin C; one makes you go strong and the other does not. Eggs from organically fed free-run chickens have much more intrinsic power than eggs from caged and chemically fed chickens. The health food movement seems to have been right all along.

Unfortunately, neither the American Medical Association nor the National Council on Food and Nutrition have a history of being enlightened in the field of nutrition. The scientific community now finally recognizes that nutrition is related to behavior and health, but this simple observation caused a controversy when Linus Pauling and I claimed twenty years ago, in *Orthomolecular Psychiatry*, that nutrition affects the chemical environment of the brain and bloodstream, influencing various behaviors, emotions and mental disorders.[1]

More recently, this author published a series of papers, the last in 1991, on a twenty-year study showing that a regimen of certain vitamins prevented the development of a neurological disorder called tardive dyskinesia, a frequently irreversible disorder which occurs in a high percentage of patients on long-term treatment with major tranquilizers.[2] In a study of 61000 patients treated by one hundred different doctors over a twenty-year period, the introduction of vitamins B3, C, E, and B6 decreased the expected rate of this terrible neurologic disorder from twenty-five percent to .04 percent.[3] (Among 61000 patients protected by high-dosage vitamin therapy, only thirty-seven patients, rather than the predicted nearly 20,000, developed the disorder.)[4]

But the paper was largely ignored in the United States because there was still no paradigm to give it credibility. The medical profession has simply been uninterested in nutrition, and organized medicine has traditionally been less than kind to innovators. It is helpful to remember that it is a foible of human nature to stoutly defend an established position despite overwhelming evidence against it; the only healthy way to deal with such lack of recognition is acceptance. Once we really understand the human condition, we will feel compassion where we once might have felt condemnation. Compassion is one of the highest of all energy attractor power patterns. As we shall see, our capacity to understand, forgive and accept is directly linked to our personal health.

XVIII
Wellness and the Disease Process

IT HAS BEEN A COMMON OBSERVATION through the ages that certain diseases are associated with certain emotions and attitudes. The medieval concept of "melancholy," for instance, connected depression with impairment of the liver. In contemporary times many physical disorders have been clearly linked with the emotions of stress.

That emotions do have physiologic consequences is well documented. In the early days of psychoanalysis, research to identify specific diseases with specific psychological conflicts gave rise to the whole field of psychosomatic inquiry. We have all heard about the connection between heart disease and type A versus type B personalities, and of how suppressed anger results in hypertension and strokes. The presumption has been that emotions affect hormonal change through neurotransmitter variations in different areas of the brain associated with controlling different organs by way of the autonomic nervous system.

In more recent years concern over the spread of AIDS has given great impetus to research on the body's immune system. Generally, it appears that that which is experienced as stress results in suppression of the thymus gland; with this the body's defenses are impaired. But the various research approaches to this topic fail to examine the relationship between belief systems and attitudes and the resultant context of perception, which determines the nature of individual experience. The etiology of stress is always related to the organism's proclivity to respond to stimuli in specific and characteristic patterns. Drawing on what we already know from the mathematics of nonlinear dynamics and attractor research, as clinically confirmed by kinesiology and acupuncture, we can derive a formulation of the basic nature of the disease process itself.

An idea or constellation of thoughts presents itself in consciousness as an attitude which tends to persist over time. This attitude is associated with an attractor energy field of corresponding power or weakness. The result is a perception of the world creating events appropriate to trigger the specific emotion. All attitudes, thoughts and beliefs are also connected with various pathways, called "meridians" of energy, to all of the body's organs. Through kinesiologic testing it can be demonstrated that specific acupuncture points are linked with specific attitudes, and the meridian, in turn, serves as the energy channel to specific muscles and body organs.[1] These specific meridians have been traditionally named according to the organs that they energize, i.e., the heart meridian, gallbladder meridian, etc.[2]

There is nothing mysterious about these vital internal communications, and they can be demonstrated in seconds to anyone's satisfaction—as we know, if you hold a particular negative thought in mind, a very specific muscle will go weak; if you replace the thought with a positive idea the same muscle will instantly go strong.[3] The connection between mind and body is immediate, so the body's responses shift and change from instant to instant in response to one's train of thought and its associated emotions.

We have referred to the law of *sensitive dependence on initial conditions*, drawing from the science of nonlinear dynamics and its mathematics.[4] We will recall that this describes the manner in which a minuscule variation in a pattern of inputs can result in a very significant change in the eventual output. This is because the repetition of a slight variation over time results in a progressive change of pattern or, sometimes, in a leap to a new harmonic when the increment increases logarithmically. The effect of the minute variation becomes amplified until it eventually affects the whole system and an entire new energy pattern evolves, which itself may, by the same process, then result in a further variation, and so on.

In the world of physics this process is called "turbulence" and is the subject of an enormous amount of research, especially in the field of aerodynamics, in a combined focus of physics and mathematics. Such turbulence, when it occurs in the attractor energy fields of consciousness, creates an emotional upset which continues until a new level of homeostasis is established.

When the mind is dominated by a negative world view, the direct result is a repetition of minute changes in energy flows to the various body organs. The subtle field of overall physiology is affected in all of its complex functions, mediated by electron transfer, neural hormonal balance, nutritional status, etc. Eventually, an accumulation of infinitesimal changes becomes discernible through measurement techniques such as electron microscopy, magnetic imaging or x-ray or biochemical analysis. But by the time these changes are detectable, the disease process is already well advanced in its own self-perpetuating resonances.

We could say that the invisible universe of thought and attitude becomes visible as a consequence of the body's habitual response. If we consider the millions of thoughts that go through the mind continuously, it is not surprising that the body's condition could radically change to reflect prevailing thought patterns, as modified by genetic and environmental factors.[5] It is the *persistence* and repetition of the stimulus which, through the law of sensitive dependence on initial conditions, results in the observable disease process. The stimulus that sets off the process may be so minute that it escapes detection itself.

If this scheme of disease formation is correct, then all disease should be reversible by changing thought patterns and habitual responses. In fact, spontaneous recoveries from every disease known to mankind have been recorded throughout history. (This phenomenon was the subject of ABC Television's 20/20 on April 8, 1994.) Traditional medicine has documented spontaneous "cures," but has never had the conceptual tools with which to investigate the phenomenon. But even thoroughly modern surgeons are very reluctant to operate on anyone who is convinced that he will die during the surgery because not infrequently such patients do just that.

It is said in Alcoholics Anonymous that there is no recovery until the subject experiences an essential change of personality.[6] This is the basic change first manifested by AA founder Bill W., a profound transformation in total belief system with a sudden leap in consciousness.[7] Such a major metamorphosis in attitude was first formally studied by the psychiatrist Harry Tiebout, M.D., of Greenwich, Connecticut, treating a hopeless alcoholic woman named Marty Mann, the first woman in AA. She underwent a sudden change of personality to a degree unaccountable through any known therapeutic method. Tiebout documented that she was transformed from an angry, self-pitying, intolerant and egocentric posture to a kind and gentle one, forgiving and loving. Her example is important because it so clearly demonstrates this key element in recovery from any progressive or hopeless disease. Tiebout wrote the first of a series of papers on this observation under the title "The Power of Surrender."[8]

In every studied case of recovery from hopeless and untreatable disease there has been this major shift in consciousness, so that the attractor patterns that resulted in the pathologic process no longer dominated. The steps necessary for recovery from such grave illness were formalized by the first 100 alcoholics who recovered; these became the well known twelve steps suggested by AA and all the twelve-step recovery groups that have followed.[9] The fact that pursuing these steps has resulted in the recovery of millions of people suggests that this experience may have a universal applicability to all disease processes. The advice Carl Jung gave Rowland— "Throw yourself wholeheartedly into any spiritual group that appeals to you whether you believe in it or not and hope that in your case a miracle may occur"[10]—may hold true for anyone who wishes to recover from a progressive disease.

In spontaneous recovery there is frequently a marked increase in the capacity to love and the awareness of the importance of love as a healing factor. We have been told that to love is to live healthily by numerous books on the best-seller list. But the mind resists change as a matter of pride. Love of our fellow man can ensue only when we stop condemning, fearing and hating him. Such radical change can be disorienting; the courage to endure the temporary discomfort of growth is also required. Recovery from any disease process is dependent on willingness to explore new ways of looking at one's self and life. This includes the capacity to endure inner fears when belief systems are shaken. People cherish and cling to their hates and grievances; to heal humanity it may be necessary to pry whole populations away from lifestyles of spite, attack and revenge.

A prime difficulty with thoughts and behaviors associated with the energy fields that calibrate below 200 is that they cause counter-reactions. A familiar law of the observable universe is that force results in equal and opposite counter-force. All attacks, therefore, whether mental or physical, result in counter-attack. Malice literally makes us sick; we are always the victims of our own spite. Even secret hostile thoughts result in a physiological attack on one's own body.

On the other hand, like love, laughter heals because it arises through viewing a small context from a larger and more inclusive one, which removes the observer from the victim posture. Every joke reminds us that our reality is transcendent, beyond the specifics of events. Gallows humor, for instance, is based on the juxtaposition of the opposites of a paradox; the relief of basic anxiety then results in a laugh. One of the frequent accompaniments of sudden enlightening realizations is laughter. The cosmic joke is the side-by-side comparison of illusion with reality.

Humorlessness, in contrast, is inimical to health and happiness. Totalitarian systems are notably devoid of humor at any level. Laughter, which brings acceptance and freedom, is a threat to their rule through force and intimidation; it is hard to oppress people who have a good sense of humor. Beware the humorless, whether in a person, institution or belief system; it is always accompanied by an impulse to control and dominate, even if its proclaimed objective is to create prosperity or peace.

One cannot create peace as such. Peace is the natural state of affairs when that which prevents it is removed. Relatively few people are genuinely committed to peace as a realistic goal. In their private lives, people prefer being "right" at whatever the cost to relationships or themselves. A self-justified positionality is the real enemy of peace. When solutions are sought on the level of coercion, no peaceful resolutions are possible.

The health-care field itself demonstrates how attempts to control only compound themselves into a burgeoning bureaucratic morass. Complexity is costly, and systems are as weak and inefficient as the attitudes that underlie their construct. Systems associated with very weak attractor fields are ineffective because of their inherent dishonesty and become wasteful and cumbersome. The health-care industry is so overburdened with fear and regulation that it can barely function. Healing from individual illness or the healing of the health-care industry itself can only occur by the progressive steps of elevation of motive and abandonment of self-deception, to attain new clarity of vision. There are not any villains; the fault is in the misalignment of the system itself.

If we say that health, effectuality and prosperity are the natural states of being in harmony with reality, then anything less calls for internal scrutiny rather than the projection of blame on things outside the system involved. Attractor patterns obey the laws of their own physics even if they are not Newtonian; to forgive is to be forgiven. As we have observed repeatedly, in a universe where everything is connected with everything else, there is no such thing as an "accident;" and nothing is outside the universe. Because the power of causes is unseen and only the manifestation of effects is observable, there is an illusion of "accidental" events. A sudden and unexpected event may appear to be random, unrelated to observable causes, but its actual origin can be traced through research. A sudden illness always has discernible antecedents; even accident-proneness involves numerous small preparatory steps before "accidents" occur.

A disease process is evidence that something is amiss in the workings of the mind, and that is where the power to effect a change resides. Treating an illness as a physical process only, within the A→B→C world of effects, does not correct the origin of the dysfunction and is palliative rather than curative. It is possible for a lifelong affliction to heal rapidly with a mere shift of attitude; but although this shift may seem to occur in a split second, it may take years of inner preparation.

We remember that the critical point in any complex system is the locus at which the least power is required to alter the whole system. A move of even one pawn on the chessboard completely changes the possibilities of the game. Every detail of the belief system that we hold has consequences for better or for worse. It is for this reason that there is no condition that is incurable or hopeless; somewhere, sometime, somebody has recovered from it through the process we have described.

It is instrumental not only in recovery but for any major advancement of consciousness to have compassion for one's self and all of mankind as we go through the painful struggles of evolution. Only thus do we become healers as well as healed. And only thus may we hope to be healed of any malaise, physical or spiritual.

Does all this mean that if we learn to operate on the level of unconditional love we will become immortal? Unfortunately, the protoplasm of the physical body is vulnerable to its own genetic programming as well as its external environment. But from the viewpoint of consciousness level 500 and above, it appears that death itself is only an illusion and life goes on unimpeded by the limitation of perception which results from being localized in a physical body: consciousness is the vital energy which both gives life to the body and survives beyond the body in a different realm of existence.

PART THREE: MEANING

XIX
The Database of Consciousness

THE GREAT SWISS PSYCHOLOGIST, Carl Jung, noting the ubiquity of archetypal patterns and symbols, deduced a "collective unconscious," a bottomless subconscious pool of all the shared experience of the race.[1] We may think of it as a vast, hidden database of human awareness characterized by powerful universal organizing patterns. Such a database, comprising all the information ever available to human consciousness, implies stunning inherent capabilities; it is far more than just a giant storehouse of information awaiting a retrieval process. Tapping into all that has ever been experienced anywhere in time, the great promise of the database is its capacity to "know" virtually anything the moment it is "asked."

This is the origin of all information obtained sub- or supra-rationally, by intuition or premonition, by divination or dream, or "lucky" guess. It is the fountainhead of genius, the well of inspiration, and the source of "uncanny" psychic knowledge, including "foreknowledge." It is, of course, the inventory drawn upon by kinesiological testing. Thinkers who are troubled by the notion of "paranormal" or non-rational knowledge usually balk at logical—or illogical—inconsistencies with Newtonian concepts of simultaneity, causality, or time and space.

It's a bigger universe than that. These same thinkers will scan the evening sky and find pleasure in identifying a favorite constellation. But there are no constellations. That familiar pattern of "stars" is made up of points of light originating in totally unrelated sources, some millions of light-years closer or farther away, some in different galaxies, some actually separate galaxies themselves; many have, millennia since, burnt out and ceased to "exist." Those lights have no spatial or temporal relationship. It is not only the shape of a dipper or bear or man, but the very pattern, the "constellation" itself, that is projected on the sky by the eye of the beholder. Yet the zodiac is still "real" because we *conceive* it, in the first sense of the word. Astrology still "exists," and for many people is a quite useful heuristic tool in explaining themselves and their relationships. Why not? The database of consciousness is an infinite resource.

The database behaves like an electrostatic condenser with a field of potentiality, rather than a battery with a stored charge. A question cannot be asked unless there is already the potentiality of the answer. The reason for this is that the question and answer are both created out of the same paradigm and, therefore, are exactly concordant. There is no "up" without an already existent "down." Causality occurs as simultaneity rather than as sequence. Synchronicity is the term used by Jung to explain this phenomenon in human experience.[2] As we understand from our examination of advanced physics, an event "here" in the universe does not "cause" an event to occur "there" in the universe. Instead, both appear simultaneously.

What is the connection between these events, then, if it is not a Newtonian linear sequence of cause and effect? Obviously, the two events are related or connected to each other in some invisible manner, but not by gravity or magnetism or a cosmic wind or an ether; they are encompassed by an attractor field of such magnitude that it includes both events. We may know this is so because otherwise the events would not be observable as events at all, much less simultaneously, or as related to each other in time.

The "connection" between two events occurs only in the observer's consciousness—he "sees" a connection and describes a "pair" of events, hypothesizing a relationship. This relationship is a concept in the mind of the observer; it is not necessary that any corollary external event exist in the universe. Unless there is an underlying attractor pattern, nothing can be experienced. Thus, the entire manifest universe is its own simultaneous expression and experience of itself.

Omniscience is omnipotent and omnipresent. There is no distance between the unknown and the known. The known is manifested from the unknown merely by the asking. The Empire State Building was born in the mind of its architect. Human consciousness is the agent whereby an unseen concept is transformed into its manifest experience, "that building," and thus frozen in time. What "happened" on Thirty-second Street in New York City in 1933 is there for all to see. What "happened" in the consciousness of its creator also stands recorded in the database for all to see to this day. Both exist complete, but in different sensory domains. By transferring concept into concrete and steel, the architect simply enabled the rest of us to experience his vision.

We "normal" humans are completely preoccupied with our function as transformers of concepts from the invisible level, ABC, to the sensorially perceptible A→B→C. Extraordinary individuals live primarily in the world of ABC (those who live beyond that, in the completely formless domain of pure consciousness itself, we call mystics). To such individuals, the origin of everything is obvious; they are uninterested in the process of making things visible and manifest. In everyday life these are the creative people who spawn new enterprises and then turn over their execution and management to others. The yet more advanced—mystics—conclude that only their ABC level of awareness is "real" and the observable world is a dream or illusion. It should be pointed out, however, that this is only another limited point of view. There is neither real nor non-real, only that which is. That which is, is so, from all viewpoints or none.

Existence without form is not imaginable, yet at the same time it is the ultimate reality, including both yin and yang, the unmanifest and the manifest, the formed and the formless, the seen and the unseen, the temporal and the timeless. Thus, the real world is simultaneously the Real world, for that which is All Possibility must include within it all which is. Creation is, therefore, continuous, or there could be no creation at all. To look for the "beginning" of creation is to proceed from an artificial notion of time. The "start" of something that is outside of time cannot be located in time. The big bang can only occur in the mind of an observer.

The universe is very cooperative. Inasmuch as the universe is not different from consciousness itself, it is happy to create whatever we wish to find "out there." The problem is with the concept of cause itself, which begs the question by presuming a time warp, a sequence, a string of events that will make sense. If we step outside of time there are no causes at all. We could say that the manifest world originates out of the unmanifest, but that again would be inferring a sequential causal series in time, i.e., unmanifest → manifest. Once beyond the warp of time, with its implicit restriction of comprehension to terms of mere sequence, there is no backwards or forwards. It is then just as valid to say, reciprocally, that the manifest universe causes the unmanifest; and at a certain level of understanding this is demonstrably true. If, for example, we look at electrons lined up on one side of a dielectric space and protons lined up on the other in an equal balance, how can we say which causes the other to line up? Similarly, though healing is a consequence of compassion, compassion is not its "cause." In an energy field of 600 or higher, almost anything will heal.

The source of all life and all form is, of necessity, greater than its manifestations; yet, it is neither different from them nor separate to any degree. There is no conceptual artifact of separation between creator and created. As scripture states, that which is, was, and always shall be.

Time, then, is a locus of the perception of a hologram that already stands complete; it is a subjective sensory effect of a progressively moving point of view. There is no beginning or end to a hologram. It is already everywhere complete; in fact, the appearance of being "unfinished" is part of its completeness. Even the phenomenon of "unfoldment" itself reflects a limited point of view. There is no enfolded and unfolded universe; there is only a becoming awareness. Our perception of events happening in time is analogous to a traveler watching the landscape unfold before him. But to say that the landscape unfolds before the traveler is merely a figure of speech: nothing is actually unfolding; nothing is actually becoming manifest. There is only the progression of awareness.

These paradoxes dissolve in the greater paradigm which includes both opposites, wherein oppositions as such are only loci of the observer. This transcendence of opposition occurs spontaneously at consciousness levels of 600 and above. The notion that there is a "knower" and a "known" is in itself dualistic, in that it implies a separation between subject and object (which, again, can only be inferred by the artificial adoption of a point of observation). The Maker of all things in heaven and on earth, of all things visible and invisible, stands beyond both, includes both, and is one with both. Existence is, therefore, merely a statement that awareness is aware of its awareness and of its expression as consciousness.

Ontology need not be speculative. It is, after all, only the theology of existence; anyone who is aware that he exists already has access to its highest formulations and beyond. There is only one absolute truth; all the rest are semi-facts spawned from the artifacts of limited perception and positionality. "To be or not to be" is not a choice; one may decide to be this or that, but to *be* is, simply, the only fact there is.

All the foregoing has been expressed at various times in man's intellectual history by sages who have moved beyond duality in their awareness. But even then, to claim that the comprehension of the non-duality of existence is superior to its realization as dual is again to fall into an illusion. There is, ultimately, neither duality nor non-duality; there is only awareness. Only awareness itself can state that it is beyond all concepts such as "is" or "is not." This must be so, because "is" can be conceived only by consciousness itself.

Awareness itself is beyond even consciousness. Therefore, it may be said that the Absolute is unknowable exactly because it is beyond knowing, i.e., beyond the reach of consciousness itself. Those who have attained such a state of awareness report that it cannot be described and can have no meaning for anyone without the experience of that context. Nonetheless, this is the true state of Reality, universally and eternally; we merely fail to recognize it. Such a recognition is the essence of enlightenment and the final resolution of the evolution of consciousness to the point of self-transcendence.[3]

XX
The Evolution of Consciousness

THOUSANDS OF CALCULATIONS and innumerable calibrations drawn from kinesiologic testing of individuals and from historical analysis indicate that the average advance in level of consciousness throughout the global population is little more than five points during a lifetime. Apparently, from untold millions of individual experiences in one's life, usually only a few lessons are ever learned. The attainment of wisdom is slow and painful, and few are willing to relinquish familiar, even if inaccurate, views; resistance to change or growth is considerable. It would seem that most people are willing to die rather than alter those belief systems which confine them to lower levels of consciousness.

If this is true, then what is the prognosis for the human condition? Is a five-point advance per generation all that can be expected? This troubling question deserves our attention.

In the first place, as we can observe from the distribution of levels of consciousness throughout the world population,

great masses of our species are at the low end of the evolutionary scale, still relying on force to compensate for their actual
powerlessness. More advanced individual cultures exhibit
more variation. The Japanese capitalized on the lessons of
World War II and collectively made a major jump in their
evolution. On the other hand, America's level of consciousness
sank as a result of the Vietnam War; what was actually learned
as yet remains to be seen.

Unfortunately our entertainment in general trades on
emotional sensationalism, and so gravitates toward violence.
Murder is nightly family fare on television; our children grow
up on a steady mental diet of it. Americans have learned to
enjoy the gruesome—the more bizarre, the better. Cruelty and
havoc are becoming status quo. In the city of Phoenix, where
an initiative requiring children to have parental permission to
carry guns recently failed, ABC News on January 1, 1993,
reported the handgun killing of a two-and-one-half-year-old by
a three-year-old. It seems that society institutionalizes certain
self-propagating levels of consciousness which become an
ingrained characteristic of various social strata.

Nonetheless, there remains free choice and thus a considerable potential for individual mobility and variety of experience, making available alternate options. From our study of
advanced theoretical physics, nonlinear dynamics and the
nature of nonlinear equations, it is clear that, at least in theory,
choice is not only possible, but inevitable. It is out of regularity
that irregularity appears; all attractor patterns are connected
to each other, if only by a single "strand," so to speak. But how
exactly do transformational choices occur? What occasions
them? Who makes them and why? This is a crucial subject
regarding which few principles have been defined.

Growth and development are irregular and nonlinear.
Practically nothing is known about the essential nature of
growth, or any "process" in nature for that matter. No one has

ever studied the nature of life itself, only its images and consequences. There simply has not been an adequate mathematics to comprehend it; linear differential equations brought us to approximations but not to essence. A simple sprouting seed performs incredible wonders through an intrinsic wizardry of which we have no understanding whatever.

As is commonly observed, growth, both individual and collective, can take place either slowly or suddenly. It is not limited by restraints, but by tendencies. Innumerable options are open to everyone all the time but are relatively infrequently chosen, because they want the context that would make them attractive. One's range of choice is ordinarily limited by one's vision.

Context, value and meaning are merely different terms for a subtle web of energy patterns within an overall organizing attractor energy field—which is itself only part of a still larger one, and so on, in an infinite continuum throughout the universe, eventually including the total field of consciousness itself. While the sheer magnitude of such a complex of energy patterns seems beyond human cognizance, its totality is nonetheless comprehended by individuals whose consciousness reaches the 600-700 range. This gives us some idea of the enormous capacity for understanding possessed by those with advanced consciousness.

The most important element in facilitating an upward movement in consciousness is an attitude of willingness, which opens up the mind through new means of appraisal to the possible validity of new hypotheses. Though motives for change are as multitudinous as the innumerable facets of the human condition, they are most often found to arise spontaneously when the mind is challenged in the face of a puzzle or a paradox. Deliberately creating such an impasse is a customary device in certain disciplines, such as Zen, to finesse a leap of awareness.

On our scale of consciousness there are two critical fulcrums that allow for major advancement. The first is at 200, the initial level of empowerment. Here arises the willingness to stop blaming and accept responsibility for one's own actions, feelings and beliefs. So long as cause and responsibility are projected outside oneself, one must remain in the powerless mode of victimhood. The second is the 500 level, reached by accepting love and non-judgmental forgiveness as a lifestyle, exercising unconditional kindness to all persons, things and events without exception. (In twelve-step recovery groups it is said that there are no justified resentments. Even if somebody "did you wrong," you are still free to choose your response and let resentment go.) Once one makes this commitment he begins to experience a different, more benign world as his perceptions evolve.

It is initially very challenging to understand that attitudes can alter the world one experiences and that there are numerous valid ways of experiencing it. But—as in viewing a hologram—what you see depends completely on the position from which you view it. Which position, then, is "reality"?

In fact, *this is a holographic universe.* Each point of view reflects a position defined by the viewer's unique level of consciousness. If you are on this side of the hologram your perception will hardly agree with that of the observer on the other side. "He must be crazy!" is a common reaction to such wide discrepancy. And the world is a set of holograms in limitless dimensions, not, as is often said, of mirrors—which are fixed in time and place and offer only a single reflection. Auditory experience, also, is part of a holographic series of attractor fields of all the sounds that ever were. The physical world is tactile, too. It has texture, color, dimension and spatial relationships such as position and shape. Each of these is again part of an underlying sequence which, with all other qualities, goes back in "end of time" to the original source of its existence, which is *now.*

A hologram, we might say, is in and of itself a process. There is nothing fixed in a three-dimensional hologram. And what then of a four-dimensional hologram? It would include all possible instances of itself simultaneously. To change seems to be to move through time, but if time itself is transcended, then there is no such thing as sequence. If all is now, there is nothing to follow from here to there. Each hologram is in itself an evolutionary projection from an endless nonlinear matrix of events which are not causally related, but instead synchronous. Then, at the perceptual level of 600 to 700, what was, what is, and what will be are comprehended wordlessly within the complete, simultaneous holographic possibility.[1] The term "ineffable" here begins to take meaning.

Let us attempt to understand all this better through an example. Imagine a "bum" on a street corner:

In a fashionable neighborhood in a big city stands an old man in tattered clothes, alone, leaning against the corner of an elegant brownstone. Look at him from the perspective of various levels of consciousness and note the differences in how he appears.

From the bottom of the scale at a level of 20, the level of Shame, the bum is dirty, disgusting, disgraceful. From level 30 (Guilt) he would be blamed for his condition. He deserves what he gets; he's probably a lazy welfare cheat. At 50 (Hopelessness) his plight would appear desperate, damning evidence that society can't do anything about homelessness. At 75 (Grief) the old man looks tragic, friendless and forlorn.

At a consciousness level of 100 (Fear) we might see him as threatening, a social menace. Perhaps we should call the police before he commits some crime. At 125 (Desire) he might represent a frustrating problem—why doesn't somebody do something? At 150 (Anger) the old man might look like he could be violent, or, on the other hand, one could be furious that such conditions exist. At 175 (Pride) he could be seen as an embarrassment or as lacking the self-respect to better himself. At 200 (Courage) we might be motivated to wonder if there is a local homeless shelter; all he needs is a job and a place to live.

At 250 (Neutrality) the bum looks okay, maybe even interesting. "Live and let live," we might say; after all, he's not hurting anyone. At 310 (Willingness) we might decide to go down and see what we can do to cheer up that fellow on the corner, or volunteer some time at the local mission. At 350 (Acceptance) the man on the corner appears intriguing. He probably has an interesting story to tell; he's where he is for reasons we may never understand. At 400 (Reason) he is a symptom of the current economic and social malaise, or perhaps a good subject for in-depth psychological study.

At the higher levels, the old man begins to look not only interesting, but friendly, then lovable. Perhaps we would then be able to see that he was, in fact, one who had transcended social limits and gone free, a joyful old guy with the wisdom of age in his face and the serenity that comes from indifference to material things. At 600 (Peace) he is revealed as one's own self in a temporary expression.

When approached, the bum's response to these different levels of consciousness would vary with them. With some he would feel secure, with others, frightened or dejected. Some would make him angry, others delighted. Some he would therefore avoid, others greet with pleasure. (Thus is it said that we meet what we mirror.)[2]

So much for the manner in which our level of consciousness decides what we see, the world we encounter as passive observers. It is equally true that having placed that construct upon the reality before us, we will react to it in a fashion predicated by the level from which we perceive. External events may define conditions, but they do not determine the consciousness level of human response. We can take the more literal scene of our current penal system as an illustration.

Placed in an identical and extremely stressful environment, different inmates react in ways that vary extraordinarily according to "where they're coming from." Prisoners whose consciousness is at the lowest end of the scale sometimes attempt suicide in jail. Others become psychotic and delusional with guilt. Some in the same circumstance fall into despondency, go mute, and stop eating. Still others sit with head in hands, trying to hide incipient tears of grief. A very frequent expression is fear, manifested either through paranoid defensiveness or blatant sycophancy. In the same cellblock we see other prisoners with a greater degree of energy rage, violent and assaultive. Pride is everywhere, in the form of macho bragging and dominance.

By contrast, some inmates find the courage to face the truth of why they are there and begin to look at their lives honestly. And there are always those who just "roll with the punches" and try to get some reading done. At the level of Acceptance, we see prisoners who seek out help and join support groups. It is not unusual for an occasional inmate to take a new interest in learning, studying in the prison library, or becoming a jailhouse lawyer (some of history's most influential books were written behind bars). A few prisoners go through a transformation of consciousness and become loving and generous caregivers to their fellows. And it is not unheard of for a prisoner aligned with higher energy fields to grow deeply spiritual, or even actively pursue enlightenment.

How we react depends upon the world we are reacting to. Who we become, as well as what we see, are both determined by perception, which can be said, simply, to create the world. It is interesting to note that the further down the scale of consciousness a person is, the harder it is for him to maintain eye contact. At the low end, visual contact is avoided altogether.

In contrast, as we go up the scale the ability to hold prolonged and finally almost endless gaze at great depth becomes characteristic. We are all familiar with the guarded glance of guilt, the glare of hostility and the unblinking open-eyedness of innocence. *Power and perception go hand in hand.*

How then does perception work; what are its mechanics? That perception is subjectively unique is evidenced by common observation: we are all familiar with the example of a mock trial in law school, wherein different witnesses relate wildly divergent accounts of the same event. The mechanism of perception is like a movie theater in which the projector is consciousness itself. The forms on the film emulsion are the attractor energy patterns, and the moving pictures on the screen are the world that we perceive and call "reality." We could say that the configurations on the film are the ABC attractor fields in mind and the moving picture on the screen is the A→B→C observed as the phenomenal world.

This schema provides a model for a better understanding of the nature of causality, which occurs on the level of the film, not the level of the screen. Because the world routinely applies its efforts to the screen of life at the level of A→B→C, these endeavors are ineffectual and costly. Causality stems from the attractor patterns of levels of energy, the ABCs of the configurations imprinted on the film of mind, illuminated by consciousness.

The nature of the stream of consciousness, its pattern of thought, perception, feeling and memory, is the consequence of entrainment of the attractor energy field by which it is dominated. It is well to remember that *this domination is volitional.* It is not imposed, but is the outcome of one's own choices, beliefs and goals.

By consensus we synchronize with a field pattern which implies specific styles of processing and influences all our decisions according to its accompanying set of values and meanings. What appears an important and exciting piece of information from the perspective of one level might be boring or even repulsive at another level; truth is subjective. That can be frightening. The current elevation of science to the status of infallible oracle is an expression of our insecure compulsion to feel there is some kind of a measurable, universally predictable objective world "out there" upon which we can rely.

But in transcending the emotional distortions of perception, science itself creates yet another conceptual distortion, due to the limitation of its parameters. Science must of necessity remove data from context in order to study it, but in the end it is only the context which gives the data its whole significance or value. The eventual discovery arrived at by advanced theoretical physics can be reached from any organized field of human knowledge: the more detailed one's analysis of the structure of "out there," the more one discovers that what one is examining is, in fact, the nature of the intricate processes of consciousness in here. There is nothing "out there" other than consciousness itself. The habitual tendency to believe otherwise is our fundamental illusion, a vanity of the human mind, which tends always to view its transitory subject as "mine."

Objectively, it can be seen that thoughts really belong to the consciousness of the world; the individual mind merely processes them in new combinations and permutations. What seem to be truly original thoughts appear only through the medium of genius and are invariably felt by their authors to be found or given, not created. It may be the case that we are each unique, as no two snowflakes are alike; however, we are still just snowflakes.

We all inherit the human condition of mind in our unasked-for birth. To transcend the limitations of mind, it is necessary to dethrone it from its tyranny as sole arbiter of reality. The vain mind confers its imprimatur of authenticity on the movie of life it happens to view; its very nature is to convince us that its unique view of experience is the genuine article. Each individual secretly feels that his experience of the world alone is accurate.

In our discussion of the levels of consciousness, we noted that one of the downsides of Pride is denial. Every mind engages in denial in order to protect its "correctness." This begets the fixity and resistance to change which prevents the average consciousness from advancing much more than five points in a lifetime. Great leaps in level of consciousness are always preceded by surrender of the illusion that "I know." Frequently, the only way one can reach this willingness to change is when one "hits bottom" by running out a course of action to its end in the defeat of a futile belief system. Light cannot enter a closed box; the upside of catastrophe can be an opening to a higher level of awareness. If life is viewed as a teacher, it then becomes just that. Unless the painful lessons of life which we deal ourselves are thus transformed, through humility, into gateways to growth and development, they are wasted.

We witness, we observe, we record apparent processions of experiences. But even in awareness itself nothing actually happens. Awareness merely registers what is being experienced; it has no effect on it. Awareness is the all-encompassing attractor field of unlimited power identical with life itself. And there is nothing the mind believes that is not fallacious at a higher level of awareness.

The mind identifies with its content. It takes credit and blame for what it receives, for it would be humbling to the mind's vanity to admit that the only thing it is doing is experiencing, and, in fact, only *experiencing experiencing.* The mind does not even experience the world, but only sensory reports of it. Even brilliant thoughts and deepest feelings are only experience; ultimately, we have but one function: to experience experience.

The major limitation of consciousness is its innocence. Consciousness is gullible; it believes everything it hears. Consciousness is like hardware that will play back any software put into it. We never lose the innocence of our own consciousness; it persists, naïve and trusting, like an impressionable child. Its only guardian is a discerning awareness that scrutinizes the incoming program.

Over the ages it has been noted that merely observing the mind tends to increase one's level of consciousness.[3] A mind which is being watched becomes more humble and begins to relinquish its claims to omniscience. A growth in awareness can then take place. With humility comes the capacity to laugh at oneself and increasingly be less the victim of the mind and more its master.

From thinking that we "are" our minds, we begin to see that we *have* minds, and that it is the mind that has thoughts, beliefs, feelings and opinions. Eventually we may arrive at the insight that all our thoughts are merely borrowed from the great database of consciousness and were never really our own. Prevailing thought systems are received, absorbed, identified with, and, in due time, replaced by new ideas that have become fashionable with us. As we place less value on such passing notions, they lose their capacity to dominate us, and we experience progressive freedom of, as well as from, the mind. This in turn ripens into a new source of pleasure; fittingly, the pleasure of existence itself matures as one ascends the scale of consciousness.

XXI
The Study of Pure Consciousness

VARIOUS ASPECTS OF CONSCIOUSNESS have been the subject of traditional philosophy, and the expressions of consciousness as mind or emotion have been the subjects of the clinical sciences, but the nature of consciousness itself has never been clinically studied in any comprehensive sense.

In medicine the presumption that consciousness is no more than a function of the brain is reflected in such statements as, "The patient regained consciousness." This routine, narrow depiction has assumed consciousness is a mundane physical phenomenon, a self-evident priority for experience about which nothing more need be said.

The one recurrent focus of interest in the subject has been speculation regarding what happens to man's consciousness at death. Does the power of life and awareness arise from a physical basis? Does the body sustain conscious life, or is it the other way around—the power of life sustains the body? Because the way the question is asked will be defined by the questioner's preconception of causality, the level of the questioner will predetermine the nature of the answer; each questioner will derive an answer representative of his level of consciousness.

To the materialistic scientist the question will appear nonsensical, a fruitless exercise in tautology. To those at the other pole, the "enlightened," the question will seem comical, and the limited perception it reveals will elicit compassion. The common man might take on faith the authority of either, or of conventional religious teachings, to answer the question.

All discussions of life, death and the final fate of consciousness must necessarily reflect differences of context. The reciprocal of Descartes' "I think, therefore I am," is, "I am, therefore I think." Because thinking takes place as form, Descartes is correct; that which has form must already have existence in order to have form. "I am" is a statement of awareness witnessing that the capacity for experience is independent of form.[1] Descartes implies that consciousness is only aware of itself when it assumes form. But the enlightened throughout history have disagreed, customarily stating that consciousness is beyond form and is, indeed, the very omnipotent matrix out of which form arises. Modern physicists concur, for example, David Bohm in his concept of an "enfolded" and "unfolded" universe.

Without consciousness there would be nothing to experience form. It could also be said that form itself, as a product of perception with no independent existence, is thus transitory and limited, whereas consciousness is all-encompassing and unlimited. How could that which is transitory, with a clear beginning and ending, create that which is formless, all encompassing and omnipresent? However, if we see that the notion of limitation itself is merely a product of perception with no intrinsic reality, then the riddle solves itself: form becomes an expression of the formless. Ontologically, consciousness is an aspect of "Is-ness," "Being-ness" and is implicit in man's definition of himself as human. Human-ness is only one expression of being-ness.

The operation of consciousness in human beings is the greater subject of our study. Although consciousness itself may be intangible, it is intrinsic to all human behavior. For purposes of this work, the problem is how to clinically explicate the connection between consciousness and behavior in an accurate and meaningful way that can be scientifically studied. Fortunately, kinesiology categorically demonstrates the physical expression of sentience through the instantaneous reaction of the body to events experienced within consciousness. The technique affords us an elegant methodology with an unmistakably established end point that can be calibrated, documented and reproduced experimentally.

Characteristics of Pure Consciousness

Our vision of consciousness is linked with our concept of self. The more limited the sense of self, the smaller is the parameter of experiencing. Restricted paradigms of reality are global in their effects. As an example, our studies of the "poor" have made it evident that "poorness" is not just a financial condition, but that the poor are poor in friendships, poor in verbal skills, poor in education, poor in social amenities, poor in resources, poor in health and poor in overall level of happiness. Poorness, then, can be seen as a quality characteristic of a limited self-image resulting in a paucity of resources.[2] It is not a financial condition, but a level of consciousness. The energy of that level of awareness calibrates at about 60.

The identification and, therefore, experience of self could be limited to an identification of self as one's physical body. Then, of course, we might well ask, how does one know that one has a physical body? Through observation we note that the presence of the physical body is registered by the senses. The question follows, what is it that is aware of the senses?

How do we experience what the senses are reporting? Something greater, something more encompassing than the physical body has to exist in order to experience that which is lesser; that something is mind. A person identifies with his body because his mind is experiencing his body. Patients who have lost sizable portions of their bodies report that their sense of self remains undiminished; such a person will say, "I am still just as much me."

The question then arises, how does one know what is being experienced by the mind? By observation and introspection one can witness that thoughts have no capacity to experience themselves, but that something both beyond and more basic than thought experiences the sequence of thoughts, and that its sense of identity is unaltered by the content of thoughts.

What is it that observes and is aware of all the subjective and objective phenomena of life? It is consciousness itself that is resonated as both awareness and experiencing. Both are purely subjective. Consciousness itself is not determined by content; thoughts flowing through consciousness are like fish swimming in the ocean. The ocean's existence is independent of the fish; the content of the sea does not define the nature of the water itself. Like a colorless ray, consciousness illuminates the object witnessed—thus its traditional association throughout world literature is with "light."[3]

Identification solely with the content of consciousness accounts for the experience of self as limited. In contrast, to identify with consciousness itself is to know that one's actual self is unlimited. When such circumscribed self-identifications have been surmounted, so that the sense of self is identified as consciousness itself, we become "enlightened."[4]

One characteristic of the experience of pure consciousness is a perception of timelessness (or timelessness of perception). Consciousness is experienced as beyond all form and time and seen as everywhere equally present. It is described as

"Is-ness" or "Being-ness" and, in the spiritual literature, "I-am-ness."[5] Consciousness does not recognize separation, which is a limitation of perception. The enlightened state is a "Oneness" in which there is no division into parts. Such division is only apparent from a localized perception; it is only an accident of a point of view.

Similar descriptions throughout the history of thought are in accord with the studies of William James as reported in the famous Gifford lectures. The experience of consciousness itself he described as rare, unique, ineffable and "beyond mind;" a thought-free state of Knowingness, complete, all inclusive, with neither need nor want, beyond the limitation of experiencing a merely individualized personal self.[6]

Another attribute of pure consciousness is cessation of the ordinary flow of thoughts or feelings, a condition of infinite power, infinite compassion, infinite gentleness, infinite love. In this state self becomes Self with a capital "S." There is an accompanying recognition of the very origin of the capacity to experience self as Self. This awareness of self as Self is the culmination of the process of eliminating limited identifications of self.[7]

The steps necessary to be taken to facilitate awareness of Self as consciousness have been well detailed historically. Numerous techniques and behaviors have been prescribed to facilitate removal of obstacles to expanded awareness; these can be found in the practice of various spiritual disciplines. The one process common to all such teachings is the progressive elimination of the identification of self as finite.[8]

Enlightenment is said to be relatively rare not so much because of the difficulty of following the necessary steps thereto, but because it is a condition of interest to very few, particularly in modern society. If we were to stop one thousand people in the street and ask them, "What is your greatest ambition in life?" how many would say, "To be enlightened."?

Contemporary Recognition of Higher Consciousness

The growing level of interest in consciousness as a scientific subject was recently evidenced by the first international conference on the subject, entitled *Toward a Scientific Basis of Consciousness*, held at the University of Arizona Health Sciences Center in Tucson, Arizona, on April 12–17, 1994. This was an international, interdisciplinary convocation of impressively credentialed scholars. However, among the numerous eminent presenters and the wide range of highly specialized subjects dealt with, there was little inquiry beyond rational/materialistic explanations of consciousness as a purely physical phenomenon.

In fact, approaches to the subject of consciousness are as varied as human experience itself. We have cited many of the cutting-edge insights of modern inquiry into this issue in passing. It may be helpful to review the evolution of contemporary thought on this matter, in order to more clearly proceed to our own conclusions.

The presence of some variety of consciousness is ordinarily considered to be the distinguishing characteristic of that which is living as opposed to that which is non-living. Life is the expression of consciousness in the observable or experiential world of form. But the totality of human experience attests that consciousness is both manifest and unmanifest. The awareness of consciousness within form is common; the awareness of pure consciousness, beyond form, is exceptional.

This "experience" of pure consciousness itself, devoid of all content, has been consistently reported throughout human history; always the reports have been the same.[9] Many who attained that state became the Great Teachers of history and have profoundly influenced human behavior. Such beings, in the course of their few short years, have been capable of creating a realization by millions of people, over millennial periods, of the contextual significance of existence. Because these teachings have not concerned the material world as experienced through the senses, they have been labeled "spiritual."[10]

Before the recent interest of scientists in the subject, the study of consciousness was exclusively the concern of spiritual teachers and their students. But in the last twenty years the considerable interest of numerous theoretical physicists has turned, as we have seen, to the correlation between advanced theoretical physics and the non-material universe. The deepening of popular cultural focus since the 1960s created a receptive audience for spinoffs of this exploration in such books as Fritjof Capra's *The Tao of Physics* (Shambhala, 1976), and Robert Ornstein's *The Psychology of Consciousness* (W.H. Freeman and Company, 1972), now classics. The occurrence of higher states of consciousness, traditionally thought to be extremely rare, grows more common as the M-field of the new paradigm spreads: recent surveys indicate 65% of respondents report having had experiences previously categorized as spiritual.

Because science is, by its very nature, concerned only with observable phenomena, it has never been attracted to spiritual concepts as a subject for consideration, despite the fact that many great scientists throughout history have personally testified to subjective experiences of pure consciousness occurring in the course of, and frequently crucial to, their work.[11] But the exploding field of nonlinear dynamics provoked curiosity and commentary regarding the nature of existence and consciousness itself, expressed in such books as *Does God Play Dice?: Mathematics of Chaos*, by Ian Steward. The new concept of a "science of wholeness" became the subject of popular works such as *Looking Glass Universe* and *Turbulent Mirror* by Briggs and Peat. Recently, astronomers, mathematicians, brain surgeons and neurologists, as well as physicists, have been caught up in a tide of enthusiasm about the significance of the new discoveries.

We have frequently pointed out that man is unable to observe or recognize an event until there is a prior context and language for naming the event. This inability, called paradigm blindness, is the direct consequence of a limitation of context.[12] Thus it was that the extension of the new intellectual substructure pervading the physical sciences only slowly created the potential for new views and approaches in the "human" sciences, such as psychology.

Although Abraham Maslow long ago discussed "peak experiences," the mainstream literature of psychology never addressed the subject of consciousness itself, with the exception of such classics as *The Varieties of Religious Experience* by William James, long the standard scientific work on the psychology of consciousness as spiritual experience. Eventually, transpersonal psychology went beyond the bounds of experimental and clinical psychology to investigate those aspects of human experience which were purely subjective. Unusual experiences or abilities once discounted as hoax or hallucination finally became the subject of parapsychology, legitimating experimental attempts to verify experiences such as extrasensory perception.

The field of psychiatry originally arose from the attempt to address the tangible etiology of the intangibles in human behavior and disease. Psychiatry, as a branch of medicine, concerned itself with pathology; therefore it dealt almost exclusively with the lower levels of consciousness and their neurophysiologic correlates. Consciousness as such remained outside the paradigms of psychiatry.

In medicine, physicians who worked from a larger paradigm of the healing process and included non-traditional modalities in their therapeutic approaches became known as "holistic" practitioners, an appellation that at first carried distinct overtones of unprofessionalism among the ranks of the medical establishment. But the contributions of pioneering individuals in this field, especially in such areas as recovery from heart attacks or the use of prayer to speed up recuperation in surgical patients, demanded serious recognition.

Elizabeth Kübler-Ross brought the attention of the professions, as well as the public, to the phenomena of dying and near-death experiences as reported by patients. Out-of-body experience also eventually became a relatively common subject, as surgical patients reported out-of-body adventures in which they witnessed their entire operations and heard everything said in the operating room.[13] Thelma Moss became well known for her work with Kirlian photography of energy fields such as those around fingertips. Her photographs of the energy body of a full leaf remaining after it had been cut in two are well known.[14] Finally even acupuncture has gained a place of some respect in the American health field, with many physicians learning the technique despite the fact that traditional medicine has not recognized any energies other than mechanical, electrical or chemical.

Holistic approaches operate from a different context of the nature of human consciousness than does traditional medicine, with emphasis on healing rather than treating. And though their connection with the theoretical breakthroughs of recent decades may not appear explicit, the alternate therapies employed by holistic health-care givers, whether physicians, alternative practitioners or lay healers—however widely they differ in their approach and method—all have one common element: all are based on techniques to influence not protoplasm as such, but *an energy field* which surrounds, courses through and conditions the human body.[15]

Outside the medical domain, the phenomenal success of the twelve-step self-help movement, to which we have frequently alluded, has impressively established that healing can be effected through the practice of *principles of consciousness*. The capacity to heal desperate conditions recognized by Jung in his work with Rowland H., the first link, as we have seen, in the long chain of healings that eventually became the world-wide Alcoholics Anonymous movement, lay distinctly within the realm of higher consciousness. The profound spiritual experience held out as hope by Jung to Rowland, very much akin to the transformations of enlightenment, was the essence of the message passed on to Bill W., the founder of AA.[16] It is notable that Bill W. characterized AA as "the language of the heart."[17]

All these trails blazed in the pioneering of theoretical and applied human wisdom have a common point of convergence. Or perhaps it might be better said that they share a common point of origin. Bill Wilson's revelation from the depths of despair did not proceed from conceptual rationality or any other introspective focus of self, but from a leap to higher consciousness, a transport of Self to a Presence of Infinite Light and Power.[18] That this transformational experience has led to the recovery of millions is merely testimony to the power of energy fields which calibrate at 600 or more. That is the level at which there is a crossover of the experience of consciousness from form to formless.

This formless power, the "Higher Power" of the world-wide twelve-step self-help movement and the basis for its millions of recoveries,[19] is the same wellspring of power to which all these far-flung branches of intellectual exploration have been not so much thrusting forward as working their way back. It is the power of pure consciousness itself.

XXII
Spiritual Struggle

FROM THE UNDERSTANDING of consciousness at which we have arrived, we can reinterpret the struggle of man's spiritual enterprise. Pure consciousness itself, that which is described as *Is-ness, Being-ness, I-am-ness,* represents the infinite potential, infinite power and infinite energy source of all existence, identified as Deity, God, Divinity. Within this potential, the Unmanifest becomes Manifest as the Avatar—Christ, Buddha, the Great Teacher, the Great Guru—whose energy field calibrates at 1,000 or more. These individuals set up attractor patterns of enormous force to which the mind, with its holographic capacity to react globally to attractor fields, is subject.

Of lesser moment, but still enormously powerful, are the "ordinary" enlightened teachers who have taught the path to the realization of the "Self." The Self has been described by the enlightened throughout time as infinite, formless, change-less, all present, unmanifest-and-manifest.[1] Herein is the Oneness, the All-ness and God-ness of all that exists, indistinguish-able from the Creator, whose power in the human realm is a giant attractor field which allows and encompasses variation (free will) so that "all paths lead to Me." Teachings and other works that treat of this have typically calibrated at 700 in our studies.

At the energy field of 600, ordinary thought ceases. Beyond temporal linear process, existence is witnessed as *Knowing-ness*, omnipresence, non-duality. Because existence has no locality, the "me/you" duality and consequent illusion of separation disappears.[2] This state is the peace beyond all understanding, infinite, unconditional love—all encompassing, all knowing, all present, omnipowerful and coincident with the Self, which is the awareness that the Manifest is one with the Unmanifest.

Truly spiritual states can be said to begin at a calibrated level of about 500 (unconditional love) and continue to infin-ity. Teachers who calibrate in the high 500s and the 600s are frequently recognized as saints; their state of consciousness is often described as sublime.[3]

It is a common experience for as yet unenlightened devotees to enter such a sublime state when in the presence of teachers whose energy fields calibrate at 550 and over, through the process of "entrainment"—the dominance of a powerful attractor field. Until the devotee himself arrives at the higher state of awareness, this state will not persist when he is out of the higher energy field of the teacher.[4] Advanced spiritual seekers often fluctuate in and out of this "presence of the Beloved" as they approach enlightenment; this loss of the higher state and descent to a lower is identified in both Eastern and Western literature as an "anguish of the soul."[5]

Spiritual work, like other intensive pursuits such as sport, can be arduous and frequently requires the development of specific tools for the task, including an extremely focused intent and unfailing concentration. The difficulty of inner work results from the great effort required to escape from the familiar gravity of lower attractor fields and move to the influence of a higher field. In order to ameliorate this struggle all religions issue proscriptions against exposing oneself to the lower energy fields; it is only from an authoritarian viewpoint that such error is depicted as "sin." A more liberal viewpoint accepts man's dalliance in lower energy fields as pardonable "failing."

But attitudes, emotions and behaviors characteristic of the energy fields below 200 do, in fact, generally preclude spiritual experience. The classical *chakra* system recognized by many spiritual disciplines correlates almost exactly with the Map of Consciousness that has emerged from our studies. The level 600 corresponds to the crown chakra, 500 to the heart, 200 and up to the solar plexus, while the lower attitudes and emotions of spite, envy, resentment and jealousy are associated with the spleen. The base chakra has to do with animal survival, absorption with which prohibits spiritual progress; thus all spiritual teachings advise against worldliness, suggesting avoidance of attachment to sex or money.[6]

The lower regions are also the locus of addictions; one can be fixated at any of the lower levels. Almost all of these energy fields and the behaviors associated with them now have given rise to specific self-help groups, all of which concur that without a spiritual context, recovery is quite unlikely. In consciousness-raising programs in general, a universal dictum is that one is powerless until one tells the truth. All spiritually oriented self-help groups require this first step. They are unanimous that an open mind and willingness are necessary prerequisites to progress; in other words, one must have reached an energy field of 200 in one's development to be healable. Lingering within the influence of fields below this entails a real danger of becoming so deeply entrained that one cannot escape. This is not always so, however; history has noted many occasions of individuals in the very depths of entrainment suddenly breaking through to a high level of consciousness.

Such sudden breakthroughs are still seen on occasion in modern society; this, as we have seen, was the precise experience of Bill Wilson which resulted in the founding of AA. This experience seems typically to be characterized by a total transformation of consciousness and liberation from the entrainment of lower attractor fields and a sudden emergence into higher awareness. (This type of experience, common in the early days of AA when its members were frequently "last-gaspers," is not reported by "high bottom" members who constitute the majority of newcomers to Alcoholics Anonymous today.)

Just as the entrainment or influence of the higher energy fields has an anabolic, or growth-enhancing, effect on a subject, entrainment by lower attractor fields has a catabolic, or destructive, effect; the most widespread example in today's culture is the influence of some forms of violent pop music. Among our test subjects, punk rock, death rock and gangster rap music made every subject go weak, confirming earlier observations made by Dr. John Diamond.[7] In a more recent study of students reported in The Arizona Republic, July 4, 1994, Dr. James Johnson of the University of North Carolina found rap music to increase tolerance for and predisposition to violence while promoting materialism and reducing both immediate interest in academics and long-term success.

A common experience observed in therapy groups and clinics is that drug abusers do not recover if they continue to listen to heavy metal rock; a one-year follow-up of inpatient and outpatient cocaine addicts from Sedona Villa, a branch of Camelback Hospital of Phoenix, Arizona, indicated that not a single cocaine abuser who continued to listen to this violent and negative music recovered.[8] Self-help groups for the addicted invariably recommend avoiding the influence (i.e., the energy fields) of former lifestyle associations. These addicts found that leaving the drug was not enough. To do so was merely to attack the A→B→C of addiction. As long as they could not make the commitment of will to entirely leave the influence of the field—of which the music, like the drug, was simply a manifestation—they could not escape entrainment to the low energy attractor, the ABC of addiction.

Recovered addicts who leave the energy field of their self-help programs rather predictably relapse.[9] Besides having relinquished the infusion of the combined power of their fellow members, their assertion that one can go it alone is a notorious symptom of an oncoming relapse, because it indicates an infiltration of arrogance and pride, calibrating at 175, well below the power of the energy field required for healing.

The same principle, of course, operates in the other direction. To seek enlightenment is to seek entrainment to the most powerful attractor patterns. The key, again, is will, a constantly repeated act of choice. Here the chaos-theory principle of sensitive dependence on initial conditions provides a scientific explanation of the traditional way of spiritual progress. In all spiritual disciplines the opening wedge predicated for advancing one's awareness is described as "willingness." History shows what has been clinically shown as well: a persistent willingness is the trigger that activates a new attractor field and allows one to begin to leave the old. We may visualize a lesser attractor field approaching a greater one, at which point the introduction of a third element (free will, the decisive consequence of choice and evolution) suddenly creates a crossover (a "saddle-pattern") and change takes place.

In Eastern spiritual disciplines it is accepted that the devotee alone, unaided by a guru, is unlikely to make much progress.[10] The AA experience is that a true alcoholic is unable to recover without the help of a sponsor. In sports great coaches are sought after because their influence inspires maximum effort. A devotee can abet his own progress by merely focusing on an advanced teacher and thereby aligning with that teacher's energy field; in our testing it was shown repeatedly that holding in mind the image of an advanced spiritual teacher made every subject go strong, irrespective of his personal beliefs.

The agency of change in spiritual struggles of personal metamorphosis is always beyond the power of the seeker. Great saints such as Francis of Assisi have typically asserted that they were mere channels of a higher power from without, taking no credit for personal initiative in achieving their state, which they attributed to Grace.[11] This is illustrative of the instrumentation whereby the newcomer from a lesser level of awareness who places himself in the influence of a higher awareness is transformed "by osmosis," (i.e., entrainment). Even casual observers frequently note this conspicuous absence of agency on the part of the person so clearly transmuted by an invisible force.

When someone suddenly goes from the influence of a lower attractor field to that of a higher, therefore, it is often acclaimed as a miracle. The unfortunate verdict of human experience is that few escape the energy fields that gradually come to dominate their behaviors. A currently popular spiritual program designed to facilitate such escape is A Course in Miracles.[12] The purpose of this course of spiritual psychology is to prepare the necessary groundwork to precipitate a sudden jump in consciousness through encouraging a total change of perception. In more traditional fashion, prayer and meditation also provide points of departure to rise from the influence of a lower energy field into a higher.

Physicians who have risen to energy fields at 500 and above have become powerful healers, accomplishing striking successes with treatments with which others are unable to achieve similar results (and thereby producing paradoxical data in many double-blind studies). Such inexplicable variances show the intervention of power unaccountable by the routine causal explanation that predominates in medicine. In a holographic world any "single" event is the result of all events in the universe; "events" as such have no self-existent reality. The universe *is* man's consciousness. It requires a comprehension beyond intellect.

The achievements of pure reason are the great landmarks of cultural history. They have made man the master of his external environment, and to some degree, on the physical plane, of his internal environment. But reason has its limits, in more ways than one. The intellectual brilliance of the 400 level, so dazzling and enviable to those in the 300s, quickly palls for those who have transcended it. From a higher perspective it is all too clear how tedious and trivial reason's infatuation with itself can become. Reason is the mirror of the mind's vanity; ultimately, there are few things more boring to observe than self-admiration.

Rationality, the great liberator which has freed us from the demands of our lower natures, is also a stern warder, denying our escape to the planes above and beyond intellect. For those entrained at the level of the 400s, reason itself becomes a cap, a ceiling in spiritual evolution. It is striking how many of history's great names calibrate at 499—Descartes, Newton, Einstein, dozens more. It is a sticking point, an enormous barrier; the fight to overcome it is the most common, and frequently the lengthiest, of spiritual struggles.

It is not unheard-of for very advanced scientists, thoroughly entrained by the influences of the level of Reason, to have sudden breakthroughs and emerge into a realm of global wholeness.[13] The world of spirituality is coincident with the world of non-deterministic science and nonlinear systems, as we have attempted to show. Our research and this presentation, in fact, are designed to facilitate rational recognition of spiritual phenomena by those who are predominantly linear and habituated to the "left-brain" mode. Perhaps the construct of our map of the anatomy of consciousness can illuminate somewhat the nature of ultimate causality by illustrating that the power of creation proceeds from the top down, rather than from the bottom up.

It is our hope, though, not to dogmatize, but to assist the reader in a process of self-revelation, as it is our desire to address not merely that figment designated as the reader's rational self, but his entire consciousness. In our study it is the total person that reacts to the test stimuli. Although the subject's mind may not be aware of what is going on, his total being certainly is, or there would be no consistency to our findings. This reminds us of the observation of advanced spiritual teachers that the devotee has only to discover...that which he already knows.

XXIII
The Search for Truth

CYNICAL THOUGH IT MAY AT FIRST SOUND, we must admit that for everyday operational purposes truth is whatever is subjectively convincing at one's current level of perception. At the lower levels of consciousness, propositions are accepted as true even when they are illogical, unfounded, and express tenets neither intellectually provable nor practically demonstrable. This is not a phenomenon restricted to the lunatic fringe. Locally, far more often than we would like to admit, innocent persons are convicted and jailed on the testimony of clearly irrational or biased witnesses. Globally, the basis for perennial wars like those of Slavic Europe or the Middle East is an insane belief in the justice of revenge, which virtually guarantees endless conflict.

With few exceptions, even religions which ostensibly represent the teachings of the "Prince of Peace" have never forbidden war or the killing of other human beings under "justifiable" circumstances—justifiable, of course, to those doing the killing; their victims will likely fail to appreciate the justification. Such self-contradictory behavior, diametrically opposed to the underlying principles of a faith, will appear less surprising if we apply critical factor analysis to calibrate the evolution, or devolution, of spiritual teachings over time.

We can look at the world's foremost religious teachings thus:

Christianity

The level of truth originally expounded by Jesus Christ calibrates at 1000, the highest attained on this plane. By the second century, though, the level of truth of the practice of his teachings had dropped to 930, and by the sixth century, to 540. By the time of the crusades, at the beginning of the eleventh century, it had fallen to its current 498. A major decline in the year 325 A.D. was apparently due to the spread of misinterpretations of the teachings originating from the Council of Nicaea. Students of religious history will find it interesting to calibrate the level of truth of Christianity as practiced before and after Paul, Constantine, Augustine, etc.[1]

It should be noted that the Lamsa translation, from the Aramaic, of the New Testament calibrates at 750, and the King James Version, from the Greek, at 500. Just as there is a wide range in the level of truth of various translations, so there is a wide variation between different Christian practices. Most major persuasions—Roman Catholicism, Anglicanism, Christian Science (and many such small denominations as the Quakers)—calibrate in the high 500s. Specialized interpretations such as that of the contemporary *Course in Miracles*, on the one hand, or the fourteenth-century mysticism of Meister Eckhart, on the other, calibrate at 600. As in the case of Islam see below) however, extreme fundamentalist groups with explicit reactionary political agendas can calibrate as low as 125.

Buddhism

The level of truth of the teaching of the Buddha was also originally at 1,000. By the sixth century A.D., the level of truth in practice had dropped to an average of 900. These teachings have deteriorated less than any other religion: Hinyana Buddhism (the lesser vehicle) still calibrates at 850; Mahayana Buddhism (the greater vehicle) calibrates at 950. Current Zen Buddhism is in the 600s.

Hinduism

The teachings of Lord Krishna calibrated at 1,000 and have deteriorated slowly over time but the truth of the current practice still calibrates at 850.

Judaism

The teachings of Abraham calibrated at 985; the practice current at the time of Moses, at 770, which is the level of truth of the Talmud. Modern Judaism calibrates at 499. The Old Testament calibrates at 475.

Islam

The level of consciousness of Mohammed was 540. The Koran calibrates at 570. The kernel of Islamic faith is an expression of loving acceptance and inner peace, but the evolution of practical dogma was intertwined from the start with the politics of territorial expansion in the form of *jihad*, or religious warfare. The truth of the teachings had dropped severely by the end of the period of the crusades. In modern times the ascendance of fanatic nationalistic religious movements characterized by paranoia and xenophobia has rapidly eroded the spiritual essence of this faith. At the present time the level of truth of the teachings of militant Islamic Fundamentalism is 130.

When we look at the decline of the level of truth of the world's great religions, we notice that those that are the most "yin" have remained relatively pure through the ages, whereas those that are more "yang" (involved in worldly affairs) have degraded markedly, until the militant extremist faction of the most aggressive religion has actually sunk below the critical level of integrity at 200. The more dualistic the creed, the greater seems to be its vulnerability to misinterpretation. Dualism promotes a split between belief and action and the disorientation of levels of truth. When this occurs, the spiritual essence can be confused in translation into physical expression. Thus, the conceptual Christian Soldier (of the spirit) becomes, through a distorted "literal" translation, a self-justified battlefield killer.

The Hindus did not fall into the error of confusing levels of interpretation; the battle described in the opening of the Bhagavad-Gita was never misinterpreted to suggest Lord Krishna teaches that believers are to engage in actual warfare. The Buddha's view—that the cause of all pain and suffering is ignorance, which he saw as the only "sin" possible, and that one's duty is to be compassionate towards others and pray for them—is hardly susceptible to such distortion.

The downfall of all lofty spiritual teachings has been their misinterpretation by the less enlightened; each level of consciousness predefines its own limited capacity for perception and comprehension. Until one has oneself become enlightened or at least experienced the higher states of consciousness, all spiritual teachings remain hearsay and are thus prone to distortion and misunderstanding. Scripture can be quoted to justify any position. The "righteous" are always dangerous because of their imbalanced perception and their consequent indifference to moral violence. Within any religion, fundamentalist sects always calibrate lowest, often operating at the same level of consciousness as criminality; their hallmark is egocentric extremism and irrationality. But with eighty-five percent of the human population below the critical level of 200, error is easily disseminated and readily accepted around the world.

Cults proliferate because the general public has no objective criterion with which to distinguish truth from falsehood. Using the tools of this study, we may identify as a cult any purportedly spiritual movement that calibrates below the level of 200. As we have seen above, cults are not just isolated, renegade phenomena; they also thrive as tolerated subgroups within the world's great religions, distorting teachings and subverting their intent.

Cults need not be formally religious at all. The ultimate cult, of course, is the anti-religion, based on anti-divinity which we know as Satanism; it has no explicit religious agenda of its own, as it defines itself through antithesis and reversal of benign principles. In one form or another, it has always been with us. As up implies down and light, darkness, man's socially organized search for truth and commitment to attaining higher spiritual levels has always implied the socially organized promulgation of falsehood and submission to the lowest energy fields. Examination of the nature of anti-religion demonstrates, in fact, the enormously destructive power of negative energy fields. Examples are unfortunately ready to hand.

The trappings of Satanism spread as fashions of a pop youth subculture, its primary vehicle being an overt musical genre. But principles are implicit in trappings, and principles generate attractor fields. The effects are all too familiar to any clinical psychiatrist practicing near an urban area. The destruction of energy fields is pathogenic. Victims become desensitized to distinctions between good and evil, a value inversion which can be clinically examined. Habitués are found to directly display "blown-out" acupuncture systems and desynchronization of the cerebral hemispheres in response to repetitive negative patterns of the associated music, the net result of which is, in effect, a hypnotic trance during which the listener is highly susceptible to the violent and blasphemous suggestion of the lyrics. In this sense, these children become literally enslaved, prone to later bouts of irrational destruction in which they, in truth, "don't know why" they act out post-hypnotic suggestions. And the influence persists.

Continued weakening of the body and its immune system long after the music stops is accompanied by an inversion of kinesiolocical response. Negative stimuli that would make a normal person go weak cause a strong response while those that would make a normal person strong now produce a weak one. Unaware that they are the victims of a potent negative energy field, the members of this culture sink into sometimes inescapable subservience to forces beyond their comprehension. Youth subjected to such physical, emotional and sexual abuse can suffer permanent damage to the brain's neurotransmitter balance, becoming adult depressives who habitually seek out abusive partners and must endlessly struggle against an inclination to suicide that is, in fact, a lingering form of posthypnotic suggestion.[2]

We may wish to deny that such a spiritual plague, reminiscent of the Dark Ages, could remain virulent in our enlightened society. But such perverse influences do not operate in a moral vacuum or arise from a social matrix that does not already incorporate preconditions for their growth. The paradox of our puritanical society is that it encourages constant seduction but denies satisfaction, so a perpetual frustration of normal outlets eventually finds release in perverse ones. If we look more closely we may find that other elements of what we call civilization in fact foster its persistence.

While the young are being programmed by specialized TV and computer games that glorify violence, their parents are being brainwashed by adult media. Kinesiolocicalal testing showed a fairly typical TV serial caused test subjects to go weak

113 times during a single episode. Each of these weakening events suppressed the observer's immune system; each weakening reflected an insult to the viewer's central as well as autonomic nervous system. Invariably accompanying each of these 113 disruptions of the acupuncture system were suppressions of the thymus gland; each insult also resulted in damage to the brain's delicate neurohormonal and neurotransmitter systems. Each negative input brought the watcher closer to eventual sickness and to imminent depression—now the world's most prevalent illness.

Subtle grades of depression kill more people than all the other diseases of mankind combined. There is no antidepressant that will cure a depression which is spiritually based, because the malaise does not originate from brain dysfunction but from an accurate response to the desecration of life. The body is the reflection of the spirit in its physical expression, and its problems are the dramatization of the struggles of the spirit which gives it life. A belief that we ascribe to "out there" has its effect "in here." Everyone dies by his own hand. That is a hard clinical fact, not a moral view.

The attempt to impose standards of would-be absolute Good and Evil is, in fact, one of the greatest moral pitfalls. But without moralizing, we can plainly state that whatever calibrates above 200 supports life and therefore may be functionally defined as good, whereas whatever calibrates below 200 is destructive, non-supportive of life and can thus be declared functionally evil. By testing we can prove that a false premise such as "the end justifies the means" is operationally evil, yet this is a routinely accepted justification for much of human behavior, from the peccadilloes of commerce to the enormities of war. Such spiritual ambiguity, leading ultimately to irretrievable confusion between functional good and evil, has always been the Achilles heel of human society.

It is this process of perversion of truth through a failure of discernment which has provided the instrumentation of the decline in the world's great religions noted above. Religions which fall below the level of 500 may preach love but they will not be able to practice it. And no religious system which encourages war can claim spiritual authority without the blatant hypocrisy that has made atheists of many honest men.

Society is collectively most vulnerable when the capacity to distinguish between attractors and imitators or to perceive nuances of differing levels of consciousness is dulled. Thus do civil abuses become law and political extremists persuade with righteous slogans. The children of violence become its perpetrators because a confused society which has lost the capacity for discernment necessary to protect its own consciousness can hardly hope to protect its young.

An individual's level of consciousness is determined by the principles to which he or she is committed. To maintain progress in consciousness there can be no wavering from principle, or the individual will fall back to a lower level. Expediency is never an adequate justification. If it is wrong to kill another human being, that principle can allow *no* exceptions, regardless how emotionally appealing a construct may be used to justify the exception. Thus, a society which condones capital punishment will always have a problem with murder. Both are products of the same level of perception. To the murderer, the killing of the victim is also a justifiable exception.

Once a principle is breached, its mutated form propagates like cancer. A society which supports killing, whether in war, by the police or by the penal system, cannot at the same time effectively stop "criminal" killing. To kill is to kill is to kill; there is no escaping the fact. The decision to kill or not is a basic issue on the path to real power. But this rudimentary step has not even been essayed by eighty-five percent of the world's population or by virtually any of its governments. Koko, the famous simian resident of the Primate Research Institute, who has worked for some years with a psychologist and developed a sophisticated sign language vocabulary, is truthful, affectionate, intelligent and trustworthy; her integrity calibrates at 250. Thus, one is safer with the ape Koko than with eighty-five percent of the humans on the planet.

Injury to man's "spiritual eye" has resulted in dimness of moral vision and blindness to truth which afflict eighty-five percent of the earth's population, who linger below the level of integrity. The great issue that confronts mankind as a whole is the healing of this spiritual blindness. The more immediate "problem" of Right and Wrong that always diverts our societal focus only exists as a function of perception based at the lower levels of consciousness. Little children must be taught dangerous behaviors are "wrong," but as they grow older discernment should replace moralism. Whether it is wrong to kill other human beings may be a moral dilemma at lower levels of consciousness; at higher levels the very question is ridiculous. Conventional morality is, therefore, only a provisional substitute for a faculty of higher consciousness. Moralism, a by-product of duality, becomes insignificant as the consciousness level rises through the 500s, and irrelevant at the level of 600.

Merely to reach a stage where one functions primarily from reason requires a major evolution in consciousness to the 400s, a very powerful level in world society. Freud, Einstein and Descartes calibrate at 499, which is also the level of humanism.[3] But reason, so vulnerable to loss of perspective through self-absorption, has in the long run never provided man any solid moral, or even intellectual, certitude. Again and again it has, to the contrary, led from the chaos of ignorance to an equally baffling cerebral maze. In a world of mass confusion we desperately need a reliable, accurate, objectively verifiable yardstick with which to measure truth. Hopefully, this study has presented such a tool. Any increased infusion of the influence of truth into the collective human consciousness gives us cause for greater hope than may be apparent from what tends inevitably to be a rather gloomy overview.

We have established that consciousness is capable of discerning any change of energy to a degree of log $10^{-\infty}$. This means that there is no possible event in the entire universe not detectable by the exquisite sensitivity of consciousness itself. The energy of human thought, though minute, is nonetheless absolutely measurable. A thought which emanates from the 100 level of consciousness will typically measure between log $10^{-800 \text{ million}}$ to $10^{-700 \text{ million}}$ microwatts. On the other hand, a loving thought at the consciousness level of 500 measures approximately log $10^{-35 \text{ million}}$ microwatts.

Although only fifteen percent of the world's population is above the critical consciousness level of 200, the collective power of that fifteen percent has the weight to counterbalance the negativity of the remaining eighty-five percent of the world's population. Because the scale of power advances logarithmically, a single Avatar at a consciousness level of 1,000 can, in fact, totally counterbalance the collective negativity of all mankind. Kinesiological testing has shown that:

One individual at level 700	*counterbalances*	70 million individuals below level 200
One individual at level 600	*counterbalances*	10 million individuals below level 200
One individual at level 500	*counterbalances*	750,000 individuals below level 200
One individual at level 400	*counterbalances*	400,000 individuals below level 200
One individual at level 300	*counterbalances*	90,000 individuals below level 200
Twelve individuals at level 700	*equal*	one Avatar at 1,000

(There are currently 12 persons on the planet who calibrate at 700.)

Were it not for these counterbalances, mankind would self-destruct out of the sheer mass of its unopposed negativity. The difference in power between a loving thought ($10^{-35 \text{ million}}$ microwatts) and a fearful thought ($10^{-750 \text{ million}}$ microwatts) is so enormous as to be beyond the capacity of the human imagination to easily comprehend. We can see from the analysis above, however, that even a few loving thoughts during the course of the day more than counterbalance all of our negative thoughts.

From a social-behavioral viewpoint, as we said, truth is the set of principles by which people live, regardless what they might say they believe. We have seen that there is subjective truth, operational truth, hypothetical truth, intellectual truth; and then there is factual data. The legitimacy of any of these is dependent on the context of a given perceptual level. Truth is not functional unless it is meaningful, and meaning, like value, is dependent on a unique perceptual field. Facts and data may be convincing at one level and irrelevant at another. Functional validity of information received also varies with the intellectual level and capacity for abstraction of the recipient. To be operational, truth must be not simply "true" but knowable; yet each level of truth is unknowable to the levels below it and has no validity beyond its own territory. Thus, we can conclude that all levels of truth as we know it, within the dimension of ordinary human function, are examples of *dependent truth*, whose veracity is totally contingent on a given set of parameters. Even our revered "scientific truth" is also truth by definition of conditions and therefore subject to dispute and error. Statistical inference has become a propaganda tool, and the statistical distortions by which anything can be proven about anything have alienated our credence.

Is there any impersonal truth, independent of individual condition or context?

Truth as detected by the research methods explicated through this book derives its validity from ultimate sources far beyond the influence of any localized perceptual field. It respects neither personality nor opinion and does not vary with any condition of test subject or environment.

Ignorance does not yield to attack, but it dissipates in the light, and nothing dissolves dishonesty faster than the simple act of revealing the truth. The only way to enhance one's power in the world is by increasing one's integrity, understanding and capacity for compassion. If the diverse populations of mankind can be brought to this realization, the survival of human society and the happiness of its members is secure.

The initial effect of taking responsibility for the truth of one's life is to raise lower energy levels to 200, the critical level at which power first appears and the stepping stone to all the higher levels. The Courage to face truth leads eventually to Acceptance, where greater power arises at the level of 350. Here there is sufficient energy to solve the majority of man's social problems. This, in turn, leads to the yet greater power available at 500, the level of Love. Knowing our own and everyone else's human foibles gives rise to forgiveness, and thence to compassion. Compassion is the doorway to grace and to the final realization of who we are and why we are here, and of the ultimate source of all existence.

XXIV
Resolution

A THOROUGH ABSORPTION of the material presented herein has been shown to be able to raise one's level of consciousness by an average of 35 points. Inasmuch as the progression of consciousness during the average of human lifetimes lived on this globe has been only five points, such an increase in individual awareness is an enormous benefit in itself. And, as advanced theoretical physics and nonlinear dynamics have shown, any individual increase also raises to some degree the consciousness of everyone on the planet.

To become more conscious is the greatest gift anyone can give to the world; moreover, in a ripple effect, the gift comes back to its source. While the level of consciousness of mankind as a whole stood at a perilous 190 for many centuries, as we have seen, in the mid-1980s it suddenly jumped to the hopeful level of 204. For the first time in his history, Man is now on safe ground from which to continue his upward march. And this promise of new hope comes none too soon.

Today, many of the subjects we have discussed are exploding in the news media: the perversion of religion to the ends of political savagery, the deepening depravity of crimes, the involvement of children in violence, moral confusion in politics and the bizarre violence of cults appear against a backdrop colored by the prevalence of lies as social tender and a of lack of consensus as to individual and collective responsibility towards one's fellow man.

This social confusion and paralysis stems from the dearth of guidelines upon which to base decisions. Hopefully this book has taken a step toward filling that void with what is, in fact, an essay at a science of Morality. By "Morality" we do not refer to petty moralistic judgments of right and wrong, but to an at once objective and personal basis from which to make decisions and evaluations regarding the highest conduct of our lives.

In a social framework, we can certainly choose to refuse passive acquiescence to any political system that falls below the level of 200, instead applying to it our newly developed faculties of examination and correction. It is now possible, for instance, to establish clear criteria by which holders of public office should be selected. Each office requires a specific minimum level of awareness in order to be effective; in general, any government official who falls below 200 will not solve problems but create them.

The larger social issue is how, in view of the dark side of mankind's behavior, one can maintain compassion. It is a relative world; everyone acts from his own level of truth and therefore believes that his actions and decisions are "right;" it is this very "rightness" that makes fanatics so dangerous. But the real danger to society does not come from overt bigotry such as white supremacism (which calibrates at 150), as such damage can at least be monitored. The really grave danger to society lies in the silent and invisible entrainment that stealthily conquers the psyche. In the process of entrainment of the public consciousness, negative attractor fields are cosmeticized by rhetoric and manipulation of symbols. Moreover, it is not the overt message of the negative input that destroys consciousness, but the energy field that accompanies it.

The extreme negativity of many popular works of pseudophilosophy, for example, is obvious if one tests these books. But even being forewarned cannot defend us against unwitting entrainment by invisible energy fields which activate when these works are read. One may think he can maintain his psychic independence by refuting the work intellectually, but mere exposure to the material has a profound negative effect that continues even after the material is intellectually rejected. It is as though there is within these negative influences a hidden virus whose invasion of our psyche goes unnoticed.

Additionally, we often relax our circumspection when encountering material that ascribes to itself the attributes of spiritual insight or religion, forgetting that every heinous crime of which man is capable has been perpetrated in the name of God. While violent cults may be clearly repellent, belief systems that masquerade as piety are far more insidious, for they corrupt by the silent entrainment of invisible attractor fields.

Here it is best to heed the traditional wisdom that tells us not to fear evil or fight it, but merely avoid it. But in order to avoid it one has to have the capacity to recognize it. Socrates said, in effect, that without such capacity, youth (including the youth that continues to reside within every adult) is corrupted by lower attractor energy fields. Though he was put to death for trying to teach this discernment, his adjuration remains: obscurity is dispelled by augmenting the light of discernment, not by attacking the darkness.[1] The final issue, then, is the problem of how we may best cultivate and preserve the power of moral discretion.

Our journey of investigation has finally led us to the most critical realization of all: *Mankind lacks the capacity to recognize the difference between good and evil.*

By humbly surrendering to this awareness, man may be forearmed. When we admit we are gullible and easily seduced by the senses and deluded by glamour, including intellectual glamour, we have at least the beginning of discernment. Fortunately, in this world of duality man has been given a consciousness which can instantly detect that which is destructive and signal it to his otherwise ignorant mind by the grossly visible weakening of his body in the presence of the inimical stimuli. Wisdom can ultimately be reduced to the simple process of avoiding that which makes you go weak—nothing else is really required.

Through frequent practice of this technique, spiritual blindness to truth and falsehood can be progressively replaced by a growing intuitive vision. Some lucky few seem born with this innate perceptivity; their lives remain clear and undamaged by negative entrainment. But for most of us life has not been so easy; we have spent a great deal of it repairing the damage done by destructive attractors which act like hypnosis. Recovering from a single addiction can take up the majority of a lifetime. And the most common and insidious addiction is to denial, which benights us through our intellectual vanity.

The intellect, contrary to its delusions of grandeur, not only lacks the ability to recognize falsehood, but grossly lacks the necessary power to defend itself, even had it the capacity for discernment. Is it irreverent, in light of history's enormous accretion of works of intellectual speculation, to say that man's vaunted capacity of reason lacks the critical faculty of discernment? The whole field of philosophy is merely evidence that man has struggled and failed for thousands of years to arrive at the simplest recognition of what is true and what is false, or the discourse would long ago have reached some consensus.

And it is clear from common human conduct that even if the intellect could reliably arrive at this basic conclusion, *it still lacks the power to stop the effect of negative fields.* We remain unconscious of the causes of our afflictions while the intellect dreams up all kinds of plausible excuses, hypnotized by these same forces. Even when a person intellectually knows his behavior is self-destructive, this knowledge has no necessary deterrent effect whatsoever; intellectual recognition of our addictions has never given us power to control them.

In scripture we are told that man is afflicted by forces unseen.[2] It is a commonplace of our century that silent, invisible rays of energy are emitted by innocent-looking objects. The discoverers of radium paid for this realization with their lives. Roentgen x-rays are lethal, and radioactive emissions kill silently, as does radon. The attractor energy fields that destroy us are equally invisible and no less powerful, though far more subtle.

When it is said that someone is "possessed," what is meant is that his consciousness has become dominated by negative attractor fields from which he cannot extricate himself. By this definition we can see that whole segments of society are so thoroughly possessed that they themselves are totally unconscious of their motives. Wisdom tells us one worships either heaven or hell and will eventually become the servant of one or the other. Hell is not a condition imposed by a judgmental God, but rather the inevitable consequence of one's own decisions. Hell is the final outcome of constantly choosing the negative and thus isolating oneself from love.

Enlightened beings have always described the general populace as being trapped in a dream; the majority of people are driven by unseen forces, and most of us are in despair over this fact a great deal of our lives. We pray to God to relieve us of the burden of our sins, and by confession we look for relief. Remorse seems woven into the fabric of life. How can salvation be possible, then, for those who have unwittingly become ensnared by such destructive influences?

In fact, even from a merely scientific viewpoint, salvation is indeed possible. In truth, it is guaranteed by the simple fact that the energy of a loving thought is enormously more powerful than that of a negative one. Therefore, the traditional solutions of love and prayer have a sound scientific basis; man has within his own essence the power of his own salvation.

Humanity is an affliction with which we all are burdened. We don't remember asking to be born, and we inherited thence a mind so limited it is hardly capable of distinguishing that which enhances life from that which leads to death.[3] The whole struggle of life is in transcending this myopia. We cannot enter into higher levels of existence until we advance in consciousness to the point where we overcome duality and are no longer earth-bound. Perhaps it is because of our collective will to transcend that we have earned the capacity to finally discover an inborn compass to lead us out of the darkness of ignorance. We needed something very simple, which could bypass those traps of the wily intellect for which we have paid such an enormous price. This compass merely says yes or no. It tells us that that which is aligned with heaven makes us go strong and that which is aligned with hell makes us go weak.

The ubiquitous human ego is actually not an "I" at all; it is merely an "it." Seeing through this illusion reveals an endless Cosmic Joke in which the human tragedy itself is part of the comedy. The irony of human experience is in how fiercely the ego fights to preserve the illusion of a separate, individual "I" even though this is not only an ontological impossibility but the wellspring of all suffering. Human reason exhausts itself ceaselessly to explain the inexplicable. Explanation itself is high comedy, as preposterous as trying to see the back of one's own head, but the vanity of the ego is boundless, and it becomes even more overblown in this very attempt to make sense of nonsense. The mind, in its identity with the ego, cannot, by definition, comprehend reality; if it could, it would instantly dissolve itself upon recognition of its own illusory nature. It is only beyond the paradox of mind transcending ego that that which *Is* stands forth self-evident and dazzling in its infinite Absoluteness. And then all these words are useless.

But perhaps from compassion for each other's blindness, we can learn to forgive ourselves. Peace can then be our assured future. Our purpose on earth may remain obscure, but the road henceforth is clear. With the consciousness level of humanity finally above 200, we may expect great transformations throughout human culture as mankind becomes more responsible for its knowledge, and thus its deeds. We have become fully accountable whether we like it or not. We are at the point in the evolution of our collective awareness where we may even assume stewardship of consciousness itself. Humanity is no longer resigned to passively paying the price of ignorance, or its communal consciousness would not have risen to its new level. From this time forth man may choose to no longer be enslaved by darkness; his destiny can then be certain.

Gloria in Excelsis Deo.

Appendix A

Calibrated Levels of Truth of the Chapters

Appendix B

Details of Kinesiologic Testing

Scientific validity depends on replicability. To insure reliable duplication of results, the kinesiologic testing technique used for all the research cited in this book is described in detail below. It is essentially the same method developed by Dr. John Diamond in his pioneering work in Behavioral Kinesiology.

Step 1

Two people are required. To determine the suitability of a test subject, the tester presses down quickly with two fingers on the wrist of the horizontally extended arm of the subject, simultaneously telling him to "resist," (i.e., against the downward pressure). A normal subject is able to resist the pressure and keep the arm extended parallel to the ground.

Occasionally there are persons who are unable to keep their arm extended when any downward pressure is applied, due to previous contact with weakening energy fields or negative health conditions; these are not suitable test subjects. Some of these subjects can recover by thumping themselves over the thymus gland (at the top of the breastbone) in a "one-two-three" rhythm, while they smile and think of someone they love. They will then "go strong" and respond normally, but the "fix" may last for only four hours and this "thymus thump" will then have to be repeated.

Step 2

Keep the testing situation impersonal; refrain from smiling or making personal comments. Keep the environment free of noise, background music or distractions such as pets or intrusive children. Remove metal objects such as eyeglass frames from the test subject's body midline. Also remove watches or jewelry, including necklaces. Be aware that aberrant stimuli such as a tester's perfume or after-shave lotion may affect the test results. To improve concentration, have the test subject close his or her eyes.

Step 3

If subjects repeatedly go weak, evaluate the examiner's voice. The occasional voice that makes others go weak disqualifies its owner as a tester under ordinary conditions.

Step 4

Do a trial run with the prospective subject. Ask the candidate to think of someone he or she loves, then press down with two fingers on the wrist of the arm extended out to the side, parallel to the ground. A normal subject will go quite strong and be able to resist firmly. Next, have the party think of someone he or she hates or fears or has a resentment toward (alternatively, Adolph Hitler). A normal subject will go very weak and be unable to resist downward pressure on his or her wrist. Run through a few more contrasting pairs of stimuli to establish consistency of response and develop a rapport between tester and subject. Some sample ideological, visual and auditory stimuli with predictable responses are:

Test Weak	Test Strong

Hate . . . . Love
Swastika . . . . American flag
Stalin . . . . Mahatma Gandhi
Gangster Rap music . . . Classical music
(For a more exhaustive list, see Chapter VII.)

Step 5

After establishing that the test subject reacts reliably and is in a normal state, proceed with the topic under investigation by making declarative statements. Questions should always be posed as a declaration of fact. It is useless to ask questions about the future as the test results will have no reliability. Always preface the investigation with the statement, "It is safe for me to make inquiry into _____ (the specific topic)." (Y/N?) The line of questioning itself can be checked by stating, "This is the correct form for the question." (Y/N?) The statement (e.g., "The accused committed the burglary." (Y/N?)) may be made by either the questioner or the test subject. Each time a question is stated, the test subject is told to resist and the tester presses down quickly with two fingers on the test subject's extended wrist.

In our research we frequently used teams of test subjects. For example, twenty, thirty, or up to 1,000 people were divided into two-person teams who took turns as tester and test subject. The whole group was asked the same question at the same time, or was divided into subgroups for independent research projects. In a group of 100 people (fifty two-person teams), perhaps one or two will have difficulty in obtaining the same results as the others. They can be taken aside to do the "thymus thump," described above, which will return their responses to normal, and they can then rejoin the group.

Using the above method, test results are one-hundred percent replicable over the course of time so that any group of people anywhere will always produce the same results; for example, the image of Adolph Hitler will make everybody go weak, even if they never heard of him or think that he is a great national hero.

Step 6

The test can also be performed by holding test objects next to the solar plexus of the test subjects. They will be found to go weak in response to artificial sweetener, pesticides, or even a picture of Hitler concealed in a manila envelope. They will go strong in response to nutritious food, beneficial medicines and nutrients, a concealed picture of Abraham Lincoln, etc.

Step 7

Test results can be verified to be independent of the test subject's knowledge, opinions, belief systems or attitudes. For example, an image of Nelson Mandela will make all test subjects go strong, even racists who resent him. The music of Bach makes everyone go strong, even if they do not personally like it, just as heavy metal music makes all subjects go weak, even if they personally prefer it.

This confirmability of results has been observed during the last twenty years by thousands of clinicians using kinesiology in their everyday clinical practices or for research. The results, in fact, are more consistent than conventional diagnostic methods used in traditional medicine (e.g., a weak heart never tests strong with kinesiology but may give an erroneous normal EKG tracing—a well-known fact).

Appendix C

Videotapes

Video demonstrations of the various subjects and techniques described herein are available from:

Veritas Publishing
151 Keller Lane
Sedona, Arizona 86336
Fax: 602-282-4789

Notes

(*See* **Bibliography,** *below, for publication data.*)

Foreword

1. American Heritage Dictionary, Houghton Mifflin, 1987.
2. See Goodheart, 1976.
3. See Diamond, 1979.
4. See Kendall, 1971.
5. Diamond, op. cit.

Preface

1. At this conference, for example, Richard Amoroso, director of the Noetic Institute, Orinda, California, stated: "Consciousness is not an abstract concept but a physical reality that permeates and powers space/time which the brain mirrors. It is a multidimensional complimentary continuum whose properties allow for the formation of physically testable hypotheses." ("Consciousness: A Radical Definition." *Toward a Scientific Basis for Consciousness; an Interdisciplinary Conference.* University of Arizona, Health Sciences Center, Tucson, Ari-

zona, April 12-17, 1994.)
2. See Hawkins, 1986.
3. Ibid. (See chapter on "Consciousness and Addiction"), 1986.
4. Hawkins, 1987.
5. Ibid. (The "Good Doctor" series.)
6. Hawkins (Audio tape series on "Consciousness and Addiction"), 1986.

Introduction
1. See Maharshi, Ramana, 1958.
2. Polls, "Happiness is Hard to Find Anywhere in the World," Time, 142:11, September 13, 1993, 56.
3. See Kosslyn and Anderson, 1993.
4. See Ruelle, 1980, for a definitive discussion.
5. See Maharshi, op. cit., 118-126.

I: Critical Advances in Knowledge
1. See Goodheart, 1976.
2. See Peat, 1988.
3. See Briggs, J., and Peat, F. D., 1989.
4. See Walther, 1976.
5. See Lorenz, 1963.
6. See Mandelbrot, 1977.
7. Geoffrey Chew originated the Bootstrap/S-Matrix Theory and is quoted in Fritjof Capra's Tao of Physics as saying that by extension the bootstrap approach may lead to the unprecedented necessity of including the study of human consciousness explicitly in future theories of matter (1975).
8. See Bohm, D., 1987.

9. As Ken Wilber has pointed out, any theory of reality must include and coincide with the perennial philosophy and an ontological order of being: 1) Matter; 2) Biology; 3) Psychology; 4) Subtle/Saintly; 5) Sage; 6) Ultimate (beyond consciousness). This is discussed in Wilber's *The Holographic Paradigm*, p. 159.

10. See Maharshi, 1958.

11. See Hawkins, 1992.

12. See Gleick, 1987.

13. The essentials of Chaos Theory are clearly explained by James Gleick in *Chaos: Making a New Science*, and by John Briggs and F. David Peat in *Turbulent Mirror*.

14. See Capra, 1975.

15. Bohm's universe is well explained by Bohm himself in an interview in *The Holographic Paradigm*, edited by Ken Wilber, 1982.

16. This state of pure awareness is Level 6 of Wilber's hierarchy and is described in detail by Maharshi, Huang Po, and Nisargadatta Maharaj in the excellent English translations of their works cited in the bibliography.

17. This was validated by Ramesh Balsekar who, after years of being Nisargadatta Maharaj's translator, arrived at the same state of consciousness, demonstrated during interviews, 1987, and in the series of six books cited in the bibliography.

18. See Hoffman, 1992.

19. See Li and Spiegel, 1992.

20. Ibid.

21. See Hoffman, 1992.

22. See Gleick, 1987.

23. This phenomenon, called "iteration," was discussed in 1960 by Edward Lorenz in his historic computer analysis of weather data.

24. The correlation between the work of David Bohm, Karl Pribam, Rupert Sheldrake and Ilya Prigogine was discussed in *Brain/Mind Bulletin* throughout Vol. IV, 1979. (*Brain/Mind Bulletin*, P.O. Box 42211, Los Angeles, CA 90042).

25. Nobelist Sir John Eccles states that the energy of mind excites the brain to response; this is expressed in his address to the 1976 Convention of the Parapsychology Association in Utrecht, Netherlands.

II: History and Methodology

1. See Hawkins, D., *The Villa Lectures*, 1987.

2. See Kendall, Kendall and Wadsworth, 1971.

3. See Goodheart, 1976.

4. See Mann, 1974.

5. See Walther, 1976.

6. See Diamond, 1979.

7. See Hawkins, D., and Pauling, L., editors, 1973.

8. This desynchronization was demonstrated at the Academy of Preventive Medicine by Diamond, 1973.

9. Kinesiologic demonstrations often result in paradigm shock for people who have an investment in strict materialism. One such observer, a research psychiatrist, responded by first trying to prove the demonstration was a fake. When he failed to do so, he walked away, saying, "Even if it's true, I don't believe it."

10. These procedures were developed over a period of several years during regular weekly testing sessions at the Institute for Advanced Theoretical Research, Sedona, AZ, 1983-1993.

11. Hawkins, D., public lectures, Sedona, AZ, 1984-1989.

12. This is well documented in the field of neuro-linguis-

tic programming.

13. Diamond, J., lectures at the Academy of Preventive Medicine, 1978.

14. Research protocol, Institute of Advanced Theoretical Research, 1992.

15. This has been repeatedly demonstrated in public and is well described in Diamond's book *Your Body Doesn't Lie*.

16. The Perennial Philosophy is an extract of the spiritual truth of all religions and reflects expanding awareness on a scale progressing from matter to protoplasm, animal life, emotional responsiveness, capacity for thought, abstract thought, archetypal awareness, higher mind, saintly love and bliss, non-duality (the sage), and ultimate pure awareness. As Ken Wilber has pointed out, these strata appear universally; any theory of reality must comprehend these axioms of existence.

III: Test Results and Interpretation

1. See Eadie, p. 114.

IV: Levels of Human Consciousness

1. See William James, 1929.

2. Personal experience of the author.

V: Social Levels of Consciousness

1. The level of consciousness of mankind as a whole remained at 190 for many centuries and then suddenly jumped to its present level of 204 after the Harmonic Convergence of the late 1980s. Did the rise in consciousness bring about the Harmonic Convergence? Did the Harmonic Convergence bring about the increase in the level? Or, did a powerful, unseen "implicate order" attractor field bring about both phenomena?

VI: New Horizons in Research

1. See Hawkins, *Consciousness and Addiction*, 1985.

2. God is both transcendent (traditional religion) and immanent (the experiential truth of the mystic).

3. *Arizona Republic*, December 20, 1993.

4. Fedarko, "The New Kingpins." Escobar was replaced as soon as he was killed. *Time*, December 13, 1993.

5. See Josephson, 1959, p. 20.

6. The based-in-fact movie which tells the whole story and its consequences was produced as *Barbarians at the Gate* and shown in November, 1993, on network television.

7. This is a traditional observation of clinicians, confirmed by the author's clinical experience over decades.

VII: Everyday Critical Point Analysis

1. See Appendix A.

2. See Brunton, *Search in Secret India*.

VIII: The Source of Power

1. This was a special area of research reported by Dr. Diamond in *Behavioral Kinesiology*, 1979.

2. Discussed at length in Weber's *Holographic Paradigm and Other Paradoxes*, 1982.

3. Bohm, D., in *Brain/Mind Bulletin*, 10:10, May 27, 1985.

4. See Sheldrake, 1981.

5. Sheldrake called for a more public approach to the scientific research. In response, prizes were awarded in the U.S. ($10,000) and Britain (£250) for confirmatory tests of the hypothesis. A Morse Code experiment supported the theory, and was reported in *Brain/Mind Bulletin*, 10:12, July 8, 1985,

by Mahlberg.

6. The mutual dependence and interpenetration of all things is observable as one leaves duality. Oneness is central to all the major religious and spiritual systems as the ultimate reality underlying and within all forms.

7. See Land and Jarman.

IX: Power Patterns in Human Attitudes

1. See Bohm, 1980.

2. See Sheldrake, 1981.

3. "Test Supports Sheldrake Theory," *Brain/Mind Bulletin*, 8:15, September 12, 1983.

X: Power in Politics

1. See Rudolph and Rudolph, 1983.

2. See Mehta, 1982.

3. See Fischer, 1982.

4. See Loczay, 1972.

5. Ibid.

6. See *Newsweek*, May 9, 1994.

7. "Crusade in Europe," *March of Time Video Series, 1939*; also Lash, 1976.

8. See Tucker, 1990.

9. This interaction between the idealism of Communism and the realities of ongoing labor wars was well presented in the PBS series *The Great Depression*, 1993.

10. Stewardship as a primary leadership role has received considerable emphasis in recent socio-political dialogue.

11. See Cuomo, *Lincoln*, 1990.

12. See Fischer, op cit.

XI: Power in the Marketplace

1. Dutton, 1990.

2. In this classic analysis of business principles, Peters and Waterman identified the sources of power as *principles* rather than business policies and procedures, management practices or technology.

XII: Power and Sports

1. *The Big Blue* (Roseanne Arquette, Jean-Marc Benn) directed by Lee Basson, produced by Studio le Clare, Paris, 1985.

2. The mottoes of *Goshin-Kan*, classical Okinawan karate, are 1) strive for good moral character; 2) keep an honest and sincere way; 3) persevere; 4) maintain a respectful attitude; 5) restrain the physical by spiritual attainment; 6) cultivate and preserve life and avoid its destruction.

3. Personal karate instruction of the author by Shihan Dennis Rao, 1986.

4. Personal instruction by Master Seiyu Oyata, 1986.

XIII: Social Power and the Human Spirit

1. Spirit is defined in the *Living Webster Encyclopedic Dictionary of the English Language* (English Language Institute of America, Chicago, 1971) as: "Latin *spiritus*: breath, air, life essence, soul; the incorporeal principle of life, the vital principle of man, conscious being as opposed to matter; vigor, courage, aliveness; character, the divine aspect of the Trinity; the principle behind action; general meaning, active principle; dominant tendency."

2. The definition of Spirit as a concept has always presented a difficult challenge to the human intellect; a full comprehension of its significance seems beyond the capacity

of the left brain (which, like a digital computer, defines how one thing differs from another). Spirit is a holistic term best grasped by the right brain (which, like an analog computer, deals with wholes and essences). The lengthy philosophical discussions which have wrestled with the idea of spirit or soul through the centuries testify to the inability of the intellect alone to deal with essence. The paradox of these philosophical debates is that any discussion at all regarding meaning utilizes essence as the very stuff of its discourse. Thus, even a discussion which rejects *a priori* idea/essence/spirit does so on the presumption of the existence of truth as the basis of the argument. If there is no such thing as reality-based spirit/essence/truth, then there is no premise for any argument against their existence either, as no argument would have a reality base. In modern times, we could say that the concept of spirit refers to Bohm's implicate order just as the concept of the corporeal refers to the explicate order.

3. What is unique about the basic premise of the U.S. government—and the source of its power—is the concept that it derives its authority by consent of the governed, who are equal by virtue of the divinity of their Creator, (e.g., "one nation under God...").

4. A calibrated comparison between the original spiritual foundations of the world's great religions and their subsequent formal expressions is presented in Chapter XXIII. There is a notably wide disparity between the two readings.

5. The preamble to every AA meeting states: "AA is a fellowship of men and women who share their experiences, strength and hope with each other that they may share their common problems and help others to recover from alcoholism. The only requirement for membership is a desire to stop drinking. There are no dues or fees for AA membership. We are self-supporting through our own contributions. AA is not allied with any sect, denomination, politics or organization or

institution and does not wish to engage in any controversy. It neither endorses nor opposes any causes. Our primary purpose is to stay sober and help other alcoholics to achieve sobriety." (Alcoholics Anonymous, P.O. Box 459, Grand Central Station, New York, NY, 1941, 1993).

6. See *Twelve Steps and Twelve Traditions*, 1952.

7. See Chapter 11 in *Alcoholics Anonymous*, 1955.

8. See Bill W., *The Language of the Heart*; Dr. Carl Jung's *Letters*, 276-281.

9. Ibid., 281-286.

10. See "Bill's Story" in *Alcoholics Anonymous*, 1955, 1-17.

11. Ibid., 171-182.

12. See *Life's 100 Most Important Americans of the 20th Century*, 66.

XIV: Power in the Arts

1. Liner notes to *Tabula Rasa*, ECM Records, 1984.

XV: Genius and the Power of Creativity

1. See Dilts, 1992.

2. Frank Lloyd Wright stated that "The Artist's perception science later verifies." (See Wright, 1949.)

3. See Galaman, 1992.

4. See Loehle, 1990.

5. See Heilbron, 1992; also Churchill, 1949.

XVII: Physical Health and Power

1. See Hawkins, D., and Pauling, L., 1973.

2. See Tkacz, C., and Hawkins, D., 1981.

3. See Hawkins, 1989.

4. See Hawkins, 1991.

XVIII: Wellness and the Disease Process

1. See Walther, 1976.

2. See Mann, 1974.

3. See Diamond, 1979.

4. See Briggs and Peat, 1989.

5. See Redington, D., and Reidband, S., 1993, *Nonlinear Analysis Reveals Link Between Health and Mind*.

6. This is emphasized in the basic book of AA, *Alcoholics Anonymous*, 1955.

7. See Bill W., *The Language of the Heart*, 1988.

8. See AA *Comes of Age*, 1957, and AA *Today*, 1960.

9. See *Twelve Steps and Twelve Traditions*, 1953.

10. See AA *Comes of Age*, 1957.

XIX: The Database of Consciousness

1. See Jung, *Collected Works*.

2. Ibid. The implication of synchronicity is that two events are not causally connected in reality but are perceived so by the observer because they are meaningful. As one's consciousness advances into the high 500s, everything begins to happen by synchronicity and the events of life unfold in perfect order and harmony with precise timing. See also Insinna, 1994: *Synchronicity Regularities in Quantum Systems*.

3. See Maharshi, 1958; Maharaj, 1973; Huang Po, 1958; and Balsekar, 1987-1991.

XX: The Evolution of Consciousness

1. See Eadie, 1992.

2. In an interesting coincidence, after this chapter was written "a 75-year-old man with a tobacco-stained white beard...(who)...would not describe himself as homeless, saying only that he was without a home temporarily while 'he waited for a friend,'" set up an impromptu camp on public land adjacent to the highway in a community neighboring the author's. During his month's residence there, Cyrus, as he identified himself, was the center of a minor controversy. Some citizens clamored for his removal as an eyesore, and the Sheriff's Department viewed him with suspicion and threatened to arrest him for trespassing. Others found him a harmless novelty or applauded his individualism; at least one local resident "offered him lodging, which he thought about, he said." He refused to request help from social-service organizations, "saying, 'I don't need any and don't want any' but he did accept kindness from individuals. People came by bringing him food, particularly sandwiches, he said." [Sedona, AZ. *Red Rock News*, November 27, 1993] On the day of the deadline given him by sheriff's deputies, Cyrus mysteriously disappeared.

3. See Maharaj, 1973.

XXI: The Study of Pure Consciousness

1. See Descartes, *Rules for the Direction of the Mind*, Great Books of the Western World, v. 31, 4.

2. See section on "Poverty," in Kaplan and Sadock's *Comprehensive Textbook of Psychiatry*, 205-287.

3. See Maharshi, 1952; Maharaj, 1982.

4. Ibid.

5. See Maharaj, 1973.

6. See James, 1929.

7. Personal experience of the author.

8. See Maharaj, op cit.; Huang Po, op cit.; Maharshi, 1952; and Balsekar, 1987-1991.

9. See Maharaj, op cit.; Huang Po, op cit.; Balsekar, op cit.
10. See *Brain/Mind Bulletin*, op cit.
11. See Chapter XV, "Genius and the Power of Creativity."
12. See Kuhn, 1970.
13. See Kübler-Ross, 1993.
14. See Krippner, 1974.
15. Ibid.
16. See AA *Comes of Age*.
17. Bill W., 1988.
18. See Chapter 1, "Bill's Story," in *Alcoholics Anonymous*, 1952.
19. See *Twelve Steps and Twelve Traditions*.

XXII: Spiritual Struggle

1. See Maharshi, 1958; Huang Po, 1958; Maharaj, 1973; Balsekar, 1990.
2. See Balsekar, 1989.
3. See Walsh Butler's *Lives of the Saints*, 1985.
4. See Maharshi, 1958.
5. "Anguish of the Soul" is a theme throughout classic Christian literature. See St. *John of the Cross*, 1958; *Meister Eckhart*, 1941; *The Way of A Pilgrim*, 1965; and Butler's *Lives of the Saints*, 1985.
6. See Krippner, 1974.
7. See Diamond, *Lectures on Behavioral Kinesiology*, NY, 1972.
8. Sedona Villa of Camelback Hospital treated over one hundred cocaine addicts a year for a five-year period (1981-1986). None of the patients who continued to listen to heavy

metal rock music recovered (follow-up survey, 1986).

9. Addicts who leave twelve-step programs relapse (clinical observation of the author).

10. See Maharshi, 1958.

11. See "St. Francis of Assisi," in Butler's *Lives of the Saints*, 1985, 314-320.

12. See *A Course in Miracles*, 1975.

13. See Capra, 1976.

XXIII: The Search for Truth

1. The fall of Christianity from calibrated 930 to 498 must be recognized as the greatest single catastrophe in the history of Western religion. Here we can see the origin of the spiritual divorce from the actual teachings of Jesus Christ that allowed the later atrocities of the Crusades and the Inquisition. A recurrent question in speculation about the historic decline of Christianity centers around the inclusion of the relatively weak (475) Old Testament in the canon of Christian scripture. What, really, does the "eye-for-an-eye" ethic of the prophets have to do with Christ's exhortation to universal love and forgiveness? It has rightly been asked why, if Jesus came to teach the Old Testament, need he have bothered coming at all?

More to the point, as in the case of Islam, the everyday practice of Christianity is most conspicuously tainted by militant fundamentalist groups that define themselves by their hates and hawk agendas primarily based on depriving others of their freedoms. It may well be this burden of vitriolic negativity which keeps current Christianity below the level of Love. It is interesting that these so-called Christians rarely quote Christ. Their repertory of polemic and self-justification is drawn almost entirely from the Old Testament; when they say "scripture," that is usually what they mean.

Had Christianity, in valuing moral behavior, kept exclusively to the tenets of the New Testament, one must wonder what the world would be like today.

2. Author's clinical experience.

3. Freud remained below the critical level of 500 because of his denial of man's spirituality, whereas Carl Jung, who affirmed the spiritual nature of man, calibrates at a much higher 560.

XXIV: Resolution

1. Socrates taught that man's purpose is to dedicate his life to the enlightenment of his soul (the light) rather than the pursuit of materialism and the senses (which leads to darkness). See Plato's *Republic*, op cit.

2. *Epistle of Paul to the Ephesians*, 6:12. "For your conflict is not only with flesh and blood, but also with the angels, and with powers seen and unseen, with the rulers of the world of darkness, one with the evil spirits under the heavens." Holy Bible, Trans. George Lamsa, (Philadelphia: A. J. Holmes Co., 1957).

3. This is often stated as a starting point from which to eventually arrive at a realization of our true nature, by teachers such as Nisargadatta Maharaj in *I Am That*, 1973.

Glossary

Chaos Theory: The science of *process* as opposed to *state*. This theory originates in the discovery of patterns within a condition of unpredictability. The view it proposes discerns global possibilities rather than local events, and entails a topologic system using patterns and shapes to visualize the intrinsic form of a complex system which, though locally unpredictable, is globally stable. Chaos theory recognizes the capacity of a complex system to simultaneously give rise to both turbulence and coherence.

In the late 1800s Henri Poincare noted that Newtonian physics was mathematically accurate if the interaction studied was between two bodies only, but that the addition of a third element made Newton's equations unreliable—only approximations could be obtained. This nonlinearity implied that any system over time could, by feedback and repetition, become unpredictable. Lorenz's 1963 *Deterministic Non-periodic Flow* provided a new paradigm of science termed Chaos Theory by James Yorke in his famous paper, "Period Three Implies Chaos." Chaos Theory encompasses such subjects as period doubling, iteration, fractals and bifurcation, and recognizes that within finite space there are an infinite number of dimensions. The first meeting on Chaos at the New York

Academy of Science was in 1977, and in 1986 the academy had its first meeting on Chaos Theory in medicine and biology.

Context: The total field of observation predicated by a point of view. Context includes any significant facts that qualify the meaning of a statement or event. Data is meaningless unless its context is defined. To "take out of context" is to distort the significance of a statement by failing to identify contributory accessory conditions that would qualify the inference of meaning. (This is a common trial strategy whereby an attorney tries to distort a witness's testimony by suppressing the inclusion of qualifying statements that would alter the implications of the testimony, demanding the witness answer only "yes or no.")

Creation: A continuous process without beginning or end through which the manifest universe of form and matter is produced by iteration, starting from three points—all that is required to create by fractals an infinite variety of forms. (This is illustrated by the now familiar complex plane of the "Mandelbrot Set.") In Sanskrit the three aspects of origination of all that is experienceable are called Rajas, Tamas and Satva. These are symbolized by the Hindu deities Shiva, Vishnu and Brahma. In Christianity these are represented by the Trinity.

Duality: The world of form characterized by seeming separation of objects (reflected in conceptual dichotomies such as "this/that" or "here/there" or "then/now" or "you/me." This perception of limitation is produced by the senses because of the restriction implicit in a fixed point of view. Science has finally gone beyond the artificial dichotomy of observer and observed characteristic of seventeenth century Cartesian duality, and now assumes that they are one and the same. The universe has no center, but is continuously expanding equally and simultaneously from every point. Bell's Theorem helped to demonstrate that this is a universe of simultaneity rather than Newtonian cause and effect over distance in an artificial time frame. Both time and space themselves are merely the measurable products of a higher implicit order.

Energy Field: In this study, a range set by parameters of the phase space of an attractor field whose pattern operates within the larger energy field of consciousness and is observable by characteristic effects in human behavior. The power of energy fields is calibrated much like voltage in an electrical system or the power of magnetic or gravitational fields.

Entrainment: A phenomenon illustrated by the principle of mode locking. When a number of pendulum clocks are placed close together, their pendulums will eventually synchronize. In human biology this is manifested when groups of women progressively synchronize their menstrual cycles. It is similar to the phenomenon wherein an adjacent tuning fork begins to vibrate at the rate of the first tuning fork. It is because of this process that troops break cadence when they cross a bridge.

Fractal: Fractal patterns are characterized by irregularity and infinite length, and strange attractors are composed of fractal curves. A classic example is the attempt to determine the length of the coastline of Britain. If one adds lengths using smaller and smaller scales of measurement, it turns out to be infinitely long. Fractal implies an infinite length in a finite area.

Hologram: A three-dimensional projection into space of the image of an object, created by projecting laser light so that half the laser beam is directed to the object and then onto a photographic plate which receives the other half of the beam directly. This creates an interference pattern on the plate so that a laser beam projected through the plate recreates the image of the object in three dimensions. It is of interest that every fragment of the photographic plate is capable of reproducing the entire image of the whole. In a holographic universe everything is connected with everything else.

Iteration: Repetition. Nonlinear iteration is present in innumerable systems. Because of this repetition, a very slight change in the initial condition will eventually produce a pattern dissimilar from the original. In a growth equation the output of the prior iteration becomes the input for the next series. For example, if a computer calculates to sixteen decimal places, the last digit is the rounding off of the seventeenth. This infinitesimal error, magnified through many iterations results in substantial distortion of the original data and makes prediction impossible. (Thus, a slight change in a repetitious thought pattern can bring about major effects.)

Left-brain: Referring to thought sequenced in the linear style commonly described as logic or reason. Processing of data in a sequence A→B→C. Analogous to a digital computer.

Linear: Following a logical progression in the manner of Newtonian physics and, therefore, solvable by traditional mathematics through the use of differential equations.

M-Fields: Morphogenetic fields, analogous to attractor patterns. In the hypothesis presented by Rupert Sheldrake, morphogenetic fields are part of the theory of formative causation, that energy fields of form evolve and reinforce each other.

Neural Network: The interlocking patterns of interacting neurons within the nervous system.

Neurotransmitters: Brain chemicals (hormones, etc.) that regulate neuronal transmission throughout the nervous system. Very slight chemical changes can result in major subjective and objective alterations in emotion, thought or behavior. This is the prime area of current research in psychiatry.

Non-duality: Historically, all observers who have reached a consciousness level over 600 have described the reality now suggested by advanced scientific theory. When the limitation of a fixed locus of perception is transcended, there is no longer an illusion of separation nor of space and time as we know them. All things exist simultaneously in the unmanifest, enfolded, implicit universe, expressing itself as the manifest, unfolded, explicit perception of form. These forms in reality have no intrinsic independent existence but are the product of perception (i.e., man is merely experiencing the content of his own mind). On the level of non-duality there is observing but no observer, as subject and object are one. You-and-I becomes the One Self experiencing all as divine. At level 700 it can only be said that "All Is;" the state is one of Being-ness; all is consciousness, which is life, which is infinite, which is God and which has no parts nor beginning or end. The physical body is a manifestation of the One Self which, in experiencing this dimension, had temporarily forgotten its reality, thus permitting the illusion of a three-dimensional world. The body is merely a means of communication; to identify one's self with the body as "I" is the fate of the unenlightened, who then erroneously deduce that they are mortal and subject to death. Death itself is an illusion based on the false identification with the body as "I." In non-duality, consciousness experiences itself as both manifest and unmanifest, yet there is no experiencer. In this Reality the only thing that has a beginning and an ending is the act of perception itself. In the illusory world, we are like the fool who believes that things come into existence when he opens his eyes and cease to exist when he closes them.

Nonlinear: Unpredictably irregular in time, "noisy," non-periodic, random, stochastic. Illustrated by mathematical series such as formalized stochastic evolution equations of the form $dx(t)\underline{dt}=F(xt)+w(t)$ where $w(t)$ is the noise term of the stochastic process. The term also describes the mathematics of chaotic signals, including the statistical analysis of time series for deterministic nonlinear systems. Nonlinear means diffuse or chaotic; not in accordance with probabilistic logical theory or mathematics; not solvable by differential equations. This is the subject of the new science of Chaos Theory which has given rise to a whole new non-Newtonian mathematics.

Oxymoronic: An expression of complexity or ambiguity in deceptively simple, apparently contradictory terms. The resolution of contradiction by juxtaposition and contrast, as in "cold fire" or "wise fool." Oxymoronic styles reflect the essence of paradox, and paradox itself arises from the contrast between different levels of abstraction, occasioned by the presentation of concepts from different contexts and points of view.

Paradigm: The dimensions of a context or field as limited by parameters which inherently predict one's perception of reality. A paradigm, generally, is a definition of one's perception of reality according to its limitations.

Phase Space: A map which affords the condensation of time-space data into a pattern in multiple dimensions. A Poincare map is the graphic depiction of a slice through a multidimensional pattern which demonstrates the underlying attractor.

Right-brain: Generally meaning holistic, enabling such functions as evaluation, intuition, and comprehension of significance, meaning and inference. Nonlinear; operating from patterns and relationships rather than through the logical sequences of Newtonian causality.

The right brain is assumed to deal with wholes rather than parts. Like an analog computer, it deals with processes and is generally capable of operating without the necessity of time reference. Right-brain perception detects essence within a complex field of data which might not otherwise lend itself to meaningful cognitive analysis—such general phenomena as "falling in love" or creativity. (The terms left-brain and right-brain originated in reference to different styles of perception which were once thought to be localized to certain cerebral areas, but as Karl Pribam has shown, the brain acts holographically rather than by precise anatomic localization.)

Scientific: The method of inquiry into nature specifically designed to derive predictable laws of physical properties. Modern scientific theory began in the sixteenth century with Descartes' *Discourse on Method*, followed by Francis Bacon's *Inductive Inquiry*. This, in turn, was followed by Newton's *Principia*. John Locke first used the term "scientific" and proposed that certainty about the interaction of physical events was based on data arrived at by physical sensation. These concepts resulted in a model of a mechanical, predictive universe, but this view was upset by modern quantum theory, which states that at the subatomic level the laws of chance replace deterministic laws.

History has noted that science does not advance by an extension of established theories, but instead takes leaps by a shift of paradigm. The inference is that science is merely a reflection of a point of view, and there is no real separation between observer and observed. Relativity theory further states that matter equals energy, depending on one's point of reference. Bohm's later *Holographic Model* predicates an explicit order based on an implicit order. Form becomes the consequence of inference, space and time are non-localized, and there is no "here" or "there" (the non-locality of quantum wholeness). The universe thus described contains an infinite number of dimensions and higher-dimension realities.

Stochastic: Random, unpredictable, nonlinear, erratic, "noisy," chaotic.

Strange Attractor: A term coined by Ruelle and Takens in 1971 in a theory which stated that three independent motions are all that is necessary to produce the entire complexity of nonlinear patterns of the universe. A strange attractor is a pattern within a phase space. The pattern is traced by the dynamic points in time of a dynamic system. The central point of an attractor field is analogous to the center of an orbit. Attractors are fractal and therefore of infinite length. The graphics of attractors are depicted by taking a cross section of a so-called Poincare map. The topographical shaping of phase space creates an attractor such as a torus, like a folded donut.

Universe: There may be seen to be an infinite number of dimensions to our universe. The familiar three-dimensional universe of conventional consensus is only one, and is merely an illusion created by our senses. The space between planetary bodies is not empty but filled with a sea of energy; the potential energy in one square inch can be said to be as great as that of the whole mass of the physical universe. David Bohm has proposed the model of enfolded/unfolded states of being, with an explicit order and an implicit order of reality comparable to the manifest/unmanifest states of reality which have been described for centuries by those who have achieved enlightenment and experienced non-duality.

In the causality model:

the A→B→C is the unfolded, explicit, manifest, discernible universe of form. The ABC is the enfolded, implicit, unmanifest potential beyond which is the formless, infinite matrix of both form and non-form—which is omnipotent, omniscient and omnipresent.

Bibliography

Abraham, R., and Shaw, C. 1984. *Dynamics: The Geometry of Behavior*, vols. I-III. Santa Cruz, Calif.: Aerial Press.

Alcoholics Anonymous. 1955. New York: Alcoholics Anonymous Publishing Company.

Amoroso, Richard. "Consciousness: A Radical Definition." *Toward a Scientific Basis for Consciousness; an Interdisciplinary Conference*. University of Arizona, Health Sciences Center, Tucson, Arizona, April 12-17, 1994.

Anonymous. 1975. *A Course in Miracles*. Huntington Station, NY: Foundation for Inner Peace, Coleman Graphics.

Anonymous. 1960. *AA Today*. New York: Cornwall Press.

Anonymous. 1957. *Alcoholics Anonymous Comes of Age: A Brief History of AA*. New York: Alcoholics Anonymous Publishing, Inc.

Anonymous. 1953. *Twelve Steps and Twelve Traditions*. New York: Alcoholics Anonymous Publishing Company.

Balsekar, R.S. 1987. *Personal Interviews*. Twentynine Palms, Calif.

———. 1988. *Experiencing the Teaching*. Calif.: Advaita Press.

———. 1989. *A Duet of One: The Ashtavatra Gita Dialogue*. Calif.: Advaita Press.

———. 1989. *Exploration into the Eternal*. Durham, North Carolina: Acorn Press, D. Sudhater.

——. 1989. *From Consciousness to Consciousness*. Calif.: Advaita Press.

——. 1990. *Pointers from Nisargadatta Maharaj*. Durham, North Carolina: Acorn Press.

——. 1989. *The Final Truth*. Calif.: Advaita Press.

Barzon, J. 1989. "The Paradoxes of Creativity." *The American Scholar*, Summer 50, 337-351.

Bendat, J.S., and Pearson, A.G. 1966. *Measurement and Analysis of Random Data*. New York: John Wiley and Sons.

Beringa, M. 1990. "The Mind Revealed." *Science* 249, August 24, 156-158.

Bill W. 1988. *The Language of the Heart*. AA Grapevine. New York: Cornwall Press.

Blakney, R.B., trans. 1942. *Meister Eckhart*. New York: Harper & Row.

Bohm, D., Hiley, B., Kaloyerous, P.N. "An Ontological Basis for Quantum Theory." *Phys. Reports* 144, 6, 323.

——, and Peat, F.D. 1987. *Science, Order and Creativity*. New York: Bantam Books.

——. 1980. *Quantum Theory*. New York: Prentice-Hall.

——. 1980. *Wholeness and the Implicate Order*. London: Routledge & Kegan Paul.

Briggs, J., and Peat, F.D. 1989. *Turbulent Mirror: An Illustrated Guide to Chaos Theory and the Science of Wholeness*. New York: Harper & Row.

——. 1993. *Fractals: The Patterns of Chaos*. New York: Simon & Schuster.

——, and Peat, F.D. 1984. *Looking Glass Universe*. New York: Simon & Schuster.

Brinkley, D. 1994. *Saved by the Light*. New York: Villard Books/Random House.

Bruner, J.S., and Posteman, L. 1949. "On the Perception of Incongruity: A Paradigm." *Journal of Personality* 18, 206.

Brunton, Paul. 1984. *A Search in Secret India*. Los Angeles: Weiser.

Butz, M. 1993. *Psychological Reports* 17, 827-843 and 1043-1063.

Capra, Fritjof. 1976. *The Tao of Physics: An Exploration of the Parallels Between Modern Physics and Eastern Mysticism.* New York: Bantam

——. 1982. *The Turning Point: Science, Society and the Rising Culture.* New York: Bantam.

Chalmers, David. "On Explaining Consciousness Scientifically: Choices and Challenges." *Toward a Scientific Basis for Consciousness; an Interdisciplinary Conference.* University of Arizona, Health Sciences Center, Tucson, Arizona, April 12-17, 1994.

Chew, G.F. 1968. "Bootstrap: A Scientific Idea." *Science* 161, May 23.

——. 1970. "Hadron Bootstrap, Triumph or Frustration?" *Physics Today*, October 23.

——. 1974. "Impasse for the Elementary Particle Concept." The Great Ideas Today. Chicago: *Encyclopedia Britannica.*

Churchill, W.S. 1941. *Blood, Sweat and Tears.* New York: G.P. Putnam's Sons.

Combs, Allan. "Consciousness as a System Near the Edge of Chaos." *Toward a Scientific Basis for Consciousness; an Interdisciplinary Conference.* University of Arizona, Health Sciences Center, Tucson, Arizona, April 12-17, 1994.

Crick, C., and Koch. 1992. "The Problem of Consciousness." *Scientific American* 267, September, 152-159.

Crusade in Europe. 1939. Marching Time. Collectors Videos.

Cuomo, M. 1990. *Lincoln on Democracy.* New York: Harper Collins.

Deikman, Arthur J. "The Role of Intention and Self as Determinants of Consciousness: A Functional Approach to a Spiritual Experience." *Toward a Scientific Basis for Consciousness; an Interdisciplinary Conference.* University of Arizona, Health Sciences Center, Tucson, Arizona, April 12-17, 1994.

Descartes, Rene. 1952. In *Great Books of the Western World*, v. 31. Chicago: Encyclopedia Britannica.

Diamond, J. 1979. *Behavioral Kinesiology.* New York: Harper & Row.

——. 1979. *Your Body Doesn't Lie.* New York: Warner Books.

Dilts, R. 1992. "Strategies of Genius," *Success*, 39, October, 26-27.

Dunn, Jean, Ed. 1985. *Prior to Consciousness: Talks with Nisargadatta Maharj.* Durham, North Carolina: Acorn Press.

——. 1982. *Seeds of Consciousness.* New York: Grove Press.

Eadie, B.J. 1992. *Embraced by the Light.* Placerville, California. Gold Leaf Press.

Eccles, J., and Robinson, D.N. 1984. *The Wonder of Being Human: Our Brain and Our Mind.* New York: Free Press.

——, ed. 1986. *Mind and Brain: The Many Faceted Problems.* New York: Paragon House.

——. 1989. *Evolution of the Brain: Creation of the Self.* Edinburgh: Routledge.

——. 1984. *The Human Mystery: The Gifford Lectures.* University of Edinburgh, 1977-78. Edinburgh: Routledge.

Fedarko, K. 1993. "Escobar's Dead End." *Time*, 142:25, December 13, 46-47.

Feigenbaum, N.J. 1981. "Universal Behavior in Nonlinear Systems." *Los Alamos Science.* 1, 4-29.

Fischer, L. 1982. *Gandhi: His Life as a Message for the World.* New York: New American Library.

Freeman, W.J., and Skarda, C.A. 1985. "Spatial EEG Patterns: Nonlinear Dynamics and Perception." *Brain Res. Rev.* 10, 147.

French, R. M., trans. 1965. *The Way of A Pilgrim.* New York: Seabury Press.

Galin, D. "The Structure of Subjective Experience." *Toward a Scientific Basis for Consciousness; an Interdisciplinary Conference.* University of Arizona, Health Sciences Center,

Tucson, Arizona, April 12-17, 1994.

Gardner, H. 1985. *The Mind's New Science*. New York: Basic Books.

Gilbert, M. 1993. *The Complete Churchill Videos*. British Broadcasting Corporation.

Glass, L., and MacKay, M.W. 1979. "Pathological Conditions Resulting from Instabilities in Physiological Control Systems." *Ann, NY, Acad. Sci.* 316, 214.

Gleick, J. 1987. *Chaos: Making a New Science*. New York: Viking Penguin.

Godman, D., ed. 1985. *Be As You Are: The Teachings of Ramana Maharshi*. Boston: Arkana.

Golaman, D., et al. 1992. "The Art of Creativity." *Psychology Today* 25, March/April, 40-47.

Goldman, A. "Philosophy of Mind: Defining Consciousness." *Toward a Scientific Basis for Consciousness; an Interdisciplinary Conference*. University of Arizona, Health Sciences Center, Tucson, Arizona, April 12-17, 1994.

Goodheart, G. 1976. *Applied Kinesiology*, 12th ed. Detroit: Privately Published.

Hardy, C. "Meaning as Interface between Mind and Matter." *Toward a Scientific Basis for Consciousness; an Interdisciplinary Conference*. University of Arizona, Health Sciences Center, Tucson, Arizona, April 12-17, 1994.

Harman, W. "A Comparison of Three Approaches to Reconciling Science and Consciousness." *Toward a Scientific Basis for Consciousness; an Interdisciplinary Conference*. University of Arizona, Health Sciences Center, Tucson, Arizona, April 12-17, 1994.

Hawkins, D. 1989. "Successful Prevention of Tardive Dyskinesia." *Journal of Orthomolecular Medicine* 4, 1.

——., and Pauling, L. 1973. *Orthomolecular Psychiatry*. San Francisco: W.H. Freeman and Company.

Hawkins, D.R. 1986. *12 Lectures on: Stress; Weight Reduction;*

Alcoholism; Illness; Health; Depression; Spiritual First Aid; Pain and Suffering; Sex; Worry, Fear and Anxiety; The Aging Process; Handling Major Crises. Farmingdale, NY: Coleman Graphics.

——. 1993. *A Map of Consciousness* (video). Sedona, Ariz.: Institute for Advanced Theoretical Research.

——. 1987. "Consciousness and Addiction," in Kiley, L., Burton, S., eds., *Beyond Addiction*. San Mateo, Calif.: Brookridge Institute.

——. 1988. *Consciousness and Addiction: The Way Out.* The Villa Lectures. Farmingdale, NY: Coleman Graphics.

——. 1983. "Expanding Love: Beauty, Silence and Joy." *Call of the Canyon*, v. II. Sedona, Ariz.

——. 1982. "Love, Peace and Beatitude." *Call of the Canyon*, v. I. Sedona, Ariz.

——. 1979. "Orthomolecular Psychiatry." *International Encyclopedia of Psychiatry, Psychoanalysis and Psychiatry.*

——. 1991. "Successful Prevention of Tardive Dyskinesia: A 20-Year Study of 64,000 Patients." *Journal of Orthomolecular Psychiatry*, January.

——. 1987. *The Sedona Series Lectures: A Map of Consciousness; Death and Dying; Hypertension and Heart Disease; AIDS; Cancer; Alcoholism and Drug Addiction; Consciousness and Addiction; Healing Relationships.* Sedona, Ariz.: The Research Institute.

Heilbron, J.L. 1992. "Creativity and Big Science." *Physics Today*, 45, November, 42-47.

Henon, J. 1976. "A Two-Dimensional Mapping with a Strange Attractor." *Com. Math Physics* 50, 69-77.

Hoffman, R.E. 1992. "Attractor Neuro Networks and Psychotic Disorders." *Psychiatric Annals* 22:3, 119-124.

Hofstadter, D.R. 1985. *Metalogical Themes: Questing for the Essence of Mind and Pattern.* Toronto: Bantam Books.

Huang Po. 1958. *The Zen Teaching of Huang Po: On Transmis-*

sion of the Mind. John Blofield, trans. New York: Grove Press.

Insinna, Ezio. "Synchronicity Regularities in Quantum Systems." *Toward a Scientific Basis for Consciousness; an Interdisciplinary Conference.* University of Arizona, Health Sciences Center, Tucson, Arizona, April 12-17, 1994.

James, W. 1929. *The Varieties of Religious Experience.* New York: Modern Library, Random House. (Longman's Green and Company).

Josephson, M. 1959. *Edison.* New York: McGraw Hill.

Jung, C.G. 1979. *Collected Works.* Princeton: Princeton University Press.

———. 1973. *Synchronicity as a Causal Connecting Principle.* R. F. Hull, trans. Bollington Ser., v. 20. Princeton: Princeton University Press.

Kelly, V.C. 1993. "Affect and Intimacy." *Psychiatric Annals,* 23:10, October. 556-566.

Kendall, H., Kendall, F., Wadsworth, G. 1971. *Muscle Testing and Function.* Baltimore: Williams and Wilkins.

Kosslyn, S., and Anderson, R., eds. 1993. *Frontiers in Cognitive Neuroscience.* Cambridge, Mass.: MIT Press.

Krippner, S. 1974. *Western Hemisphere Conference on Kirlian Photography.* Garden City, NY.

Kübler-Ross, E. 1991. *On Life after Death.* New York: Celestial Arts.

———. 1993. *Questions and Answers on Death and Dying.* New York: Macmillan.

Kuhn, T. 1970. *The Structure of Scientific Revolutions.* Chicago: University of Chicago Press.

Laczey, E. 1972. *Gandhi: A Man for Humanity.* New York: Hawthorne.

Lampanski, R. 1981. *Lampanski's Hidden Hollywood.* New York: Simon & Schuster.

Lamsa, G., trans. 1957. *Holy Bible from Ancient Eastern Manu-*

scripts. Philadelphia: A.J. Holmes Co.

Land, G., Jarman, B. 1992. *Breakpoint and Beyond*. New York: Harper Business.

Lee, T.D. 1981. *Particle Physics and Introduction to Field Theory*. Switzerland: Harwood Academic Pubs.

Li, E., and Spiegel, D. 1992. "A Neuro Network Model of Associative Disorders." *Psychiatric Annals* 22:3, 144-145.

Libet, Benjamin. 1984. *Brain* 106, 623-642. (Physiology Dept., University of California at San Francisco.)

"Life's 100 Most Important Americans of the 20th Century." 1990. *Life Magazine*, 13:12, Fall.

"Lincoln, Abraham." 1984. In *The New Encyclopedia Britannica*, 15th Ed. Chicago.

Loehle, C. 1990. "A Guide to Increase Creativity in Research." *Bioscience* 40, February, 123-129.

Lorenz, E.N. 1963. "Deterministic Nonperiodic Flow." *Journal of Atmospheric Science* 20, 130-141.

——. 1979. "Predictability: Does the Flap of a Butterfly's Wings in Brazil Set off a Tornado in Texas?" *American Association for the Advancement of Science*, December 29.

——. 1964. "The Problem of Deducting the Climate from the Governing Equations." *Tellus* 16, 1-11.

Losh, J.P. 1976. *Roosevelt and Churchill*. New York: W. W. Norton.

Lowinsky, E.A. 1964. "Musical Genius: Evolution and Origins of a Concept." *Musical Quarterly* 50, 321-340 and 476-495.

Maharaj, Nisargadatta. 1973. *I Am That*, v. I and II. Bombay: Chetana.

Marharshi, Ramana. 1958. *Talks with Sri Ramana Maharshi*, v. I-III. Madras, India: Jupiter Press.

——. 1972. *The Spiritual Teachings of Ramana Maharshi*. (Forward by Carl Jung.) Boulder, Colo.: Shambhala.

Mandelbrodt, G. 1977. *The Fractal Geometry of Nature*. New

York: W.H. Freeman & Co.

Mandell, A.J. 1985. "From Molecular Biologic Simplification to More Realistic Central Nervous System Dynamics." In Cavenar, et al., eds. *Psychiatry: Psychological Foundations of Clinical Psychiatry.* New York: Lippincott.

Mann, F. 1974. *The Meridians of Acupuncture.* London: William Heinemann Medical Books Limited.

Maslow, A.H. 1971. *The Farther Reaches of Human Nature.* New York: Viking.

McAlear, N. 1989. "On Creativity." *Omni* 11, April, 42-44.

Mehta, V. 1982. *Mahatma Gandhi: and His Apostles.* New York: Penguin Books.

"Mind's Chaotic Periods May Lead to Higher Order." *Brain/Mind Bulletin* 18, September, 12.

Monroe, R. 1971. *Journeys Out of the Body.* New York: Anchor/Doubleday.

"Musical Composition." In *The New Encyclopedia Britannica,* 15th Edition.

Nathanson, D.L. "About Einstein." *Psychiatric Annals* 23:10, October, 543-555.

——. 1993. "Understanding Einstein: New Theories, New Therapy." *Psychiatric Annals* 23:10, October.

Nome, Bhagavan. 1988. *Personal Inteviews.* Santa Cruz, Calif.

"Nonlinear Analysis Reveals Link Between Heart and Mind." 1993. *Brain/Mind Bulletin* 18:12, September.

Peat, F.D. 1988. *Artificial Intelligence.* New York: Baen.

——. 1988. "Time, Structure and Objectivity in Quantum Theory." *Foundation of Physics,* December.

Peers, E.A., trans. 1958. *St. John of the Cross: Ascent of Mount Carmel.* Garden City, NY: Image Books/Doubleday & Co.

Penrose, Roger. "Quantum Coherence and Consciousness." *Toward a Scientific Basis for Consciousness; an Interdisciplinary Conference.* University of Arizona, Health Sciences

Center, Tucson, Arizona, April 12-17, 1994.

Peters, T.J., and Waterman, R. H. 1982. *In Search of Excellence.* New York: Warner Books/Harper & Row.

Plato. *The Republic.* In Great Books of the Western World, v. 7. Chicago: Encyclopedia Britannica, Inc., 1952.

Prigogine, I., Stengers, I. 1984. *Order Out of Chaos: Man's New Dialogue.* Toronto: Bantam.

Raspberry, W. 1994. "Rap Music Shares Same Qualities as Nicotine: Dangerous, Addictive." *The Arizona Republic,* July 4, 1994.

Ray, M., and Rinzler, A., eds. 1993. *The New Paradigm in Business: Emerging Strategies for Leadership and Organizational Change.* New York: Tarcher/Perigee.

Redington, D., and Reidbond, S. 1993. *Journal of Nervous and Mental Disease* 180, 649-665; 181, 428-435.

Ring, K. 1984. *Heading Toward Omega.* New York: Wm. Morrow.

Rosband, S.N. 1990. *Chaotic Dynamics of Nonlinear Systems.* New York: John Wiley and Sons.

Rudolph, S.H., and Rudolph, L.I. 1983. *Gandhi: The Traditional Roots of Charisma.* Chicago: University of Chicago Press.

Ruelle, D. 1989. *Chaotic Evolution and Strange Attractors: The Statistical Analysis of Time Series from Deterministic Nonlinear Systems.* New York: Cambridge University Press.

——. 1980. "Strange Attractors." *Mathematical Intelligence,* 2, 126-137.

Schaffer, W.M., and Kot, M. 1985. "Do Strange Attractors Govern Ecological Systems?" *Bioscience* 35, 349.

Scott, Alwyn. "Hierarchical Organization in the Brain—Emergence of Consciousness." *Toward a Scientific Basis for Consciousness; an Interdisciplinary Conference.* University of Arizona, Health Sciences Center, Tucson, Arizona, April 12-17, 1994.

Sheldrake, R. 1981. *A New Science of Life*. London: Victoria Works.

———. 1981. Essay in *New Scientist* 90, June 18, 749, 766-768.

———. 1981. "Formative Causation." Interview in *Brain/Mind Bulletin* 6, August 3, 13. Los Angeles.

Simonton, D.K. 1988. "What Produces Scientific Genius?" *USA Today* 117, June, 11.

Smale, S. 1980. *The Mathematics of Time: Essays on Dynamical Systems*. New York: Springer-Verlag.

Stewart, H.B., and Thompson, J.M. 1986. *Nonlinear Dynamics and Chaos*. New York: John Wiley & Sons.

Steward, I. 1989. *Does God Play Dice?* Cambridge: Bazel, Blackwell.

Stone, A.M. 1993. "Implications of Affect Theory for the Practice of Cognitive Therapy." *Psychiatric Annals* 23:10, 577-583.

Tcaz, C., and Hawkins, D. 1981. "A Preventative Measure for Tardive Dyskinesia." *Journal of Orthomolecular Psychiatry* 10, 120-123.

The Anti-Stalin Campaign and International Commission: A Selection of Documents. 1956. New York: Columbia University, Russian Institute.

Trimble, V. 1990. *Sam Walton*. New York: Dutton.

Tritton, D. 1986. "Chaos in the Swing of a Pendulum." *New Scientist*, July 24.

Tucker, R.C. 1990. *Stalin in Power*. New York: W. W. Norton.

Tuckwell, H.C. 1988. *Introduction to Theoretical Neurology: Nonlinear and Stochastic Theories*. New York: Cambridge University Press.

Varvoglis, Mario. "Nonlocality on a Human Scale: PSI and Consciousness Research." *Toward a Scientific Basis for Consciousness; an Interdisciplinary Conference*. University of Arizona, Health Sciences Center, Tucson, Arizona, April 12-17, 1994.

Walsh, M., ed. 1985. *Lives of the Saints.* New York: Harper & Row.

Walther, D. 1976. *Applied Kinesiology.* Pueblo, Colo.: Systems DC.

Weisburd, S. 1987. "Neural Nets Catch the ABCs of DNA." *Science News,* August 1.

"What is Consciousness?" Interviews with C. Koch, T. Winograd, and H.P. Moravat. In *Discover* 13, November, 95-98.

Wilber, Ken, ed. 1982. *The Holographic Paradigm and Other Paradoxes: Exploring the Leading Edge of Science.* Boston: Shambhala.

——, Engler, J., and Brown, D.P. 1986. *Transformations of Consciousness.* Boston: Shambhala.

Winfree, Arthur. "Is It Impossible to 'Measure' Consciousness?" *Toward a Scientific Basis for Consciousness; an Interdisciplinary Conference.* University of Arizona, Health Sciences Center, Tucson, Arizona, April 12-17, 1994.

Wing, R.L. 1986. *The Tao of Power. An Introduction to the Tao Te Ching of Lao Tsu.* Garden City, NY: Doubleday.

Wright, R.L. 1949. *Genius and the Mediocracy.* New York: Drell, Sloan and Pierce.

Yorke, J.A., and Tien-Yien, L. 1975. "Period Three Implies Chaos." *American Math Monthly* 82, 985-992.

Zukav, Gary. 1982. *The Dancing Wu Li Masters: An Overview of the New Physics.* New York: Bantam.

About the Author

DAVID R. HAWKINS has practiced psychiatry since 1952 and is a life member of the American Psychiatric Association. A widely respected therapist and lecturer, his national television appearances include **The MacNeil/Lehrer News Hour, The Barbara Walters Show,** and **The Today Show.** He has authored numerous scientific papers and videotapes, and co-authored the book **Orthomolecular Psychiatry** with Nobelist Linus Pauling. His diverse background as a researcher and teacher is noted in his biographical listing in **Who's Who in America.**

Dr. Hawkins currently divides his time between his practice, books in progress, and direction of **The Institute for Advanced Theoretical Research** in rural Arizona.

Power Versus Force is the culmination of a life's work. Believing the evolution of that work has paralleled his personal spiritual evolution, Dr. Hawkins recounts that history in the following autobiographical note.

–Ed.

WHILE THE TRUTHS REPORTED in this book were scientifically derived and objectively organized, like all truths, they were first experienced personally. A life-long sequence of intense states of awareness, beginning at a young age, first inspired and then gave direction to the process of subjective realization that has finally taken form in this book.

At age 3, there occurred a sudden full consciousness of existence, a sub-verbal but complete understanding of the meaning of "I Am"—followed immediately by the frightening realization that "I" might not have come into existence at all. This was an instant awakening from oblivion into a conscious awareness of being itself. In that moment the personal self was born and the duality of Is and Is-Not entered my subjective awareness.

Throughout childhood and early adolescence the paradox of existence and the question of the reality of the self remained a repeated concern. The personal self would sometimes begin slipping back into a greater impersonal Self, and the initial fear of non-existence, the fundamental fear of Nothingness, would recur.

In 1939, I was a paperboy in rural Wisconsin with a seventeen-mile route. One dark winter's night I was caught miles from home in a twenty-below blizzard. My bicycle fell over on the ice, and the fierce wind ripped the newspapers out of the handlebar basket and blew them across the ice-covered, snowy field. I broke into tears of frustration and exhaustion; my clothes were frozen stiff. To get out of the wind, I broke through the icy crust of a high snow bank and dug out a place to crawl into. Soon, the shivering stopped, and there was a delicious warmth, and then a state of peace beyond all description. This was accompanied by a suffusion of light and a presence of infinite love which had no beginning and no end and which was undifferentiated from my own essence. I became oblivious of my physical body and surroundings as my awareness fused with this all-present illuminated state. My mind grew silent; all thought stopped. An infinite Presence was all that was or could be, beyond time or description.

After what might have been eons, I was drawn back to an awareness of someone shaking my knee; then my father's anxious face appeared. I felt most reluctant to return to the body and all that entailed, but I loved my father dearly, and because of his anguish, I chose that. In a detached way, I sympathized with his fear of my death, although at the same time the concept of death seemed absurd to me.

I did not discuss my subjective experience with anyone. There was no context available with which to comprehend it; I had never heard of spiritual experiences other than those reported in lives of the saints. But after this experience the accepted reality of the world began to seem only provisional; traditional religious teaching lost significance, and, paradoxically, I became an agnostic. Compared to the light of divinity which I had felt bathing all existence, the god of traditional religion shone dully indeed. I had lost religion but discovered spirituality.

During World War II, I was assigned to hazardous duty on a minesweeper and often brushed close to death; but unlike the other crew members, I had no fear of it. It was as though death had lost it authenticity. After the war, fascinated by the complexities of the mind and wanting to study psychiatry, I worked my way through medical school. My training psychoanalyst, a professor at Columbia University, was also an agnostic; we both took a dim view of religion. The analysis went well, as did my career, and I became quite successful.

I did not, however, settle quietly into professional life. I succumbed to a progressive and fatal illness which did not respond to any treatments available. By age thirty-eight, I was in extremis, and knew I was about to die. I didn't care about the body, but my spirit was in a state of extreme anguish and despair. As the final moment approached, the thought flashed through my mind, "What if there is a God?" So I called out in prayer, "If there is a God, I ask him to help me now." I surrendered to whatever God there might be, and went unconscious, and when I awoke, a transformation of such enormity had taken place that I was struck dumb with awe.

The person I had been no longer existed. There was no personal self or ego, only an Infinite Presence of such unlimited power that it was all that was. This Presence had replaced what had been "me," and my body and its actions were controlled solely by the Infinite Will of the Presence. The world was illuminated by the clarity of an Infinite Oneness which expressed itself as all things revealed in their infinite beauty and perfection.

For nine months this stillness persisted. I had no will of my own; unbidden, my physical entity went about its business under the direction of the infinitely powerful but exquisitely gentle will of the Presence. In that state, there was no need to think about anything. All truth was self-evident; no conceptualization was necessary or even possible. At the same time, my nervous system felt extremely overtaxed, as though it were carrying far more energy than its circuits had been designed for.

I was unable to function effectively in the world. Along with all fear and anxiety, all ordinary motivations had disappeared. There was nothing to seek, as all was perfect. Fame, success, money were meaningless. Friends urged me to be pragmatic and return to my practice, but I had no ordinary motivation to do so. However, I discovered that I could perceive the reality that underlay personalities; I saw how the origin of emotional sickness lay in people's belief that they *were* their personalities. And so, of its own, my practice resumed and eventually became huge.

People came from all over the United States. I eventually had fifty therapists and other employees, two thousand out-patients, a suite of twenty-five offices, research and electro-encephalic laboratories, and treated a thousand new patients a year. I was invited to appear on radio and network television shows—*The MacNeil/Lehrer News Hour, The Today Show, The Barbara Walters Show,* etc. In 1973, I reported the work I was doing in a traditional format in the book *Orthomolecular Psychiatry,* with Nobelist Linus Pauling as co-author. This work, ten years ahead of its time, created something of a stir.

The overall condition of my nerves improved slowly, and then another phenomenon commenced—a sweet, delicious band of energy continuously flowing up the spine and into the brain, where it created an intense sensation of continuous pleasure. Everything in life happened by synchronicity, evolving in perfect harmony, and the miraculous was commonplace. The origin of what the world would call miracles was the Presence, not my personal self. What remained of the personal "me" was only a witness to these phenomena. The greater "I," deeper than my own self or my own thoughts, determined all that happened.

The states I was experiencing had been reported by others; I began investigating spiritual teachings, including those of the Buddha and enlightened sages, Huang Po and more recent teachers such as Ramana Marharshi and Nisargadatta Maharaj, and thus confirmed that these experiences were not unique. Suddenly, the Bhagavad-Gita made complete sense; eventually I experienced the same spiritual ecstasy reported by Sri Rama Krishna and the Christian saints.

Everything and everyone in the world was luminous and exquisitely beautiful. All living beings became Radiant, and expressed this Radiance in stillness and splendor. It was apparent that all mankind is actually motivated by inner love, but has simply become unaware; most lives were lived as though by sleepers unawakened to the awareness of who they really were. All those around me looked as though they were asleep, but incredibly beautiful; I was in love with everyone.

I had to stop my habitual practice of meditating for an hour in the morning and then again before dinner because it would intensify the bliss to such an extent that I could not function. An experience similar to the one I had in the snow bank as a boy would recur, but it became increasingly difficult to leave that state and return to the world. The incredible beauty of all things shone forth in all their perfection, and where the world saw ugliness, I saw only timeless beauty. This spiritual love suffused all perception; all boundaries between here and there, then and now, or me and you disappeared.

I spent the years in inner silence, and the strength of the Presence grew. I had no personal life; my personal will no longer existed; I was an instrument of the Infinite Presence, and I went about and did as it willed. People felt an extraordinary peace in the aura of that Presence. Seekers sought answers from me, but as there was no such individual as David any longer, I saw what they were doing was finessing answers from their own Self, which was not different from mine. As I looked at each person, my Self shone forth from their eyes. How did I get into all these bodies, I wondered.

The miraculous happened, beyond ordinary comprehension. Many chronic maladies from which I had suffered for years disappeared; my eyesight spontaneously normalized and I no longer needed my lifetime bifocals. Occasionally I would feel an exquisitely blissful energy, an Infinite Love, suddenly begin to radiate from my heart toward the scene of some calamity. Once I was driving on a highway when this exquisite energy began to beam out of my chest; as I rounded a bend, there was an auto accident, the wheels of the upturned car still spinning. The energy passed with great intensity into the occupants of the car and then stopped of its own accord. Again, as I was walking down the streets of a strange city, the energy started to flow down the block ahead of me, and I arrived at the scene of an incipient gang fight. The combatants fell back and began to laugh, and the energy stopped again.

Profound changes of perception came, without warning, in improbable circumstances. While dining alone at Rothman's on Long Island the Presence suddenly intensified until every thing and person, which had appeared separate in ordinary perception, melted into a timeless universality and oneness. In the motionless Silence I saw that there are no "events" or "things" and that nothing actually "happens," because past, present and future are merely an artifact of perception, as is the illusion of a separate "I" subject to birth and death. As the limited, false self dissolved into the universal Self of its true origin, there was an ineffable sense of having returned home, a state of absolute peace and relief from all suffering. For it is only the illusion of individuality that is the origin of all suffering; when one realizes that one *is* the universe, complete and at one with all that is, forever without end, then no further suffering is possible.

Patients came from every country in the world, and some were the most hopeless of the hopeless. Grotesque, writhing, wrapped in wet sheets for transport from far-away hospitals, they came hoping for treatment for advanced psychoses and grave, incurable mental disorders. Some were catatonic; many had been mute for years. But in each patient, beneath the crippled appearance, I clearly saw the shining essence of love and beauty, perhaps so obscured to ordinary vision that he or she had become totally unloved in this world.

One day a mute catatonic was brought into the hospital in a strait-jacket. She had a severe neurologic disorder and was unable to stand. Squirming on the floor, she went into spasms, her eyes rolled back in her head. Her hair was matted; she had torn all her clothes, and uttered guttural sounds. Her family was fairly wealthy, and therefore she had been seen by innumerable physicians over the years, famous specialists all over the world. Every treatment had been tried on her, and she had been given up as hopeless by the medical profession.

I looked at her and asked non-verbally, "What do you want me to do with her, God?" I then realized that I was just to love her; that was all. Her inner self shone though her eyes, and I connected with that loving essence. In that second, she was healed by her own recognition of who she really was; what happened to her mind or body didn't matter to her any longer.

This, in essence, occurred with countless patients. Some recovered in the eyes of the world, and some did not, but whether a clinical recovery ensued didn't matter any longer to the patients. Their inner agony was over; as they felt loved and at peace within, their pain stopped. This phenomenon can only be explained by saying that the Compassion of the Presence recontextualized each patient's reality so that he or she experienced healing on a level that transcended the world and its appearances. The inner peace in which I existed encompassed us both, beyond time and identity.

I saw that all pain and suffering arises solely from the ego and not from God. This was a truth which I silently communicated to the minds of my patients. When I intuited this mental block in another mute catatonic who had not spoken in many years, and said to him, through my mind, "You're blaming God for what your ego has done to you," he jumped off the floor and began to speak, much to the shock of the nurse who witnessed the incident.

But the work became increasingly taxing, eventually overwhelming. Patients were backed up and waiting for beds to open, although the hospital with which I was affiliated had built an extra ward to house my patients. I felt an enormous frustration in the face of the tide of human suffering that I could only counter one patient at a time. It was like bailing out the sea. I felt that there must be some way to address the causes of the common malaise, the endless stream of spiritual distress and human suffering.

When I first encountered kinesiology, I was instantly amazed at the potential I saw. It was the "wormhole" between two universes—the physical world, and the world of the mind and spirit—an interface between dimensions. In a world full of sleepers lost from their source, here was a tool to recover, and demonstrate for all to see, that lost connection with the higher reality. I proceeded to test every substance, thought, concept I could think of, and had my students and research assistants do the same. Then I noticed a strange thing. Whereas all subjects went weak from negative stimuli such as fluorescent lights, pesticides and artificial sweeteners, students of spiritual disciplines who advanced their level of awareness did not go as weak as ordinary people did. Something important and decisive had shifted in their consciousness—apparently as they realized they were not at the mercy of the world, but rather were affected only by what their minds believed. Perhaps the very process of progress toward enlightenment could be shown to increase man's ability to resist the vicissitudes of existence.

I was more and more powerfully struck by the capacity to change things in the world by merely envisioning them; I saw how love changed the world each time it replaced un-love. The entire scheme of civilization could be profoundly altered by focusing this power of love at a very specific point. Whenever this happened, history bifurcated down new roads.

It now appeared that these crucial insights could be not only communicated with the world, but visibly and irrefutably demonstrated. It seemed that the great tragedy of human life had always been that the psyche is so easily deceived; discord and strife have been the inevitable consequence of mankind's inability to distinguish the false from the true. But here was an answer to this fundamental dilemma, a way to recontextualize the nature of consciousness itself and make explicable that which otherwise could only be inferred.

It was time to leave my life in New York with its Fifth Avenue apartment and estate on Long Island; I had discovered something more important. Before I could make my ideas concrete, I needed to perfect myself as an instrument. I left that world and everything in it and took up a reclusive life in a small town where the next seven years were spent in meditation and study.

But overpowering states of bliss would return unsought, and eventually I realized that I had to teach myself to be in the Divine Presence and still function in the world. I had lost track of what was happening in the world at large. In order to do research and writing, it was necessary to stop all spiritual practice and focus on the world of form. I started reading the paper and watching television to catch up on the story, who was who, and the nature of the current social dialogue. I didn't know who was running for office or who Princess Di was, either, but I found it a pleasure to become reacquainted.

Exceptional, subjective experiences of truth–the province of the mystic, who affects all mankind by sending forth energy of his level into the collective consciousness–are not understandable to the majority of mankind, and therefore are of limited meaning except to other spiritual seekers. I sought now to be ordinary because just being ordinary in itself is an expression of divinity; the truth of one's real self can be discovered through the pathway of everyday life. To live with care and kindness is all that is necessary. The rest reveals itself in due time. The commonplace and God are not distinct.

And so, after a long, circular journey of the spirit, I returned to the most important work, which is to bring the Presence that has moved my life perhaps at least a little closer to the grasp of as many of my fellow beings as I can reach.

The Presence is silent and conveys a state of peace that is the space in which and by which all is and has its existence and experience. It is infinitely gentle and yet like a rock. With it, all fear disappears. Spiritual joy occurs on a quiet level of inexplicable ecstasy. Because the experience of time stops, there is no apprehension or regret, nor pain, nor anticipation; the source of joy is unending and ever present. With no beginning or ending, there is no loss or grief or desire; nothing needs to be done; everything is already perfect and complete.

When time stops, all problems disappear; they are merely artifacts of a point of perception. As the Presence prevails, there is no further identification with the body or mind. When the mind grows silent, the thought, "I am," also disappears, and Pure Awareness shines forth to illuminate what one is, was, and always will be, beyond all worlds and all universes, beyond time and therefore without beginning or end.

People wonder, "How does one reach this state of awareness?" I can only share my own experience, and note that few follow the steps because they are so simple. First, my desire to reach that state was intense. Then began the discipline to act with constant and universal forgiveness and gentleness, without exception. One has to be compassionate towards everything, including one's own self and thoughts. Next came a willingness to hold desires in abeyance and surrender personal will at every moment. As each thought, feeling, desire or deed was surrendered to God, the mind became increasingly silent. At first, I turned over whole stories and paragraphs, then ideas and concepts. As one lets go of wanting to own these thoughts, they no longer reach such elaboration, and begin to fragment while only half formed. Finally, I could turn over the energy behind thought itself, before it even became thought.

The task of constant and unrelenting fixity of focus, allowing not even a moment of distraction from meditation, continued while doing ordinary activities. At first this seemed very difficult, but as time went on, it became habitual, automatic, requiring less and less effort, and finally effortless. The process is like a rocket leaving earth. At first, it requires enormous power, then less and less as it leaves the earth's gravitational field, and finally it moves through space under its own momentum.

Suddenly, without warning, a shift in awareness occured, and the Presence was there, unmistakable, all encompassing. There were a few moments of apprehension as the self died, and then the absoluteness of the Presence inspired a flash of awe. This breakthrough was spectacular, more intense than anything I had ever known. It has no counterpart in ordinary experience. The profound shock entailed is cushioned by the love that is with the Presence. Without the support and protection of that love, one would be annihilated.

There followed a moment of terror as the ego clung to its existence, fearing it would become nothingness. Instead, as it died, it was replaced by the Self as Everything-ness, the All in which everything is known and obvious in its perfect expression of its own essence. With nonlocality came the awareness that one is all that ever was or can be. One is total and complete, beyond all identities, beyond all gender, beyond even humanness itself. One need never again fear suffering and death.

What happens to the body, from this point, is immaterial. At certain levels of spiritual awareness, ailments of the body heal, or spontaneously disappear. But in the absolute state, such considerations are irrelevant. The body will run its predicted course and then return from whence it came. It is a matter of no importance; one is unaffected. The body appears an "it," rather than a "me," another object like the furniture in the room. It may seem comical that people still address the body as though it was the individual "you," but there is no way to explain this state of awareness to the unaware. It is best to just go on about one's business, and allow Providence to handle the social adjustment. However, as one reaches bliss, it is very difficult to conceal that state of intense ecstasy. The world may be dazzled, and people come from far and wide to be in the accompanying aura. Spiritual seekers and the spiritually curious may be drawn, as may be the very ill, seeking miracles; one may become a magnet and a source of joy to them. Commonly, there is a desire at this point to share this state with others and to use it for the benefit of all.

The ecstasy that accompanies this condition is not absolutely stable; there are also moments of great agony. The most intense occur when the state fluctuates and suddenly ceases for no apparent reason. These times bring on periods of intense despair, a fear that one has been forsaken by the Presence. These falls make the path arduous, and to surmount these reversals requires great will. It finally becomes obvious that one must transcend this level or constantly suffer excruciating "descents from grace." The glory of ecstasy, then, has to be relinquished, as one enters upon the arduous task of transcending duality until one is beyond all oppositions and their conflicting pulls. But while it is one thing to happily give up the iron chains of ego, it is quite another to abandon the golden chains of ecstatic joy. It feels as though one is giving up God, and a new level of fear arises, never before anticipated; this is the final terror of absolute aloneness.

In my own case, the fear of nonexistence was formidable, and I drew back from it repeatedly as it approached. The purpose of the agonies, of the dark nights of the soul, then became apparent—they are so intolerable that their exquisite pain spurs one on to the extreme effort required to surmount them. When vacillation between heaven and hell becomes unendurable, the desire for existence itself has to be surrendered. Only once this is done, may one finally move beyond allness or nothingness, beyond existence or nonexistence. This culmination of the inner work is the most difficult phase, the ultimate watershed, where one is starkly aware that the illusion of existence one here transcends is irrecoverable. There is no returning from this step, and this specter of irreversibility makes this last barrier appear the most formidable choice of all.

But, in fact, in this final apocalypse of the self, the dissolution of the sole remaining duality—that of existence and non-existence—identity itself dissolves in universal divinity, and no individual consciousness is left to choose. The last step, then, is taken by God alone.

–*David R. Hawkins*

The author was Knighted for this work by the Danish Crown. Officiated October 1996 by Crown Prince Valdemor into the Soverign order of St. John of Jeruselem (Established in the year A.D. 1070).

Index

Correct Calibration Techniques-

(All calibrations in ***Power vs Force*** were made in reference to the scale on pages 52 and 53.

Ask ***"On a scale of 1 to 600 where 600 represents enlightenment, this_____calibrates at_____"***. The scale is relative only and the numbers were chosen arbitrarily. Unless a specific scale is used as reference the numbers obtained would be arbitrary. Anyone can make up their own scale.

If a specific scale is not specified readers may get astounding numbers over 1000 and progressively higher and higher numbers, with subsequent readings. On the above scale no person who ever existed on this planet ever scored over 1000 and they were all the great Avatars.